GARABANDAL

The Warning and the Great Miracle

The Divine Reset That Will Correct
the Conscience of the World

By Ted Flynn

Maxkol Communications

Cover pictures: Purchased at Shutterstock
Published and printed in the USA
Copyright ©2023 MAXKOL
ISBN Number: 978-0-9668056-8-0
Design Layout: Paul McNamara Design

Publisher:
MAXKOL, All Rights Reserved.

For bulk or case orders contact: tflynn333@icloud.com

Available on Amazon and Kindle

Distributor:
Signs and Wonders for Our Time.
P.O. Box 345
Herndon, Virginia. 20170
E mail: signsorders@gmail.com
Web site: Sign.org
Phone:703.707.0799

DEDICATED TO

Our Lady of Mount Carmel

"But of that day and hour no one knows,
not even the angels of Heaven, nor the Son,
but the Father only."

MATTHEW 24:36

"For when they shall say, peace and security;
then shall sudden destruction come upon them,
as the pains upon her that is with child,
and they shall not escape."

I THESSALONIANS 5:3

"Then the fire of the Lord fell, and consumed the
burnt offering, and the wood, and the stones, and the dust,
and licked up the water that was in the trench.
And when all the people saw it, they fell on their faces;
and they said, "the Lord, He is God; the Lord He is God.
And Elijah said to them, "seize the prophets of Baal,
let not one of them escape..."

I KINGS 38-40

Acknowledgments

If a person's life is considered successful by the quality of their relationships with family and friends, I am in the category of blessed. There have been many good people that I have had the pleasure of being around for a lifetime. The Lord said, "I have come to give you life, and give it more abundantly." I am living proof of that verse. All that can explain it is grace.

Garabandal embodies so many of the reasons why Heaven is about to bring the Warning, the Miracle, and the Permanent Sign to the world. Heaven often uses the Mother of Jesus to communicate to mankind with modern day epistles at apparition sites with the promises made to the Church, that the Lord will never abandon His people.

Many thanks to the disciples and master craftsmen who helped in the process of making this book a reality. Maureen Flynn for the conversations on the specific aspects of Garabandal, and apparitions in general. Several people have had a hand in the molding process. Everyone had great value, and in alphabetical order.

Father Joseph Esper did a deep dive of thought, correction, structure, and guidance to the relevance of the subject matter bringing coherence to very dense and serious subject matter. His comments, suggestions, and thoughts were incorporated throughout.

Colleen Flynn made many suggestions that I knew were right, where I would go off on a tangent, she would bring me back inside the ropes. It sure felt good writing it, but the story is about the messages of Our Lady to the world. Colleen's insights were valuable, and it was appreciated. She kept the book going in the right direction.

Team Flynn. Danny & MTM. It is hard to have more appreciation for Danny, Meredith, Liam, Evan, Emma, and Clara. The source of joy brings one to an altered state when they are near. You just look forward to waking up earlier when they are around, because you know the day is going to be epic with activities and memories.

Martin Hartigan. Few in the world see the big picture as clear as Martin. His past career in large multi-lateral lending and social policies for a lifetime at the highest levels in the world enabled him to see the inner machinations, how the globalists work in public, with a separate agenda in private. He also is a devoted soul to the apparitions of Our Lady globally. These two traits are not commonly found in people.

Team Kopp. I have more appreciation than most when someone in a family takes on a job, because it is a joint effort for the whole family. While one is working, the other is doing something else picking up the slack. Debbie Kopp went through every single page of a very rough draft where 98. 8653% of her changes were incorporated. Terry and Debbie Kopp have been an advocate for our apostolate from the very beginning, and their contribution to the welfare of our family is without measure. When you are around the Kopp's, good things happen. They follow the Scriptural admonition, "let your good deeds be done in private."

The miracle of Chriss Rainey. Books would just show up on my doorstep that were never asked for, that were exactly what was needed at that moment to make a point in a chapter. It could not have been better if it was pre-planned. Her review was very helpful with suggestions and edits. Chriss' reading list looks like a college professor that advises post doc Ph.D. students in political philosophy.

Friends along the way who have been an encouragement and helping are Jason Azarkhish, Bill and Donna Bradt, Oscar Delgado, John and Ilo Duckett, Jon Gorog, Father David Gunter, Bob and Meg Malafronte, Dave and Joan Maroney, Stu Mayberry, Dr. Tom Petrisko, Dr. Antone Raymundo, Jim Shea, Father Ron Stone, Dr. Bryan Thatcher, Amy Young, and the Saint Joseph Prayer Cenacle.

A special thanks to Barry Hanratty in memoriam who gave me permission to use his material without reservation wherever I saw fit. Barry was very aware of our interest and writings on Garabandal for thirty years. His only request was to cite the source coming from his writings and magazines over the years. In Signs and Wonders for Our Times over the last several decades we have posted numerous articles always with credit and notation. His sole interest in life was making the messages of Garabandal known to a wider audience and my wife and I have spoken widely on the messages since 1993. For those wishing to keep abreast of stories on Garabandal, write:

Garabandal Journal
P.O. Box 1796
Saint Cloud, MN 56302-1796
Attn. Dick Kodet

It is hard to find a more wondrous topic to write on where only superlatives fill one with awe on the subject matter as we watch promised events come to pass that will leave people speechless. What a privilege writing about the Daughter of the Father, the Mother of the Son, the Spouse of the Holy Spirit, the Immaculate Conception, and the Queen of Heaven and earth.

Thank You All.

— TED FLYNN

December 8, 2023 Feast of the Solemnity of the Immaculate Conception

Contents

THE ENEMY HEAVEN FIGHTS

A Red Sea Moment for the World: Heaven Sees the Pain and Intervenes— An Act of Mercy and Hope

"By their fruits you will know them."

MATTHEW 7:20

I first heard of the apparitions of the Blessed Mother at Garabandal, Spain, in 1984, and have been fascinated by them ever since. I met a neighbor at church who had family who was involved on a personal basis with a key individual in the Garabandal story by the name of Joey Lomangino, and a friendship was established between our families. Joey was blinded in an accident of youth, and over time became known as the "apostle of Garabandal." I then learned more about what happened in that small Spanish village in northern Spain. Due to that family having a very ill daughter, they were praying for a healing, given the promise that all would be healed who went to Garabandal for the day of the prophesied Great Miracle. The father of the family was an asset fund manager who had gone so far as to plan a private plane to bring his sick daughter to Garabandal in the likelihood of the Miracle. Many people are still waiting in joyful hope for the events prophesied to happen. Families are in prayer for the events to come to pass for two principal reasons. First, for the healing of a loved one where medicine and science have failed them. Second, the problems mankind face are now so large, they see little hope for the world other than Divine intervention.

Here is just one of the several reasons for the realization of Garabandal—HOPE. Garabandal is a beacon of HOPE, MERCY, TRUST, and GRACE for people who know and believe what was said there because they see society crumbling from the interior with no human solutions on the horizon. Garabandal explains the *why,* and *why now* for a world in pain

1

to persevere. Garabandal gives them the assurance that God has a plan for the salvation of mankind. The promises provide a clear vision of the future with their practice of faith, of a society around them tries to crush their very physical existence. The village of Garabandal is out of Heaven's playbook for the current downward slide towards Gomorrah. The promise made by the Blessed Mother is that all who journey to the nine pines at the time of the Miracle, in the Cantabrian Mountains of northern Spain, will be healed. The reason they will journey there is rooted in love for another. As the Lord said, "*For my thoughts are not your thoughts, neither are your ways my ways, declares the Lord. As the Heavens are higher than the earth, so are my ways higher than your ways and my thoughts than your thoughts*" (Isaiah 55:8-9).

What has been said by one of the visionaries, "The miracle at Fatima is nothing in comparison with what will happen here. The miracle here will be much greater, more tremendous than Fatima. It will cause such an impression that none of those who see it will be able to leave with doubts. It would be well if all the world were here, since that way there surely would be no chastisement, since everyone would believe."

My wife, Maureen, and I have written and spoken on Garabandal in books, our magazine, *Signs and Wonders for Our Time*, (Sign.org), *MaxKol Communications (publishing)*, conferences, films, on pilgrimages to Garabandal, and at other venues for 35 years. We have never doubted the authenticity of the apparitions for reasons cited in this book. We have met hundreds of people who all have their own stories to tell about Garabandal, and they are not shy about telling them. In this period of time, we have met as many as twenty people who claim they have experienced the Warning, the Illumination of Conscience, a Judgment in Miniature, or a Life Review. The phrase is used interchangeably and really means the same thing. They all refer to what was described at Garabandal — the Warning, and called the "aviso" in Spanish. All the stories are remarkably similar, and they say that it often takes years for them to process it. People all say it is the single most dramatic life altering event they have ever experienced. Priests, seminarians, and everyone in between tell their stories. We have filmed them, written their stories, and they have spoken at events we have sponsored in the Northern Virginia region.

The graces these people have received are incalculable as they each speak how knowing what was said at Garabandal has positively impacted their personal spirituality. Garabandal is a bright spot for many, because it provides a vision of a bright future for mankind, bringing restoration to the brokenness of the world. It is very possible Garabandal will experience (and has to a certain degree) what is called the three states of truth. First, it will be ridiculed. Second, it will be violently opposed. Third, it will be accepted as self-evident.[1]

Some have had a difficult time with the Illumination of Conscience when they have experienced it. Some have less emotional trauma, some greater, depending on how they lived their lives. One thing is certain: each individual says it changed every aspect of their life, and made them a better person. I will tell just two stories in this book about a Filipino man named Stanley Villavicencio, who died for three days and came back to life, and a Catholic priest who experienced the Warning. There could have been many more testimonies, but their stories are emblematic of others. The doctor who witnessed what Stanley went through immediately quit the medical profession and became a priest. This is an example of grace coming to a world that has run out of human solutions for its ills. The Warning and the Miracle must be seen from God's eyes, and the need for it, as an event of GRACE and MERCY, and the solicitude of a loving Mother in Heaven. If not seen through this lens, it cannot be comprehended. It is the world of the supernatural, in which the laws of reason do not always apply.

My family first visited Garabandal in 1994. We sponsored a trip to the site after the publication of *The Thunder of Justice* (1993, revised 2010), a book that had two large chapters on Garabandal that explained what happened there. In Fatima, Portugal, I met John Haffert (Co-founder of the Blue Army). The first question John asked me was, *"So, when is the Warning and the Miracle?"* John knew a lot about private revelation and had written extensively about Fatima, as well as other apparition sites. John wrote a book on Fatima circa 1975 titled, *There is Nothing More,* published by the Blue Army. After a lifetime of study and observation on Fatima, John felt there was nothing more to say. The events at Fatima happened as Our Lady said they would, and the prophesied events came to pass. This is similar to the story of Garabandal. The Garabandal apparitions began in 1961 and ended in 1965. There has been no more narrative from the Blessed Mother since then about the apparitions, or at least anything anyone knows about. **Those who are familiar with the messages can now see in clearer focus that what was spoken about is now easier to see what the four young visionaries prophesied.** That should be proof enough if one is intellectually and spiritually honest, and not bound by a predisposed prejudice or judgment on a singular element they may hold about the apparitions.

Jesus said, *"You will know them by their fruits"* (Matthew 7:20). Believing in Garabandal has never caused scandal, and to the contrary, it has been a source of inspiration and encouragement to people. We are watching in real time the destruction of the culture, the family, the state, and the Church. This fact is irrefutable as one watches the dismantling of Christianity in Western Civilization. The issue of why the Blessed Mother comes is the most basic concept in all life: She comes as a mother to save her children. She warns them of impending danger and provides solutions to the woes of fallen man. Innocence does not have a chance any longer unless God intervenes. This is the short answer of why the Warning is necessary for humanity, and it is explored in detail throughout this book. Our Lady said, "This will now be made evident by the very events themselves which are about to take place in the Church and in the world."[2] We are also told in Scripture, "Where sin abounds, grace abounds all the more" (Romans 5:20). To those not aware that Heaven is in control and has a plan, this is reassuring. The Lord hears the cries of His people.

What happened in Fatima is potentially a replay at Garabandal prophetically. Fatima spoke of bloodshed if Our Lady's messages were not obeyed. At Garabandal, the Blessed Mother spoke of the further destruction of the Church, if her messages were not heeded, as she had also asked at Fatima. Heaven in its own design gives mankind free choice to make its own decisions.

There are some legitimate areas of concern and confusion of what was supposed to happen post 1965 and towards the end of the apparitions. These issues are addressed in order to present the full picture that should intellectually satisfy a doubter, and maybe even a hardened skeptic. To answer all questions and tell the story conclusively, and leave no stone unturned, would require 800 pages, which would close the door on a scoffer.

I am also reminded of the words of the apostle John in the very last verse of the Gospel of John. John wrote: *"But there are also many other things which Jesus did; were every one of them to be written, I suppose that the world itself would not contain the books that would be written."* The Blessed Mother appeared over 2,000 times over a four-year and four-month period in Garabandal to four young girls. The volume of messages and dialogue was substantial. The conversations many times lasted several hours between Our Lady and the young girls. What they heard and did not announce or write down, we will never know.

Barry Hanratty, writer and editor on all things Garabandal, is the individual who made the stories known through his magazines, while living and publishing with an austere lifestyle to keep the messages alive and in front of people for fifty years. It is important that writers and readers look to the early published documents on the subject because many people have mixed and matched the Garabandal messages with messages from other apparition sites, and come to conclusions that were never mentioned in the early writings of the visionaries. This is common in the study of apparitions, because Heaven often says similar things to the visionaries that are fundamental to the faith at numerous other sites. As Sergeant Joe Friday in the 1950's TV series *Dragnet* used to say arriving at a crime scene, *"Just the facts ma'am."*

When the Church discerns an apparition as either true or false, it does not look to see if it coincides with other messages from somewhere else, even if that apparition has been approved by the Church. Each apparition must stand on its own without the support of another to validate it. There are unquestionable similarities of Garabandal and other apparition sites, but they are dealt with factually, making no predictions. I do use the writings of some mystics, visionaries, and saints that use language very supportive of the Warning, but this is intentionally kept to a minimum.

The earliest material concerning the messages of Garabandal is sometimes hard to pinpoint, as so much of the written material uses identical language or contains the exact same story from different decades — sometimes with differing interpretations. The Third Secret of Fatima is just one instance where more information has come out over time than was ever divulged in the very early messages. This exact same situation has happened at Garabandal, and what was originally said in the very early years. There is the distinct possibility that Mari Loli (one of the four visionaries) did tell a priest about the Warning being in an even numbered year, or it may be an anecdotal story uttered in a casual conversation. These matters are addressed. The timely issue of a pope going to Moscow, and a Synod, near the time of the events are also critically examined.

Another issue involves what may appear as redundant material presented about the Warning. Often, the language is naturally similar as each of the visionaries experienced for the most part (especially regarding the Warning) the same appearances by Our Lady. However, no one really knows what each were told in private conversations. All of the visionaries have a different way of saying things because of the uniqueness of the individual. Stories on the same subject may appear redundant, but more is always added to the story to make it more complete when said by one of the other girls. This gives the reader a more comprehensive understanding of what Our Lady said. With each of the four visionaries there is slightly different language with added insight. There are nuggets provided that add to the overall story and give it more substance. This puts the entire moment they experienced with Our Lady in context in their own language. Also, Our Lady sometimes said things to one visionary and not the other(s).

There are several glaring issues that have possibly been embellished over time. We know a person can tell another something, and by the time it reaches the tenth person, it is often unrecognizable from the original version of the story. There may be some of that here. The issues of a pope going to **Moscow**, and a *"great event in the Church"* near the time of the Miracle over the years has been translated to an *"ecclesial event."* The event could be a positive or negative, we just don't know. What does a *great event* really mean? Another issue discussed at length is a **synod**, and a possible **schism** (the word was used in the apparitions) that could trigger a downward spiral in the Church. Another is whether the **Miracle is in the month** of March, April, May, or June. Still another topic discussed is **"four more popes,"** yet once **"three popes" were mentioned,** and then *"el fin de los tiempos"*—the end of times. Which one is correct? Everyone has an opinion based on the information they have, but it may not be as conclusive and convincing as we would all hope it to be.

There has been a parlor game for many years attempting to predict the month of the Miracle. This started in earnest several years before the Jubilee of the year 2000, and then slowed down after that. The Warning and the Miracle have not happened and here we are now decades later. Do the

Warning and the Miracle happen in the same calendar year, or just **within one year** as originally stated? Is the Warning in an **even numbered year** as it was indicated decades after the apparition? There is greater plausibility that events are nearer than before due to current circumstances throughout the world conforming to the messages. One sign is the persecution of believers we see in many parts of the world, and increasingly evident in the USA as well. This is always a sign indicating dictatorship and tyranny.

There is also considerable narrative on Communism, the potential for a schism in the Church, Freemasonry, an event of reunification in the Church, and the Spanish Civil War. The world becoming Communist was mentioned by Our Lady during the apparitions, and this is examined. For a person living in Spain, this may be more relevant because they had family members who lived through the Spanish Civil War. Garabandal began twenty-two years after the end of Spanish Civil War (1939). These facts have enormous relevance of WHY the Blessed Mother said what she said, and helps explain our current situation. You cannot understand modern-day Spain, until you understand the significance of the Spanish Civil War. The gaps are filled in on the enemy that Heaven fights, and they are entities and people with names. Our Lady comes for a reason, and has an agenda.

These issues are explored in significant detail throughout the book, and hopefully they will bring clarity to what was said by the visionaries. Did the girls release some information in general conversations over the last sixty years? Maybe, maybe not, but the real answer may be probably. Over time there is more flesh on the bone of what was originally released from 1961-1965, the actual years the apparitions were happening. What can be said, is that, if Garabandal is authentic, we are getting a lot closer to civilization changing in front of our eyes.

Even the most spiritually insensitive person likely senses the world is in a death spiral morally, and economically, by every index used by the social sciences. When a country is in debate on what constitutes a biological male versus a female, and there is disagreement on that issue, it shows just how much the devil has infiltrated society, and the degree of confusion we have reached. Homosexuality is not new in the world, nor is drag. They are as old as the oldest profession. What is new in all of world history is the transgender movement where science now enables individuals to alter their sex through surgery and hormone therapy. The chaos this is causing to people is Luciferian. Social pressure on insecure souls with no spiritual formation is just increasing the number of people subscribing to its theory and practice. The demons have been unleashed on earth, and this is a direct sign of the end times. The normalization of sexual perversion and deviant behavior is well past the tipping point. It is only an intoxicated brain, lacking intellectual honesty and discernment after generations of apostasy, that could subscribe to it.

Saint Paul addressed this pagan culture saying, *"God gave them over to depraved minds"* (Romans 1:28). In other versions of the bible, the word *reprobate* is used. We are now living the same characteristics of society as Saint Paul described in Romans 1 about the behavior of pagans.

Sin has hypnotized many through darkened intellects that advocate the practice of heinous sin. However, one thing seems to be certain at the moment. The barbarians are now inside the gates of the Church and many other prominent institutions. The ideologues on the left are now so strident in their actions, they would rather burn down the existing system than work within it, and this is precisely what they are doing. They refuse to accept the Divinity of Christ in their lives and submit to a Divine Order.

People and entities who promote this diabolical ideology now have a scorched earth policy. It is the moral equivalent of General William Tecumseh Sherman marching from Atlanta to Savannah, Georgia, during the Civil War, burning and destroying any resemblance of the past to make sure the south never fought again. Covid was a massive transfer of wealth, and fires throughout the world will transfer more wealth and property to state control. If the Marxists cannot get their way, they will now simply burn down the past to introduce the future they want to implement. Just one passionate phrase that typifies this ideology is from a group of transgender, homosexuals and drag queens marching in New York City during June 2023, which was pride month: "We're queer, we're here, and we're coming for your children." For decades, there has been a hidden and unspoken evil agenda to indoctrinate the next generation of children. This community is now so brazen, nothing is being held in secret any longer. Evil is now being brought to the light. The new normal for people will be increasingly bizarre phenomena all around them.

As we watch the political, social, and cultural fabric of our society disintegrate before us at an accelerated pace, we may rightly assume Satan's final assault has come from the continued attack on the issue of gender ideology. Religious institutions of all denominations and affiliations, and people of faith, will continue to be confronted with decisions of conformity to the culture, or standing for Divine truth, and facing the consequences of their decisions in this world or in the next. The legalization of abortion made evident the *"end times"* are upon us, and the mutilation of God's biblical creation of man and woman leaves no doubt we are in the final battle. There is no place left for Satan to turn to level his evil debauchery upon humanity. In a long history of rebellion against God, it will be Satan's final utterance of *"Non Serviam"* — I will not serve. All perversions going forward will merely be an extension of this grievous sin embraced by disordered confused minds, and lost souls. Like birth pangs the difficult times are increasing in intensity and severity. The very issue of what it means to be human and created by God is being challenged, mocked, and scandalized by Satan. We must ask, **Why** is the Blessed Mother appearing with these messages and why **Now?**

If believers have been silent, or fearful of what others may think about their view on abortion, and been silent in the marketplace and schools, and now fearful for the same reasons about transgender mutilation, they are spiritually dead. It reminds one of the oft used phrase of Edmund Burke, *"The only thing necessary for the triumph of evil is for good men to do nothing."* Or, as Archbishop Fulton J. Sheen once said, *"The refusal to take sides on great moral issues is itself a decision. It is a silent acquiescence to evil. The tragedy of our time is that those who still believe in honesty lack fire and conviction, while those who believe in dishonesty are full of passionate conviction."*

It is now Satan's hour and this is precisely the reason Heaven has its own design for a **Divine Reset,** as sin is so virulent and aggressive around us. Jesus Himself was clear when He said, *"but whoever causes one of these little ones who believe in me to sin, it would be better for him to have a great millstone fastened around his neck and to be drowned in the depths of the sea"* (Matthew 18:6). That leaves little room for interpretation of what Jesus thought about harming children. The sex trafficking industry is now larger than the illegal arms trade, and approaching money in the illegal drug trade at approximately $150 billion per year.

This is the fight we are in at the moment, and the time of reversal of this extreme evil may be close. The evil being heaped upon children from an early age doesn't give them a fighting chance for normalcy or the intentions of God in their lives. This reason alone is enough for Heaven to act in such a profound way that Garabandal promises. Come Lord Jesus, save and protect your children.

There is a great deal of narrative on the enemies Heaven is fighting. People experienced the problems mandated vaccines caused in families, but until they understand how the imminent introduction of Central Bank Digital Currency (**CBDC**) creates the potential for much greater government tyranny, where unelected government bureaucrats gain control of us to put us all in a *"digital cage,"* they haven't experienced the worst of it yet. Ultimately, the agenda of the globalists is to create a digital gulag for people of the world. This issue is addressed in a section called, The Enemy Heaven Fights — Central Bank Digital Currency (CBDC). The World Health Organization (WHO) will soon roll out the vaccine passport or ID system, wherein nations effectively cede the sovereignty and rights of their citizens on health matters to United Nations types of institutions and unelected bureaucrats. This subject alone deserves another book on how developed and organized government and businesses are on these issues. Few understand how ferocious this will be for the population of the world. Whether it be the vaccine passport, the Synod document altering established traditional Catholic doctrine, CBDC, or some new untested injection to fight off death, globalists and government agencies are continually telling people, "It's for your own good."

Mankind continues to pursue the elusive utopian model of living without God, and will have to endure the negative consequences of the resulting dystopia. The unbelievers will not be fazed by its actions or consequences, because they have little to no understanding of its motives, nor its negative ramifications. They will be told it is good for everyone to participate as it is for their own security, as well as for the betterment of mankind. Heaven too has an agenda, because it is aware of the evil in our midst, and that is the reason for the Warning and the Miracle. When Our Lady appears, she is coming with a loving desire and agenda to save her people. Our Lady is engaged in a prominent role as Genesis 3:15 states, *"I will put enmities between thee and the woman, and thy seed and her seed: she shall crush thy head, and thee shall lie in wait for her heel."*

When navy aviators and fighter pilots are training, they practice a drill in case they ever have to eject and ditch their plane over water in the dark of night. While in the water, if the pilot is disoriented and doesn't know which way is up or down, they are trained to release some air from their lungs, see which way the bubbles go, and follow them upwards. Likewise, for us, our refuge is the Sacred Heart of Jesus and the Immaculate Heart of Mary. Sticking to the fundamentals of the faith and being obedient is paramount. If we are not firmly rooted in the faith, and especially prayer, we will struggle when the storm gets more intense. Advice for those living in the midst of the confusion that surrounds us, don't look right, don't look left: look up — for there your salvation lies.

Jesus said, *"My sheep listen to My voice, I know them and they follow Me"* (John 10:27). Is it a coincidence the first saint of the new millennium is Saint Faustina Kowalska whose message of Divine Mercy encourages us not to become despondent or despair in difficult times? It will only be a solid faith rooted in foundational principles that will bring us to the New Times promised, and Garabandal will be a big part of that.

CHAPTER 2

Garabandal — The Divine Reset

*And I will work wonders in the Heavens above, and signs on
the earth below; blood, fire, and a cloud of smoke.*

ACTS 2:19

*It is the most beautiful story of humanity since the days of Christ.
It is like a second life of the Virgin on earth. And we can never be grateful
enough for it. We have to pray much and have much patience...
it is necessary to pray that the Church will become aware of the
importance of Garabandal.*

SAINT POPE PAUL VI AND HIS SENTIMENTS ON GARABANDAL

*My mercy is so great that no mind, be it of man or of angel,
will be able to fathom it throughout all eternity.*

DIVINE MERCY IN MY SOUL, THE DIARY OF SAINT MARIA FAUSTINA KOWALSKA

Those familiar with Signs and Wonders Magazine, and the writings of
my wife Maureen and I, know we have had a particular interest in
the apparitions of the Blessed Mother at Garabandal since the early 1980's.
Garabandal has a uniqueness all its own, which we have written about
extensively. My wife and I released a book in 1993 (revised in 2010), titled,
***The Thunder of Justice: The Warning, the Miracle, the Chastisement, The
Era of Peace.*** The story and messages of Garabandal were the heart and the
soul of the book. Garabandal is a fascinating story historically, prophetically,
scripturally, and mystically. It pieces together a beautiful mosaic of
Heaven's language to its people. Garabandal points to future events that are
complementary to other elements in the Catholic faith, as well as significant
events that are in the Old Testament. If one understands that God, the Blessed
Mother, and the Host of Heaven, have a plan for the salvation of all mankind

in our troubled times, then Garabandal and its promises make even more sense. Recently, there has been heightened interest in Garabandal because there are more religious, geopolitical, and spiritual events converging that make the events prophesied more plausible. Russia/Ukraine, China/Taiwan, the Korean Peninsula, Israel and the Muslim world, and other significant factors enable an individual to know the world could change in an instant with a nuclear event that could catapult the interconnected world into a state of complete chaos. Attempting to predict the exact date of an event is never wise, but it appears what was prophesied at Garabandal is inching closer to reality. One could use the logic of Blaise Pascal (1623-1662), and his famous wager looking at the information provided in this book. Pascal's pragmatic approach to religion said in essence, *"If God exists, then I have everything to lose. If I do not believe, if He does not exist, I have lost nothing."*

I first visited Garabandal with my family in 1994, and again in 2017 along with a pilgrimage to Fatima (100th anniversary). My second visit to Garabandal was a more eye-opening experience because I had learned so much more during that interval of time since my first visit. What was most noticeable in 2017 was how little life had changed in the village. More accurately, we all were stunned by it. The tiny church had not been updated or expanded, and only a few dozen more homes were built in the surrounding area. For pilgrims, there were only two public bathrooms. Two! It was eerie in its simplicity and tranquility, and remoteness from the noise of the world, understanding what is expected to happen there at some point in the future.

The miraculous occurrence that is prophesied to happen in Garabandal will be unprecedented. The lack of amenities and facilities in the village may be a part of the much bigger story when the predicted Miracle does happen. Although our group had been to Fatima just a few days before Garabandal, most of the two bus-loads of people felt that the future of the prophetic was here in this remote hamlet in northern Spain few have actually visited. Fatima was true, and events happened as prophesied, exactly to the letter. Russia did spread her errors throughout the world as the Blessed Mother said in 1917 to three peasant children. Fatima became the cornerstone of apparitions for the 20th Century as it had been approved by the Magisterium of the Church. That is now history, and the Holy Spirit, being dynamic and not static, moved on with new things to teach.

Fatima opened up the 20th Century for renewed reception of Our Lady's words. Our Lady continued her apparitions as a mercy to humanity in the form of modern day epistles at Beauraing, Belgium, (1932), Banneux, Belgium (1933), Divine Mercy, Poland (July 1934 earliest notes written) Our Lady of All Nations, Amsterdam (1945), Montichiari, Italy (1947), Flame of Love, Hungary (1961), Garabandal, Spain (1961), Akita, Japan (1973), Medjugorje, (now Bosnia, formerly Yugoslavia) 1981, Kibeho, Rwanda (1981)… and the list of love and mercy continues to all humanity on a continual basis.

Opposing Armies—Satan's vs. Heaven's Reset

And you shall remember your wicked ways, and your doings that were not good: and your iniquities, and your wicked deeds shall displease you.
It is not for your sakes that I will do this, saith the Lord God, be it known to you: be confounded, and ashamed at your own ways, O house of Israel.

(EZEKIEL 36:31-32)

At the time of this writing, the Great Reset is all over the news, with the elites having power to determine the welfare of future generations. Those wanting government control of people from cradle to grave, determining who lives and who dies, and administratively ramming their agenda for global governance are growing more powerful. It is a Luciferian plan to enslave mankind for the dominion of the world. We hear it now ad nauseam. This creep of an agenda has been gradual for many generations. If one understands that the plan is population control and climate legislation as the vehicles created to implement their programs, news would have made more sense from the beginning for those willing to listen. The perfect scenario came together with the man-made creation of Covid 19, enabling the vehicle for medical tyranny with a preplanned pandemic, to usher in new social and financial instruments to create more data points for surveillance and governmental control. The age-old Masonic battle cry still proves to be true, *"Out of chaos, comes order."*

We now live in a world where the standard operating procedure is glorifying the guilty and framing or cancelling the innocent, while elites are protected by immoral and unjust laws that support a totalitarian agenda, which always requires an identifiable enemy. As Saint Augustine said, "I think that a law that is not just, is not actually a law." The tangible enemy of bureaucrats is now someone who disagrees with unjust and heinous governmental policies. The plan that makes all despots giddy with joy as Chairman Mao Zedong once said, *"A lie repeated a hundred times becomes the truth."* In current times with news and social media bombarding our senses all day, it now seems like 10,000 times. Day after day as people watch the news, we are being fed lies so big and outrageous, there is no longer a rational response that can penetrate senses. We are living a dystopian nightmare where Heaven has no alternative but to step in, lest all be lost. George Orwell's predictions in his book *1984*, have proven to be prophetic.

The Warning and the Great Miracle of Garabandal will be Heaven's Reset to offset the evil in our day. Due to the interconnectivity of the community of nations that is so well organized, Heaven will have its own global solution.

A promise so great awaits us, there are barely words to describe the majesty of it all. In message number 83, October 18, 1975, the Blessed Mother to the Marian Movement of Priests simultaneously gave the blueprint for humanity and the Church. It is titled **Be Joyous**, and partially reads,

"My adversary will one day think that he is celebrating a complete victory: over the world, over the Church, over souls. It will be only then that I will intervene — terrible and victorious — that his defeat may be all the greater when he is certain in his conviction that he has conquered once for all.

"What is in preparation is so extraordinary that its like has never happened since the creation of the world. That is why everything has already been predicted in the Bible. The terrible struggle between me, the Woman Clothed with the Sun and the Red Dragon, Satan, who has now succeeded in seducing many even with the error of Marxist atheism, has always been foretold to you...**Above all, my complete victory has already been clearly foretold.** You, my sons, have been called to live through these events. It is now time for you to know this, that you may be consciously prepared for the battle. This is now the time for me to begin disclosing part of my plan.

"First of all, it is necessary that my enemy having the impression of conquering everything, of having everything now in his hands. That is why **he will be permitted to penetrate even into the interior of my Church,**

and he will succeed in plunging the sanctuary of God into darkness. He will reap the greatest number of victims from the ministers of the sanctuary. This will in fact be a time of great falls on the part of my beloved sons, my priests.

"Satan will seduce many of them by pride, others by love of the flesh, others by doubts, others by unbelief, and still others by discouragement and loneliness. How many will have doubts about my Son and about me will believe that this is the end of my Church (83:c-l).

"Conquer temptation and fear, of discouragement, of sadness. Distrust paralyzes your activity and greatly benefits my Adversary (n).

"The weapons that I will use to fight and win this battle will be your prayer and suffering (83z).

"And so then, you too will be on the cross with me and my Son Jesus, close to His Mother and yours. And then I myself will do everything, because God has arranged this be my hour, my hour and yours, O sons consecrated to my Immaculate Heart (83 A)."

The late Pope Benedict XVI wrote, "All will seem lost, but at the right time, right at the dramatic stage of the crisis, the Church will be reborn… for it will no longer be the Church of those who seek to please the world, but the Church of the faithful to God and His eternal law. Renaissance will be the work of a small remnant, seemingly insignificant but nevertheless indomitable, who have undergone a purification process. Because that is how God works. Against evil, a little flock stands…."

When one sees in the modern era what the Blessed Mother and the Host of Heaven are looking to accomplish at authentic and time-tested apparition sites, there is more of a complete understanding of what is happening in the world. The messages of Garabandal address these issues. They show what Heaven is doing to bring us to a new Era of Peace, a New Jerusalem, a New Epoch, a New Era — New Times. This will not be the end of the world, but a line of demarcation where world events transition to a New Time. We have seen transitions in history like Charlemagne and the creation of the Holy Roman Empire, after the Bolshevik Revolution, the French Revolution, the American Revolution, the American Civil War, World War 1 and II, and many others. Garabandal will be much larger, with a far bigger and broader global impact. No prior event has ever touched every person on earth at the same time.

The prophetic events that are to occur at Garabandal are breathtaking and will defy natural law. At the time of this writing, there are five Cardinals and many bishops who are openly saying they see signs of *"the end times"* in our midst. More people of all faiths believe we are in *"the end of times,"* and are willing to openly discuss it. Even the secular press now speak in terms that we are now battling evil. Due to the extreme evil in our world, they have come to the logical conclusion that what is happening is not of human origin. The earth is vomiting due to such grievous sin and is groaning in agony (Romans 8:22), and the Lord will not idly standby before Grace makes a move to remedy the situation. Some are obdurate, blind and insensitive to the sin in our midst, while others see that Heaven has an agenda. Not the end of the world, as one may say in an attempt to discredit the argument, but the end of an age, an era, or epoch of time. Similar to the age of the Old Testament under Mosaic Law that shifted to a New Testament with the Incarnation and Resurrection of Jesus Christ. Once the redemption of man took place with the birth of Jesus, life and Scripture took on a new dimension as the Jews became the elder brothers in the faith. With the Warning and the Great Miracle, we will enter the period of a New Era, a New Time!

What is the Lord doing? Is there a timetable? What are we to expect? No one knows the precise answers to these questions, but we are potentially not far off from momentous changes, if what has been spoken about is true. What we are being told is that before the events, there will be chaos and war in the world. What you once knew is no longer, and the safety net of government is largely gone, or at least disintegrating rapidly, and not working as originally designed. With the monstrous deficits governments are running with reckless printing of fiat currencies, this cannot go on much longer.

We are moving forward in a new direction. What worked in the past is not working now, and plans are afoot for global government that will add new dimensions to our lives at a bewildering and rapid pace. Most people will wilt under the changes and bend a knee to tyrannical leaders, and not be able to adapt and cope unless they have solid spiritual formation prior to the events. The globalist goal is to give people a social credit score as in Communist China to monitor all activities. Systems are now in place to execute that plan. This globalist goal is in direct preparation for the Antichrist. The goal is Agenda 2030 under the United Nations, with the ideology of the World Economic Forum (WEF), and other large multi and transnational bodies behind it. Previously, it had been called Agenda 2020, but the date was just pushed out further to 2030 to give advocates of transforming the world with a new tangible goal and vision for the future to effectuate radical change. Every area of life will be affected, and no one will come away unscathed from the changes.

If one were to look at the world, mankind has run out of answers to govern itself. It is not a question of looking at the glass half full, it is seeing that mankind is on the precipice of destruction, and due to the interconnectivity of the world, it is more serious now than in the past. A spark from just about anywhere could ignite a world-wide maelstrom that could generate a massive tsunami of destruction. There would be uncontrollable wars were it not for the grace of Heaven to stop the carnage. The Blessed Mother told Sister Lucy of Fatima, *"Wars are a punishment for the sins of mankind."* The anxiety and commotion of our times are birthing a New Era that will lead us to an Era of Peace.

Satan knows his time is short, thus the flurry of evil in our day. It is like watching a major sporting event in the last two minutes. Both teams know it is down to the final minutes, thus the frenetic activity. Garabandal will be a Divine Reset countering the Great Reset designed by men, and it will be on Heaven's terms, like the world has never seen. It will offset the evil of our day, and it will happen in an instant, changing the world as we know it. People will soon speak of time before the Warning and Miracle and after the Warning and the Miracle. It will be like we now designate centuries and millennia as Before Christ (BC) and Anno Domini (AD). The Miracle and the Permanent Sign will be things for people to know and remember, and history will speak of them.

Heaven has an agenda and it is filled with grace. We can either accept it, or fight it. It is a personal choice. If a person is unsure whether Garabandal is true, wisdom would say to remain quiet to not quench the work of the Holy Spirit. If it is not true, it won't matter. But if it is true, nothing you can do or say will stop it. This would be a similar situation of Rabbi Gamaliel when he spoke to the Jews who did not know what to do after the death of Jesus. As they fought amongst themselves at Pentecost, addressing the Sanhedrin he said, "What I suggest, therefore, is that you leave these men alone and let them go. If this enterprise, this movement of theirs, is of human origin it will break up of its own accord; but if it does in fact come from God you will not only be unable to destroy them, but you might find yourselves fighting against God" (Acts 5:38-39).

What is prophesied to take place at Garabandal is of such mind-numbing scope, it is impossible to fully comprehend in its totality. The events will be God's ultimate acts of mercy on a scale the world has never seen before.

This book will present a short synopsis of what happened and what is expected to happen when Our Lady came and foretold future events for the world and the Church. Due to the poverty of space, many poignant and important aspects of the story cannot be told. The point of this narrative is principally on the Warning, and the Great Miracle — and **WHY the apparitions took place is crucial to understand.**

The Village and the Beginnings

San Sebastian de Garabandal was a tiny village of about 300 people and about 70 small stone homes in the Diocese of Santander, when the Blessed Mother first appeared in 1961. At the time of the apparition there wasn't a motor with moving parts in the entire village and only one telephone. The townspeople were simple and devout. The homes had no electricity or running water, and heat was created only from home fireplaces or animals living near the homes. Less than one-quarter of a mile to the north of the tiny local church, are the nine pines where the Blessed Mother frequently appeared. These pines which tower over the village are tucked in a valley that is a natural amphitheater where millions could comfortably sit and look down on them. It is this spot where the Great Miracle is prophesied to happen.

The story of Garabandal began on the evening of June 18, 1961, when the Archangel Michael appeared to four young girls. The Archangel made eight silent appearances during the following twelve days. The visionaries were: Conchita Gonzalez (age twelve), Jacinta Gonzalez (age twelve), Mari Cruz Gonzalez (age eleven), none of whom were sisters (second cousins), and Mari Loli Mazon (age twelve). On July 1, St. Michael finally spoke to announce that on the following day the Blessed Virgin Mary would appear to the girls as Our Lady of Mount Carmel. The Blessed Mother then appeared on July 2, 1961 to the children. This was the **Feast of the Visitation** of Mary to Elizabeth, Mother of John the Baptist (more modern church calendar). In the old Latin rite calendar this was the *Feast of the Ark of the Covenant.*

The Ark of the Covenant contained the signs of God's presence among His chosen people, and was a physical sign of the Lord's covenant with His people. Throughout the times of the Hebrew people, the Ark would accompany them into battle, and Our Lady is showing us she is leading us into battle as the Ark of the New Covenant.

During her series of visitations at Garabandal, Our Lady was only visible to the four girls and one priest, but she had much to do in San Sebastian de Garabandal, and had things of exceedingly grave importance to tell all humanity. She let us know the sequence of events, unprecedented in human history, which will bring about the *"End of the Times."* She told us what must be done as she knew the fate of all humanity is at stake, just as in the days of Noah. The village became very crowded that day.

It was just before 6:00 PM, when the four girls were making their way up the "calleja" (lane or pathway, and in this instance, it was rocky) when they suddenly exclaimed, *"The Virgin!"* The Mother of Jesus appeared sent by God with an Angel on each side. She told the girls that one of these was St. Michael. The girls did not seem to recognize the other angel who was dressed like St. Michael and looked almost identical. Years later, Jacinta said that she was very sure that the other angel was St. Gabriel.

During this rather lengthy visit from Heaven, the four girls had a very relaxed and familiar conversation with the Blessed Mother. They told the Lady all sorts of things they had been doing in their village. The Lady smiled at their words.

From Conchita's Diary:

"We had not yet arrived at the scene of the apparitions when the Blessed Virgin appeared with an angel on each side. One of the two angels who accompanied her was Saint Michael. The other I didn't recognize. He was dressed exactly like Saint Michael. They looked like twins. Beside the angel, who stood at the Blessed Virgin's right and at the same height as she, was a large eye which seemed to be the eye of God.

"That day we talked a lot with the Blessed Virgin, as she did with us. We told her everything. We told her that we went out to the fields, that we were tanned from the sun, that we put the hay in the stacks, etc. And she laughed as we told her all these things." (It was the first apparition of Our Lady of Garabandal (July 2, 1961). Garabandal was going to be converted into a place touched by the presence of Our Heavenly Mother.

"Her hands are open and there is a scapular hanging from the right hand: the scapular is brown. Her hair is long, a dark chestnut brown color, wavy, parted in the middle; the face somewhat elongated; the nose also somewhat long, and fine; the mouth, very beautiful with lips a little full; the color of her face tan, much lighter than that of the angel, different. The voice, very beautiful, a voice very unusual. I don't know how to explain it. There is no other woman who resembles the Virgin, either in voice or in anything. Sometimes she carries the Baby in her arms. He is very small, like a newborn baby with a round face the same color as the Virgin's. He has a very small mouth, and hair slightly long. She is dressed in something like a blue tunic. Her face was oval with a fine nose. The girls said, "No other woman looks like her or sounds like her."[3]

Interior Calls Preceding Ecstatic Raptures

The girls' visions were preceded by three interior calls (llamadas), each becoming stronger than the last. After the third call they would run where the visions first began and crash to their knees on the jagged rocks, and entering into a Heavenly rapture. Coming from different places in the village, they would all arrive at the same time. Their heads were thrown back, the pupils of their eyes dilated and their faces imbued with an angelic countenance. Phenomena frequently occurred that defied natural law as they would fall to their knees in spiritual ecstasy. The girls found it hard to explain this interior call, and how they knew to show up for a meeting with Our Lady.[4]

They were insensitive to pin pricks, burns, physical contact or bright spotlights shone directly into their eyes. Their weight factor changed so much that two grown men had great difficulty in lifting one 12-year-old girl, and yet the girls could lift each other with the greatest of ease to offer a kiss to the Virgin.

Bookends — Two Key Messages

"Immediately after the tribulation of those days, the sun will be darkened, and the moon will not give its light, and the stars will fall from the sky, and the powers of the heavens will be shaken. And then the sign of the Son of Man will appear in Heaven, and all the tribes of the earth will mourn, and they will see the Son of Man coming upon the clouds

of Heaven with power and great glory. And He will send out
His angels with a trumpet blast, and they will gather His elect from
the four winds, from one end of the heavens to the other"

(MATTHEW 24:29-31).

1961. Our Lady revealed the first key message for the world. She told the girls to announce the message publicly on **October 18, 1961.** On this day, the children made known the message, "Many sacrifices must be made, much penance must be done. We must pay many visits to the Blessed Sacrament… but first of all we must be very good… **if we do not do this, punishment awaits us… already the cup is filling, and if we do not change, we will be punished."** That message given to the young girls was heavily centered on conversion and amendment of life. The Blessed Mother had a continual theme as to the urgency of our times and what would happen, IF man does not repent.

The message continued, "If you ask pardon with a sincere soul, He will pardon you. It is I your Mother, who through the intercession of Saint Michael, wish to say that you amend, that you are already in the last warnings and that I love you much and do not want your condemnation. Ask us sincerely and we will give to you. You should sacrifice more. Think of the Passion of Jesus." Our Lady appeared wearing the Brown Scapular, an indication we should wear it, and taught the children how to pray the Rosary. Her greatest emphasis was placed on the Eucharist and prayers for priests.

1965. On January 1, 1965, the Blessed Virgin told Conchita that the Archangel Michael would appear to her on the following June 18th to deliver a final message in Mary's name for the entire world, because her first message was not heeded. Saint Michael appeared to Conchita while she was in ecstasy, which lasted approximately sixteen minutes. **On June 18, 1965** the following message was delivered to the world." As my message of **October 18th** (1961) has not been complied with and has not been made known to the world, I am advising you that this is the last one. **Before the cup was filling up. Now it is flowing over. Many cardinals, many bishops, and many priests are on the road to perdition and are taking many souls with them. Less and less importance is being given to the Eucharist.**

"You should turn the wrath of God away from yourselves by your efforts. If you ask His forgiveness with sincere hearts, He will pardon you. I, your mother, through the intercession of Saint Michael the Archangel, ask you to amend your lives. You are now receiving the last warning."

There are several very important things contained in the above message. First and foremost, beyond temporal concerns, is the importance of fidelity and obedience to the faith. Where there is no fidelity, there will be adverse consequences for humanity. It states clearly if people do not change, there will be punishment. Also, some cardinals and bishops are leading souls to perdition. Not just priests, but bishops and cardinals. **These are profound statements with broad implications** for the Church, the family, and the culture. It would be wise to reflect on these two messages and what they mean for us today. At the time those messages were given, the challenges to the Church with the changes that Vatican II brought had not been implemented, and the sexual scandal involving clergy had not unfolded. The gathering of bishops from all over the world at Vatican II took place during the middle of the apparitions at Garabandal. This is a profound commentary beyond measure of what Heaven saw in advance and alerted the world. However, the seeds of destruction had already been securely planted in the seminaries of the world previously to bring the Church in an entirely different direction.

The Essence of the Story

When the messages were given at Garabandal, it was a primary source of information to caution the world about Heaven's plan for the salvation of mankind — and to prepare the world for what is coming. It had been expected that Pope John XXIII would reveal the Third Secret of Fatima in 1960, but he did not, to the disappointment of the faithful. Is it a coincidence that just a year later the Blessed Mother came to Garabandal, and gave messages specifically addressing the importance of the Eucharist and the Priesthood? At the same time Vatican II was in session, and many in the Church were meeting behind the scenes, there was a rogue element deliberately and in stealth, undermining Magisterial tradition. This was similar to what became known as the Saint Gallen Group that met in private in Saint Gallen, Switzerland in the years before the election of Pope Francis.

For many people in the Church, the truth about the Third Secret of Fatima is as elusive as the location of the Ark of the Covenant. Many believe the Church has never officially released the message in total. We know a portion of it deals with a pope dressed in white being killed. Yet, that has not happened.

There is still continued dialogue on the exact contents of the Third Secret, as well as the issue of the Consecration of Russia which is still a contentious point among many people of good will. It is a never-ending story that grows. Pope Francis consecrated the world from Rome mentioning Ukraine on October 13, 2013, yet never mentioned just the name Russia as Our Lady asked. Russia was central to Mary's call for consecration at Fatima in 1917, and Russia and Communism are central to Garabandal as well. The Blessed Mother has said to the Marian Movement of Priests, it is now *"My Time,"* due to the lack of cooperation of God's people to fulfiill her plan for peace.

There are still powerful forces within the Church blocking the full release of the Third Secret. The political maneuverings inside the Vatican are as significant as any issue in the Church over the last several hundred years. Why? Because many insiders, sources, and apparition sites over the last several decades have told us the Third Secret deals with Communism, the destruction of the Church from within, deep apostasy inside the Church, widespread calamities such as *"fire from heaven,"* millions of humanity perishing, and Satan reaching the very summit of the Church. One must ask, what is the "summit" of the Church?

There is widespread opposition to the Secret being released for obvious reasons. Cardinal Ratzinger (Pope Benedict XVI) while head of the Congregation for the Prefect of the Faith (CDF), having read the Third Secret of Fatima, said the Church-approved messages of Akita, Japan and Fatima "are essentially the same." No messages in the entire history of the Holy Roman Catholic and Apostolic Church are as apocalyptic and severe as those from Akita, Japan where it was said, "The living would envy the dead." Pope Benedict XVI while speaking at Fatima on May 13, 2010 made an interesting point when he said, "May the seven years which separate us from the centenary of the apparitions hasten the fulfillment of the prophecy of the Triumph of the Immaculate Heart of Mary to the glory of the Most Holy Trinity." This put the centenary at 2017.

CHAPTER 3

Like Three Acts in the Same Play

"I consider that the sufferings of this present time are not worth comparing with the glory that is to be revealed to us. For the creation waits with eager longing for the revealing to the sons of God."

ROMANS 8:18-19

The prophecies of Garabandal tell us that three of the greatest supernatural events in the history of mankind are to take place:

WORLD-WIDE WARNING: It will come from God. All will experience it.

GREAT MIRACLE: God will perform a great miracle.
What it is exactly is not known, but we have been told it will be
much greater than the miracle of the sun at Fatima.

PERMANENT SIGN: After the great Miracle,
a sign, something that has never been seen before on earth,
will remain forever in "the nine pines" of Garabandal.

CHASTISEMENT: This punishment is conditional upon
the response of mankind to these messages.

Our Lady's messages at Garabandal promised three supernatural events, and possibly a fourth. The Warning will be seen and felt by everyone in the world, but the Miracle and Permanent Sign will take place specifically at Garabandal. A fourth may be a chastisement that is contingent for the entire world, depending upon the response to the Warning. Conchita wrote in a letter on January 1, 1965, **"Our Lady said that a Warning would be given to the entire world before the Miracle in order that the world might** amend itself. It will come directly from God and be visible throughout the entire world."

The Transition of Civilization Takes Place, Two Events to Come — The First Will be the Warning, Followed by the Miracle

Conchita wrote on June 2, 1965: **"The Warning, like the chastisement, is a fearful thing for the good as well as the wicked. It will draw the good closer to God and warn the wicked that the end of times is coming. These are the last warnings."** Conchita explained that the Warning is a purification to prepare us for the Miracle. She believes that after it occurs, we will be near the end of times. Each person on earth will have an interior experience of how he or she stands in the light of God's Justice. Believers and non-believers alike will experience the Warning. Mari Loli said, "We will see it and feel it within ourselves and it will be most clear that it comes from God." Jacinta Gonzalez said: "The Warning is something that is first seen in the air, everywhere in the world, and immediately is transmitted into the interior of our souls. It will last for a very little time, but it will seem a very long time because of its effect within us. It will be for the good of our souls, in order to see in ourselves. The good that we have failed to do, and the bad that we have done. Then we will feel a great love towards our heavenly Parents and ask forgiveness for all our offenses. The Warning is for everybody because God wants our salvation. The Warning is for us to draw closer to Him and to increase our faith. Therefore, one should prepare for that day, but not await it with fear. God does not send things for the sake of fear but rather with love. He does it for the good of all His children so they might enjoy eternal happiness and not be lost."

Something that is seldom spoken of is that Lucia, Francisco, and Jacinta, the young visionaries at Fatima described something similar: seeing oneself in the Divine Light of Truth. On the very first apparition of May 13, 1917, Our Lady revealed Divine Mysteries in an aura of light exactly how the visionaries of Garabandal speak of it. Lucia wrote, ***"We were able to see ourselves in God, Who was this Light, more clearly than we see ourselves in the best of mirrors."*** All three of the children witnessed themselves as God would see them, and more importantly, what God was asking of them. Each of their faith grew after this event, and they took their spiritual life more seriously. Garabandal speaks of a Warning, and it singularly speaks of a great Miracle at the nine pines, and both events are designed by Heaven so people can amend their lives and take their faith more seriously, which is exactly the impact it had on the three young children at Fatima.

Just two months after the first apparition, on July 13, 1917, all three Fatima visionaries witnessed a vision of Hell. The impact that this would have on nine-year old Francisco Marto (nine is very young) is hard to imagine. Heaven decided it would be beneficial for these very young children to see Hell. Today, if one were to speak of Hell, many would consider it extreme or even cruel to reveal to a child as the faith has become so sanitized. Yet, Heaven thought otherwise in 1917. Up until his premature death of the Spanish flu on April 4, 1919, Francisco spent his remaining time praying the Rosary and consoling God for the sins of mankind. He would often make visits to the Blessed Sacrament to see *"the Hidden Jesus."*

Why an illumination of conscience at Fatima is seldom mentioned is puzzling. It can validate other apparitions where there are similar events. One can see consistencies if there is a cumulative knowledge of what happens when the Blessed Mother appears.

Father Joseph Brennan, O.C.S., an early writer on Garabandal, summarized the prophetic statements made by saints, blessed, and popes said, "They foretell a time of unprecedented and terrible confusion and suffering unlike anything that has ever been experienced in human history. It will affect every area of human life."

The events prophesied are of supernatural deliverance where there is no answer for mankind unless it is by the hand of Almighty God Himself. The mission of Jesus was and still is to deliver men from the bondage of sin. The memorial of His sign is a testament to what He says will happen for His glory, and for the benefit of his people. God speaks through signs to show His people He can be trusted, that He is true to His promises.

The Warning will be our Damascus Road moment like that of Saul, who became the Apostle Paul, when he was knocked from his horse and penetrated by the same light we will soon endure. Saul was on his way to Damascus to persecute the new Christian converts. Saul's self-righteous bigotry was so strong, it took the Lord Himself to knock him to the ground (Acts 4:9) In a glorious vision, Jesus revealed to Saul that he was assailing not only the members of the Church, but persecuting Jesus Himself. The blinding light of the Risen Christ convicted him of his sin. Saul heeded the warning Jesus had given him; he repented, and became the Lord's faithful follower. A follower of Jesus in Damascus named Ananias was told in a vision to lay hands on Saul to restore his sight, and fill him with the Holy Spirit (Acts 9). Saul, who approved of the stoning of the first Christian martyr Saint Stephen, soon became the great Paul, after the *"illumination of soul."* The same grace granted to Saul will penetrate every human heart in a sudden burst of Divine light. Saint Paul became the first "visionary" of the New Testament as his teaching came from infused knowledge in the desert of Arabia for three years (Galatians 1:17). Saul had never met or walked with Jesus, and his teachings came directly from the Holy Spirit through a gift of grace. Many of us who have our own insular views on what God may or may not do will shortly be knocked off our horse as well.

The Complete Transformation of a Soul, The Warning/Illumination of Conscience/Life Review/Judgment in Miniature is a worldwide event where everyone in the world will see the state of their soul as God would judge them, based upon the life they have lived. It brings one's thinking to *The Four Last Things:* DEATH, JUDGMENT, HEAVEN, HELL. We will know that it is God communicating in absolute love, and there will be no rebuttal. There will be no exceptions to this. After speaking to numerous people over the last thirty years who have experienced a near-death experience (NDE), which is often like a life review, I have learned it often takes them years to emotionally and intellectually sort it out and put the event into words. The Warning will be more profound than a near death experience.

Believers who know the messages of Garabandal have been waiting many years for the events prophesied at Garabandal to come to pass. But, one thing is certain, with the speed of events in an interconnected world, and with all of the chaos and flash points possible for world conflict, things could happen in an instant.

The **Warning and the Miracle** will be a line of demarcation in history. The choice of living for God and the pursuit of virtue or sin will be more evident as the veil of Satan's lies will be clearer for all to see who just experienced the Warning. As the Jews wandered in the desert after they left four hundred years of captivity in Egypt, it was not long before they forgot what God had done for them. Shortly thereafter they were making a golden calf in the desert (scholars say six weeks).

Manna and quail were falling from the sky to feed the migratory people heading to the promised land, yet they were soon offering up a pagan rite.

It will be the same after the Warning for some, where many will forget the graces of the Warning, and continue in their sinful ways.

The Warning is a Purification to Prepare the World for the Miracle

There is great speculation on what the Warning will entail. Conchita said it will be like **"two heavenly bodies colliding."** Conchita explained "that the Warning is a purification to prepare us for the Miracle. Each person on earth will have an interior experience of how he or she stands in the light of God's Justice. Believers and non-believers alike will experience the Warning." Conchita said, "Those living in a state of grace will have less severe impact." Mari Loli said, **"We will see it and feel it within ourselves, and it will be most clear that it comes from God."**

The Lord in His infinite love and mercy for humanity continues to provide every opportunity for His people to make amends. Evidence from many sources in the world today, indicates that the day of reckoning may be soon upon us. Just as prophets like Amos, Ezekiel, Jeremiah, Jonah, and Isaiah warned the people of impending judgments, we too are being warned. **The great multiplicity of Our Lady's apparitions shows the urgency of our times.** The Warning and Miracle will be events on a scale unprecedented in the world and the Church. There are miraculous things like days of darkness that are written about **several** times in Scripture, but the Warning and Great Miracle will be new to mankind. If one includes the Permanent Sign left at Garabandal until the end of time, it will be like three acts in one play, all over a short period of time.

Whatever the Warning actually is, we know it is a major event. Pedro Regis a visionary from Brazil provides what may be a glimpse into the event when he says,

> "God will speak to mankind by extraordinary signs. A great sign will be given to humanity, but if men and women don't repent, the wrath of God will fall upon humanity. People will see something like the sun visible in the sky for many hours. All eyes will see it."[5]

Pedro continues "Rejoice for all of your names are written in Heaven. All of you know that the Lord will manifest His Mercy to mankind. He wants to save you. The Lord will show mankind a great sign. **A great cross will be seen in the whole world. People will be able to contemplate it and the**

Lord will bless their lives. It will be a grand chance for the conversion of humanity.[6]

"The Lord will show His power in favor of mankind. The Lord loves you and calls you. God will send a great sign to mankind and all eyes will see it. Gold will be in the heights, and flames will cross the sky."[7] Again Pedro speaks of this event, "The great sign will be seen by all. A great cross will illuminate the sky and all eyes will see it. This will be a great chance for everybody to repent and return to the God of salvation and peace.[8]

The above message from Pedro Regis is similar to the message of Saint Faustina (Diary Number 83) when the Lord told her, "The Sign in the Heavens … the cross will be seen in the sky…"

Just when it appears all is lost, Heaven will not abandon its children. By and large some people may know of these events coming our way through friends and family, but it tends to be almost exclusively Catholics that have been receptive to it. Why? Because it has been the Blessed Mother as the Prophetess of our age saying it, preparing us for many years about what is to come. Other denominations, who do not understand her role in these times are generally not open to what she says at apparition sites, thus their lack of awareness or openness to Garabandal – at least for now. She has been appointed by the Most Holy Trinity for her task at this point in time, as we move to the culmination of the battle. Satan's cohort is battling God's cohort for the soul of mankind. In Revelation 12, the Woman Clothed with the Sun is in battle as the Queen of Heaven and Earth, as Satan makes his last gasp. Many Catholics, including some clergy, reject the messages when she speaks, or will only address her messages in hushed terms for fear of being marginalized by their congregations or confreres. The faithful will often venerate her as a symbol in history, but they will shun her when someone speaks of her majesty and mission in the world. Many believe her activity stopped at Fatima and refuse to address the last 100 years. Soon, there will be no getting around what she has been saying, as we will know the appointed time by the events themselves. As theoretical and practical atheism have taken over the culture, the messages of Garabandal will show mankind an alternative.

CHAPTER 4

The Nights of Screams

The First Night of Screams

Over time, more information has been gleaned, and interviews given about the forthcoming events of Garabandal. One such event where information came over time was called the Nights of Screams. Both nights happened at 10:30 pm. The first night of screams lasted 50 minutes and took place on June 19, 1962. Jacinta, Mari Loli, and Mary Cruz saw visions **where Russia would have dominion over the world, and Communism would rule Europe. Priests would go into hiding, churches would be destroyed, and there would be many martyrs.** The girls were shown in a vision, that rivers would turn red with blood, the Church would be persecuted and decimated, its buildings will no longer exist as they once did, professing your faith would be very difficult, and the Sacraments would be difficult to receive. The girls were heard crying out, **"Stop telling us those things! Wait, Wait! Everyone should confess…. They should get ready!"** When it appears all is lost, the Warning would come. Barry Hanratty wrote in the *Garabandal Journal,* "Their tear-stained faces and incoherent speech immediately afterwards attested to the trauma experienced by Jacinta, Mari Loli and Mari Cruz during the first night of screams, and it doesn't appear that they gave many details of what they experienced for quite some time."

Shortly afterwards, Jacinta and Mari Loli confirmed the coming Chastisement.

> "The Virgin told us, that we do not expect the Chastisement. That without expecting it, it will come, since the world has not changed. And she has already told us twice, and we do not pay attention to her, since the world is getting worse. And it should change very much, and it has not changed at all. Prepare yourself. Confess, because the Chastisement will come soon. And the world continues the same …."

The Second Night of Screams

On June 20, 1962, on the Vigil of Corpus Christi, there was another horrifying vision that lasted for three and a half hours. The girls saw destructive things happening in the world at a future time. Mari Loli Mason said, "We saw rivers change into blood...fire fell from the sky...and something worse still which I am not able to reveal now..." Three of the girls were shown the Great Chastisement of fire that would come if humanity reverts to its evil ways after the grace of the Great Miracle. The girls were heard saying, **"Oh! Don't let this happen, don't let this come. May everyone go to confession first! Forgive us! Don't let this happen!"**

June 23, 1962: Our Lady gives Jacinta and Mari Loli the following important message:

> "The Virgin has told us: that the world continues the same, that it has not changed at all; that few will see God; so few they are, that it is causing the Virgin great sorrow. How unfortunate that the world does not change! The Virgin has told us that the Chastisement is coming. As the world is not changing, the cup is filling up. How sorrowful is the Virgin, although she does not allow us to see it. Since the Virgin loves us so much, she suffers alone, since she is so good. Everyone be good, so that the Virgin will be happy! She has told us that those who are good should pray for those who are evil.
>
> Yes, we should pray to God for the world, for those who do not know Him.
>
> Be good, be very good."

With the coalition of the NATO nations and the US providing munitions and more sophisticated military hardware to Ukraine, and China aiding Russia, the actions and the rhetoric of world war are increasingly alarming to the entire global community. Europe and the world are at a crucial point. When Conchita visited Saint Pio (padre) in his monastery in Italy at San Giovanni Rotondo, he told Conchita that the Miracle of Garabandal will accompany "the blood of Europeans and oceans of blood."

Padre Pio wrote Conchita a letter and said,

> "I give you only one counsel: Pray and make others pray, because the world is at the beginning of perdition. They do not believe in you

or in your conversations with the Lady in White… **They will believe when it will be too late."**

Abortion Referenced by Our Lady

Among the many prophecies of Garabandal was one that only came to light with the publication of Albrecht Weber's book, *Garabandal — The Finger of God*, released in 1993 (revised in 2000). Weber was in Garabandal on the day of Conchita's last apparition on November 13, 1965, and had a conversation with the visionary. The following excerpt from his book deals with some of what the visionary told him:

She (Conchita) spoke quite openly about the developments by which men in the near future would rebel against God. On the day after Our Lady's last appearance at Garabandal, Conchita asked the author how someone can kill a child without killing the mother? The author spontaneously answered, "Now, what gave you that idea"?

Conchita: "Well, the Blessed Mother spoke about this and she let me know that this will happen with the overflowing of the chalice." In the second message of June 18, 1965, the Virgin said, "Before the cup was filling up. Now it is flowing over."

Conchita said this trembling, without being able to visualize what it really implied. She said it disturbed her very much but that she felt ridiculous because she had not understood at all how this could happen. The Blessed Virgin had not explained it to her, and up until that moment, nobody had been able to explain it to her at all.

Conchita would learn soon enough when abortion became legalized, even in her own country.[9]

The Mass Suppressed and Priests in Hiding

One of the powerful prophecies of Garabandal is that a time would come when the **Mass will be suppressed, and priests will go into hiding.** The word **suppressed** should be examined. The various definitions range from emotive, all the way to violent. They are to *"put down by authority of force, to press down, to exclude from consciousness, all the way **to decimate**."* There are places in the world where priests are persecuted and much worse. Those who follow the Traditional Latin Mass (TLM) have been marginalized, as well as priests who wish to celebrate it. The Mass did change after Vatican II, and people that go to the TLM are aware of the hostility Pope Francis has to it. There are people who attend the TLM today who feel that this prophecy has been fulfilled as the TLM has already been suppressed. There are two separate issues. One is suppression and the other is much more serious with priests having difficulty saying the Mass, and having to go into hiding. It would logically seem that priests going into hiding would indicate serious social unrest, with a tyrannical government imposing unjust laws. However, to date, it has been the Church that has made it increasingly difficult for priests to celebrate the TLM.

Russia Suddenly and Unexpectedly Overruns a Great Part of the Free World

Mari Loli was often asked, "Since you are not allowed to tell me the exact year of the Warning, perhaps you could tell me approximately when it will happen? "Loli would respond, **"It will be at a time when the world will most need it."**

Loli continued, **"When Russia will suddenly and unexpectedly overrun a great part of the free world.** God does not want this to happen so quickly. In any case, the Warning will come when you will see the **Holy Mass cannot be celebrated freely anymore; then it will be that the world will most need the intervention of God."**

For those following Garabandal and other Catholic prophecies, Russia is still the country to watch. During the most recent Russia/Ukraine war, a Russian general said, "It would take us all of about six minutes to get into Poland." Poland is a country that has produced some of the great saints of the twentieth century: Saint Faustina, Saint Maximilian Kolbe, and Saint John Paul II to name just a few. The country happens to be sandwiched between two aggressive nations, namely Russia and Germany. For hundreds of Russian tanks to roll over eastern Europe and further west is quite plausible.

Mari Loli did not know the date of the Warning, only the year. Conchita alone knows the day of the Miracle. Mari Loli also said that the Blessed Mother told her prior to the Warning and the Great Miracle, "A time would come when it would look like the Church was finished, when priests would have difficulty saying Mass and talking about holy things. There would come a time when the Church would give the impression of being on the point of perishing. It would pass through a terrible test. Priests would supposedly have to hide in order to say Mass. It is then that the world will be in most need of God's intervention." When she asked Our Lady how this would happen, Our Lady called it "**Communism.**" This has happened in many countries already. Whether or not it will be more widespread remains to be seen. The trend is that the world is increasingly negating the role of God.

It is much easier to manipulate and control an individual who does not acknowledge the truth of Christianity, which is precisely why it must be removed by a tyrannical totalitarian government. Christianity breeds independent thought, contrary to godless tyrants and allegiance to a Higher Power (which all dictators consider a threat). We have seen the brutality of Communist regimes from the USSR and China and other brutal dictators, but Communism is simply a government where God cannot be publicly acknowledged or displayed — in any form. Through sophisticated social engineering, much of the West, and the world at large, exhibit a form of atheism — or communism as it comes to everyday living. A world without God is the Socialist, Marxist, Atheistic, Communist, Masonic global elite goal.

The Blessed Mother once told Conchita, "**It would be like an invasion of Communism.**" Premier Mikhail Gorbachev said the event that toppled the USSR was the nuclear disaster at Chernobyl April 26, 1986. The ramifications of Soviet incompetence spreading throughout western borders was no longer acceptable to the West, and Gorbachev was firm when he said it was this event that led to the 1992-1994 downfall of the USSR. As the world watches the destruction of Ukraine and the issues that it is causing world-wide, a major event from anywhere in that region could escalate to catastrophe

In 1988, on the 1,000-year anniversary of Kiev/Rus, General Secretary of the Communist Party of the Soviet Union Mikhail Gorbachev said the mistake of the Bolshevik Revolution was they tried to remove God from the Russian soul too abruptly. He said this was not possible in a short period of time, and it was the significant longitudinal reason the revolution failed. What a striking truth he articulated. Gorbachev later said, speaking from the Presidio in San Francisco, California, that Communism needed more of the approach of socialism with small steady incremental changes, because with this strategy the people would not notice what the government was really doing. "If we had followed that incremental approach," Gorbachev said, "we would have achieved our goals much more easily."

The girls described **the times of tribulation "as the return of Communism."** Four young mountain children in the early 1960's would not have had any understanding of what Communism meant. In political philosophy, Communism does not necessarily have to be violent, although it usually is. Communist ideology for generations has been embedded in the classroom, indoctrinating youth without using the word. It is much more sophisticated than outright preaching a communist doctrine. Communism has been socially engineered through language manipulation. We increasingly see a world that does not want God in peoples' lives — especially the classroom. The spiritual, moral, and sexual assault against children in our culture is unprecedented in world history. Many classrooms across the world are cesspools of impurity, with a lack of any moral formation, teaching courses that promote and nurture an atheistic, godless ideology. Many countries, especially in the West, have outright reverted to teaching pagan practices. The progressive Marxist epistemology is that God is not wanted in the culture. This would constitute Communism returning on a much wider scale than what we have seen in the past in Bolshevik Russia or under the purges of Mao in China, using violence to coerce the masses.

According to Garabandal, Communism is still an element that must be addressed as real. It has a crucial role in the fulfillment of what is yet to happen on an on-going basis. On September 29, 1978, esteemed Jesuit and scholar of Garabandal, Father Francis Benac, S.J., interviewed Mari Loli at her home in Haverhill, Massachusetts. He had a particular focus on addressing Communism. The following questions were asked:

Father Benac: Did the Blessed Virgin speak of Communism?

Mari Loli: Our Lady spoke several times of Communism. I don't remember how many times, but she said a time would come when it would seem that Communism had mastered or engulfed the whole world. I think it was then that she told us that priests would have difficulty saying Mass, and talking about God and divine things.

Fr. Benac: Did Our Lady ever speak of people being put to death?

Mari Loli: What Our Lady said is that priests would have to go into hiding, but I didn't see whether they were killed or not. She didn't exactly say they would be killed, but I am sure they would be martyred.

Fr. Benac: Your mother told me that one night you were upstairs with your father and that you cried and cried for one hour. Afterwards your father said to her: "I have seen the most touching sight. Loli was crying the whole time while saying, **Oh, it is going to be bad like that in the Church?** People are going to suffer like that? Oh, make me suffer!" Do you remember what you said at the time?

Mari Loli: It was all related to Communism and what is going to happen in the Church and to the people because all these things are to have repercussions amongst the people. When the Church suffers confusion, the people are going to suffer too. Some priests who are communists will create such confusion that people will not know right from wrong.[10]

Are We Close to the Warning?

How much closer to this year of the Warning could we be? At this point in America, many leading political figures are far more Communist than socialist. Worldwide, America has lagged other countries in implementing Communist principles, but now seems eager to catch up. Many are promoting a Communist ideology, demanding faith be removed from the culture in every way possible. If politicians don't directly say it, they will often try to legislate it into reality, while they personally benefit from the largesse a capitalist structure affords them. The **"Invasion of Communism"** is gaining ground in the USA faster than at any time since the Great Depression of the 1930's. A world that submerges into moral relativism where sin does not exist fits a cleaner definition of Communism. Today we have people who do not obey the commandments of God, yet will attend church paying more attention to cultural and state norms than Biblical truth. In essence, a state run, politically acceptable faith void of God, is increasingly the situation in the U.S. Language engineering and social manipulation are key to controlling the populace and maintaining a godless narrative. We are seeing Our Lady's prophecy on Communism being fulfilled with state control of social and political structures. Inch by inch this goal has been achieved over several generations. Taking prayer (1962), and then the Bible (1963) out of the classroom by order of the United States Supreme Court saying it was unconstitutional, was a significant step to fulfill this agenda. In many ways, these two decisions sealed America's fate to the carnage we see today.

The events happening near a Synod may be another indication the time is getting closer, as we are presently in the midst of a three-year Synod on Synodality, which officially ends in October 2024.

The Warning in Perspective

Fear of God is a good thing, as Holy Scripture tells us, but the fear of God that is good is not the kind of fear that obsesses us, causes us to worry constantly, and ultimately robs us of our peace of mind and heart. The fear of God that is good is the fear that draws virtuous souls to God and prompts sinners to amend their lives. **The "fear" of the Lord** translates to **"awe of the awesome majesty"** of God. This is precisely the purpose that Conchita ascribed to the Warning. It will cause a holy respect for God.

CHAPTER 5

Is the Warning the Second Pentecost?

Message number 383 of the Marian Movement of Priests is titled, *The Holy Spirit Will Come.* The Blessed Mother says something absolutely breathtaking on the significance of the Warning. She said it is the **Second Pentecost.** The message was delivered on the Solemnity of Pentecost, May 22, 1988, in Heede Germany.

"This is the day which recalls the descent of the Holy Spirit upon the Apostles, gathered together in prayer with me in the Cenacle of Jerusalem. On this day of Pentecost of the Marian Year, consecrated to me, I am calling upon you to unite your prayer to that of your heavenly Mother, to obtain **the great gift of the Second Pentecost.** The time of the Second Pentecost has come.

"The Holy Spirit will come as a Heavenly dew of grace and of fire, which will renew all the world. Under His irresistible action of love, the Church will open itself to live the new era of its greatest holiness and will shine resplendently with so strong a light that it will attract to itself all the nations of the earth. The Holy Spirit will come, that the Will of the Heavenly Father be accomplished and the created universe once again reflect His great glory. The Holy Spirit will come, to establish the glorious reign of Christ, and it will be a reign of grace, of holiness, of love, of justice and of peace."

"With His divine love, He will open the doors of hearts and illuminate all consciences. Every person will see himself in the burning fire of divine truth. It will be like a **judgment in miniature.** And then Jesus Christ will bring His glorious reign in the world. The Holy Spirit will come, by means of the Triumph of my Immaculate Heart. For this, I am calling upon you all today to enter into the Cenacle of my Heart. Thus you will be prepared to receive the gift of the Holy Spirit which will **transform you** and make you the instruments with which Jesus will establish His reign."

The message above has enormous similarity of language and concepts to the Warning that is described at Garabandal. The locutions of the Marian

Movement of Priests addresses in elegant and majestic language Heaven's master plan for transforming the people of the world. The book *Our Lady Speaks to Her Beloved Sons,* shares public messages that Our Lady gave through Father Stefano Gobbi to priests and laity of her movement from July, 1973, to December 31, 1997 the last of which is titled, *All Has Been Revealed to You,* when she said, "I have given you the full and entire truth."

The apostles were frightened men after the crucifixion of Jesus and feared for their lives due to persecution. After receiving the Holy Spirit on Pentecost, they left the Cenacle room and went to the streets like roaring lions for the faith with no fear of man. The apostles were infused with the Holy Spirit in a supernatural way. This will be a similar event with the Second Pentecost. **All people in the world will see themselves in the "burning fire of divine truth, through a judgment in miniature, and illuminate all consciences"**[11] making them different people immediately. The promises continue. It is said, **"What will come to pass is something so very great that it will exceed anything that has taken place since the beginning of the world. It will be like a judgment in miniature, and each one will see his own life and all he has done in the very light of God."**[12]

Our Lady is Mother and Queen of the Universe. At this time in history, as the Ark of the New Covenant, she has taken a more exalted role speaking to her people, in her time and her Heart. The safety for the future is in her Immaculate Heart, under the guidance of the Most Holy Trinity. After the Second Pentecost happens, believers will be working with preternatural gifts, as the apostles did after the first Pentecost. As the Jews sprinkled blood on the door posts in Egypt for their safety so the angel of death would pass over them, the Blessed Mother tells us our safety and refuge in these times, lies in her Immaculate Heart.

The Warning is Worldwide

Father Joseph Pelletier (1912-1986), the late Marian scholar, author on Garabandal, and professor at Assumption College, Massachusetts, asked Conchita several questions and offered further insight about the events of Garabandal. Conchita's answer on June 19, 1965, is as follows: "Here in writing is the Warning that the Blessed Virgin gave me when I was alone at the pines on January 1st of this year, 1965. The Warning that the Blessed Virgin will give us is like a chastisement. Its purpose is to draw the good nearer to God and to warn the others. I cannot reveal what the Warning will consist of. The Blessed Virgin did not tell me to announce it. Nothing further. God would like that through this warning, we amend our lives and that we commit less sins against Him." To the question posed by Marian and Garabandal scholar Father Laffineur, whether the Warning would cause death, Conchita said, "If we die from it, it would not be from the Warning itself, but from the emotional shock that we would experience in seeing and feeling the Warning."

Statements were made by Conchita in response to questions put to her:

Q. Will the Warning be a visible thing or an interior thing or both?

Conchita. The Warning is a thing that comes directly from God. It will be visible all over the world, in whatever place anyone might be.

Q. Will the Warning reveal our personal sins to every person in the world and to persons of all faiths, including atheists?

Conchita. Yes, the Warning will be like the revelation of our sins, and it will be seen and felt equally by believers and non-believers, and people of any religion whatsoever.

In reply to a question whether the Warning might be a comet that was approaching the earth, Conchita said: "I don't know what a comet is. If it is something that depends on man's will, I answer — no. If it is something that God will do, it is quite possible." When the woman (interviewer) expressed fear, Conchita replied: "Oh, yes, the Warning will be very fearful, a thousand times worse than earthquakes." To an **inquiry concerning the nature of the Warning, Conchita answered: "It will not burn** our flesh, but we will feel it bodily and interiorly." She added, "We shall comment on this later. All nations and all persons will experience it in the same way. No one will escape it. Even the nonbelievers themselves will experience the fear of God. Even if you hide in your room and close the blinds, you will not escape it. You will feel and see it just the same. Yes, it is true. The Blessed Virgin gave me the name of the phenomenon. **"It begins with an A,** but she did not tell me to reveal it to anyone."

As the woman again expressed her fear, Conchita added: "Oh, but after the Warning, you will love the good Lord very much." To the question, what about the Miracle, she said, **"The Miracle will not delay in coming."**

Conchita added an interesting observation: "Although it is taking time to come, it will not be late. God's time is always the appropriate time."

It Begins with an A

The issue of what could begin with the letter "A" has been something that no one has ever come up with a reasonable answer to. Many have thought it could be an *Asteroid* as we are told there will be an event that would be like *"two stars colliding"* at some point — and it **will be seen and felt.**

There is a serious contender for what A means and it ties into several hundred years of Catholic prophecy. There is a comet coming towards earth by the name of Atlas, which is not an asteroid. However, we have been told what is coming has never been seen in the world before. Conchita has said it is not a comet, but like a comet, and something that has never been seen before. Below are some data points on this comet.

A. The comet is called Tsuchinshan – Atlas C/2023 A3

B. It was found by Chinese observatory Tsuchinshan and the Atlas Robotic Early Warning system in early January 2023. China named the comet. It is approaching earth at 80.74 kilometers per second.

C. It will come by again in another 80,000 years.

D. It will be closest to earth on Sunday, **October 13, 2024,** and will still be 44.3 million miles away.

E. It might outshine every star in the night sky and light up earth.

F. It will be the biggest comet in decades, and people will see it with the naked eye in the morning sky.

G. Comets are unpredictable, and data is not always accurate as comets approach earth. Historically, a great deal of the speculation on exactly what MAY happen fizzles out over time.

H. Atlas in Greek mythology is a Titan who holds up the heavens or sky for eternity.

There is also speculation about a prophecy saying it could be a worldwide rainbow, as the word for rainbow in Spanish is **Arcoiris.** A rainbow is very plausible, as it is a sign of **Mercy.** We have seen a rainbow in Genesis with Noah's Ark, Exodus, Ezekiel, and Revelation. It is not a new concept for God to use a rainbow as a symbol to communicate with His people. As Almighty

God can do anything, perhaps both an Aurora and an Arcoirus could occur simultaneously all around the world, visible to the observer day or night.

The problem is that a rainbow would only be seen in the daylight, and the world is not all light or all dark all at the same time. We have been told the Warning will be felt, and a rainbow is not felt. The word Abanico is another Spanish word for colors in a spectrum. Saint John Bosco on the Feast of the Epiphany in 1870, spoke of The Rainbow of Peace on Earth – l'iride di pace.[13]

Another thought is Aurora, or an Aurora Borealis, or Aurora Australis — the natural occurrence of light in the sky. Asteroid begins with an A. On October 13, 2029, a large asteroid named Apophis will be closest to the earth

Sister Lucia of Fatima said, "When you see a night illumined by an unknown light, know that this is the great sign given to you by God that He is about to punish the world for its sins, by means of war, famine, and persecution against the Church and the Holy Father." On the night of January 25-26, 1938, the sky became blood-red, likened to a blaze of fire, filling the evening sky throughout much of the world. Fire engines headed to the direction of the light as it was so bright, yet never found fires. Sister Lucia knew this was the sign that persecution would soon arrive for the sins of mankind. World War II soon followed, where an estimated 60 million people died in all theaters of the war. Heaven communicates through signs.

An important note should be added: When Conchita describes the Warning as being "like fire," she means that in some way or ways it resembles fire, but it is not fire. According to Conchita, the Warning and fire have two things in common, "they can be seen and felt, and they are very terrifying. The Warning will be seen and felt by all men and will cause great fear in men's hearts, a fear so great that it could conceivably cause some to die.

The Warning — Conchita

Conchita told us **that the Warning will be like two heavenly bodies or stars colliding that make a lot of noise and a lot of light, but they don't fall.** We are going to see it. It will horrify us because at that very moment we will see our souls how God sees us. In that moment, we are going to see our conscience, everything wrong that we are doing, and the good that we are not doing. It will be as though we are in agony, but we will not die by its effects, but perhaps we will die of fright or shock in seeing ourselves as we truly are.

During an interview, Conchita said the duration of the Warning is about five minutes. In an interview in October 1968, in answer to a question about the Warning, Conchita said: "The Warning is something supernatural and will not be explained by science. **It will be seen and felt.**"

The Warning—Mari Loli

Mary Loli said: "When the Warning occurs, everything will stand still, even planes in the sky, but just for a few moments. At the moment everything stops, the Warning will occur. The Warning will last just a few minutes. It is important we prepare ourselves because it is a terrible thing. It will make us feel all the wrong we have done. Everyone will experience it wherever they may be, regardless of their condition or their knowledge of God. It will be an interior personal experience. It will look as if the world has come to a standstill, however, no one will be aware of that as they will be totally absorbed in their own experience. It is going to be something like an interior feeling of sorrow and pain for having offended God. God will help us see clearly the harm we are causing Him, and all the evil things we do."

Our Sins Revealed, The World Changes in an Instant

Since the publication of *The Thunder of Justice (1993)*, numerous people who have experienced the Warning have shared their own personal experience of the Warning. Priests, seminarians, and lay people have all experienced the same thing. All speak of seeing their lives like a slow-moving motion picture. Everything that has happened in a person's life is seen, and the person knows there is no excuse or rebuttal for sins before Almighty God—the light of Divine Truth. In what seems to be a great deal of time, but actually not, some have fallen to the floor and wept for hours as they have seen sins in their life. In every instance observed, it has been the single biggest life-changing event they have ever experienced. With no exceptions, everyone speaks of this *Illumination of Conscience* the same way, as the defining moment of their lives. All speak of unconditional love and purity in their midst, which gives them virtually no way to refute their sins. All know they are in the presence of God and His judgment.

The Warning will be the first dramatic sign to all that this Era of Time is coming to a close. It is not God's wish that we be among those who refuse to repent in time. Not in all the ages is it ever His wish that even a single one of His little ones be lost.

The March/April, 2012 issue of the *Garabandal Journal*, Barry Hanratty, editor and founder of the Journal, offered more insight on the Warning. It reads, "The Warning begins, according to Conchita, as a sighting in the **sky but not a comet, meteor or anything of a physical nature, since it will be supernatural and 'will not be explained by science.'** From the sky this presence descends into every soul to do its terrible (but beneficial) work. Conchita tells us: 'Everyone in the whole world will see a sign, a grace, or a punishment within themselves. They will find themselves all alone in the world, no matter where they are at that time, alone with their conscience right before God.'

Mari Loli said, "It will look as if the world had come to a standstill, however, no one will be aware of that as they will be totally absorbed in their own experience." Then, at this moment, frozen in time, will come the reckoning. Conchita continues, "They will see all their sins and what their sins have caused." She also said that in addition to seeing the evil of our sins, we will also see all the good we have failed to do. She goes on, "It will not burn our bodies but we will feel it both physically and interiorly."

The following is from **The Warning — 1965, The Garabandal Events.**[14]

> Before 1964 was over, Garabandal entered into a phase of reactivation: something that now, from a perspective of the passing years, could be described in the jargon of sports as the final stretch or the last lap. On December 8th, the Feast of the Immaculate Conception, the girl received the singular favor of another encounter, in a locution, with the Mother of Heaven. A month later, on January 12, 1965, she spoke about it briefly to Father Laffineur: "On the day of the Immaculate Conception, the Virgin congratulated me on my saint's day and she told me that I would see the Angel St. Michael on the coming June 18." A few days later, on January 24, Conchita wrote again to this priest (whom she familiarly called grandfather): "I don't remember whether I mentioned in my last letter that on June 18, I am going to see the Angel St. Michael. The Virgin told me this during a locution on my saint's day, the feast of the Immaculate Conception."

And so, in the unfolding of Garabandal, the year 1965 began under the favorable sign of the return of St. Michael, which had significant implications since the great Archangel was not for minor matters; and his visit, announced so far in advance, certainly could not be of the routine type. He who had come four years previously to start everything in motion, could well return now to bring it to a close.

The coming year would be important. It was the holiday evening of January 1 and daylight was fading. Two children from the village, Joaquina (12 years of age) and Urbano (9), were tending their herd of sheep, which they were leading over the little flat area by the Pines. On coming to the Pines, the children stood staring open-mouthed, discovering Conchita, solitary and enraptured, beneath a pine tree. How many times had a similar scene taken place there and in the village! They observed her as closely as the wandering of their sheep permitted. The visionary, with her gaze fixed upwards, appeared to be in mysterious conversation, since she was speaking and listening.

Only later, piece by piece, were some segments learned of all that had transpired during that exceptional ecstasy. In her letter of January 12, Conchita told Father Laffineur: "On January 1, I saw the Virgin at the Pines." Conchita said nothing about the vision; however, in another letter of February 2, while answering the priest's questions, she explained more:

"The Virgin appears to be the same age as the first time I saw her (July 2, 1961); the same as in these past years: about 18 years old. She wears a white robe and a sky-blue cloak. A prodigious light, which doesn't hurt the eyes, radiates from her and surrounds her completely. Apart from the ecstasy that I am going to have on June 18, I don't know whether the apparitions will begin again, either for me or for the four of us all. The Virgin will give a new message, since she said: Hardly any attention was given to the other (that of October 18, 1961). Therefore, the Virgin is going to give a final message."

A Warning for the Whole World

Conchita wrote,

"The Warning that the Virgin is going to send us will be like a punishment to bring the good close to God, and to warn the others either to change their ways or receive what they justly deserve. I'm not going to reveal what the Warning consists of; the Virgin didn't say that I should tell it. And concerning this, there is nothing more to add. God wishes that as a result of the Warning we amend our lives and commit fewer sins against Him!"

Father Laffineur, having read these words, asked Conchita if the Warning would cause people to die. She then added: "The Warning itself will not cause death, but one could die from the effect that it will have by seeing and feeling it." If the information written by Conchita for Father Laffineur was brief and delayed, it was not that way what she said to her aunt and godmother, Maximina Gonzalez. She spoke to her aunt when she was still under the effect of what she had just learned at the Pines on January 1: "Before the Miracle, there will be a Warning, so that the world can amend its ways." Hearing this, Maximina wanted to know more. The niece explained the Warning to her the best she could. From those explanations, the aunt remembered the following, which she wrote down: She told me we were going to suffer a horrible disaster some day in all parts of the world. None of us will escape this: the good, so that they may draw nearer to God; the evil, so that they may amend their lives. She didn't tell me what it was, but that she was expecting it any day, it is horrible, that it is a thing clearly from Heaven. People in every part of the world will suffer from it. I said to her: "Why don't you publish it so the world may know what is going to happen to it?" And she told me that she was tired of giving warnings for the world when no one pays attention.

She said the Virgin told her people certainly believe there is a Heaven and a Hell, but think little about those things. The Virgin also told her that when we suffer this punishment, all of which we have caused ourselves by our sins, that we should not feel the suffering and pain for ourselves, but rather that we should suffer everything for her Son, since He is very offended by what we do. I asked her how long this catastrophe would last, and she said that she didn't know but that we could suffer it either in the night or in the day. I asked her, "Will we die?" And she answered, "I think if that happens it will be from fright.

"And if we were in the church praying"?

"I also think the church would be the best place to endure it, there near the Blessed Sacrament, so He could support us, give us strength, and help us to suffer it better. Since you've told me this, I've done nothing but look at the sky, to see if I can see anything. I, too, and when I go to bed, I look and have great fear. Though on the other hand, I have a desire for it to come, to see if we amend our lives since we don't seem to realize how much we offend Our Lord.

Well then, when we see it coming to us, we can all go to church.

I myself would consider doing that! But perhaps it will come upon us in the darkness and we won't be able to."

'How horrible it will be if I could tell it is as Conchita told it to me... She said that if she didn't already know what the Chastisement was, she would say nothing could be worse than the Warning.'

From this testimony, written and signed by Maximina, it appears adequately clear that the Warning that was revealed to Conchita on January 1, 1965, will have the following characteristics:

- It will be of a terribly afflictive and impressive nature.
- It will have a universal scope; that is, it will reach everyone, in all parts of the world.
- It will be recognized as being supernatural, something that man himself could not do, leaving him no choice but to implore the mercy of God.
- It will come with a purpose of salvation: in order that the good may draw nearer to God, and the bad take their amendment of life seriously.
- It will certainly come, and before the Miracle, but no one knows the day or the hour.
- Its time, probably, will be a time of mysterious darkness.
- At that time, there will be no other refuge or relief except prayer.

Waiting for the Day

News of Garabandal being the site of amazing phenomena was spreading throughout the world, and new visitors continued arriving in the secluded little village. Everyone wanted to know what had happened firsthand from the visionaries themselves. The girls could not always acquiesce to the people's wishes, either because the flood of inquisitive people was at times overwhelming, or because the girls had duties which they could not neglect, or because their parents placed obstacles in the way of the persons who came. Usually, the visionaries tried to please everyone. Obviously, they could not put everything in writing.

A Different Atmosphere

The atmosphere that had descended on the mountain village was lamentable; it was described by the French witnesses in *L'Etoile dans la Montagne:*

"There is dissension between the families of the visionaries and we noticed no small amount of envy — discussions, criticism, suspicion, imprudence to the point of impertinence even regarding the visit of the Angel…But one is aware, through all of this, of a badly disguised desire that 'finally something is going to happen' after more than two years in which nothing has happened! During these days of confusion, especially on May 16, 1965 it became increasingly known that Conchita had been holding an important secret since January 1. So it appears, at least, in the notes of Dr. Ortiz: 'Placido went up to Garabandal, and Maximina relayed the conversation she had with Conchita in which she had been told that a sign (the Warning) would come before the Miracle.'

The news or announcement, if it were divulged to the village, certainly made no impression. Almost everyone's attitude remained the same: doubting and dubious. They shrugged their shoulders: We will see what happens, if anything.

Conchita, on the other hand, showed herself more certain than ever. On May 23, the Sunday before the Ascension, Mr. Ruiloba (an interested party to the apparitions) once again was walking through Garabandal. He met Father Valetin (pastor), who was quite worried about some plans attributed to Pajares and 'Tobalina (chancery secretary and vicar general) who governed the Diocese of Santander and from the priest he learned that Conchita was continuing to repeat that the Angel would definitely return on the date announced: June 18 (the year was 1965).

"But are you really sure," the pastor had said to her, "that it is not a lie or something that you imagined."

"Do you think that the Virgin would lie." (Conchita said)

"No, of course not."

"Well, the Virgin told it to me..." (Conchita said).

Finally, the door slowly opened, and in the doorway stood the girl, pale, heavily bundled up, but with her best smile for everyone.

Mr. Poch Soler (another interested party in the early literature) continues:

At two o'clock in the afternoon of June 18, we managed to speak with Conchita. I confess that this was most moving moment of my career as a journalist. Never has a person filled me with such respect and confidence at the same time...The interview took place in the kitchen of her home. Present were her mother and her two brothers, two strong men of the north who maintained the place. She held out her hand and apologized for making me wait to get the interview.

"Are you happy!" I asked.

"Very happy, Senor. I feel a great joy."

"Why?"

"Because today I will see the Angel and that's marvelous."

"Have you noticed the number of people who are here!"

"I haven't stopped thinking of them!"

"And how do you feel about this enormous crowd?"

"My joy is difficult to put into words. How happy Our Lady will be!"

"Are you sure you will see the Angel today?"

"Very sure."

"At what time?"

"I cannot say, since I don't know. I don't know the hour, but I have a feeling that it will be rather late."

"What do you feel when the Virgin appears to you?"

"A strong constriction that comes up from my chest to my throat. And then there is a marvelous light."

"What do you think the Angel will say?"

Such an environment could not fail to produce moments of near hysteria. Some inundated Conchita with medals, scapulars and holy cards, hoping she would touch them and kiss them. Others approached for her autograph, to take her picture…A woman raised a paralytic son in her arms, imploring Conchita to kiss him.

The evening advanced, without Conchita announcing the time of the apparition. It became darker. But how sure it is that faith which moves mountains! No one gave up or abandoned his post… Eight o'clock came, then nine, then ten…They were praying without ceasing; supplications and hymns in every language rose up to Heaven…

…until a trembling of emotion seized everyone: At the door of Conchita's house a priest came out, and calling for silence, spoke to the crowd: "This is from Conchita. Everyone should go to the Calleja (*the rocky way to the Pines*), to what is called the cuadro, since the ecstasy will be there."

The frenzy stirred up by these words could not be described. A stampede was set into motion with everyone intent on getting the best place for observation. Aniano Fontaneda wrote in his letter to Father Ramon Andreu:

Everybody wanted to be the first to get there; they almost ripped my clothes off as they shoved me on all sides. Many were knocked to the ground. I lifted up Mercedes Salisachs (noted author) and others who had stumbled and fallen going up the hill.

Encounter With the Angel

At the *cuadro*, order had been restored in the crowd. Almost everyone was praying in a loud voice, in two choruses, the French and the Spanish alternating. What an extraordinary night! There was an unprecedented luminosity with innumerable stars shining as never before, even without a moon. Suddenly all lifted up their heads. From the northwest, a new star shot up, brighter than the others. It traced a great circle and returned to its starting point.

Two minutes later, another star; splendid but brighter than the first, appeared straight above Conchita's house, advanced slowly in the sky and suddenly disappeared above the Pines.

Everyone was talking with the person next to him about these extraordinary phenomena, when at the bottom of the lane, in the light of the starry night and the flashlights, Conchita appeared, protected by a squad of police guards. The young girl was walking so fast that her guards were out of breath (*L'Etoile dans la Montagne*).

Reporter Poch Soler saw the scene like this:

At a quarter to midnight, Conchita, followed by some priests and seven police guards, went up to the Calleja in a completely normal state. She advanced with her gaze fixed. The flashes from the photographers' cameras were firing away at her. A police guard asked her: "It is here, Conchita?"

"No, Senor, a little higher up."

On coming to the designated spot, the girl plummeted to her knees on the sharp stones of the lane. The ecstasy had begun.

The moment is exciting. Conchita's eyes are fixed on the sky. She laughs and pronounces some words in a very low voice…But immediately her expression changes completely and tears run down her cheeks. The lights for the TV cameramen and the photographers' strobes shine directly into her eyes wide open, but she doesn't blink or make the least motion. The ecstasy is absolute.

The witness of *L'Etoile dans la Montagne* tells of it:

"The ecstasy was smaller to those that we had previously observed in the village, in the seer's kitchen or her room. There were signs of the cross made with an indescribable piety and majesty, a face resplendent with an interior light, an angelic smile and moments of solemn seriousness, whispering with lips open and the silence of a soul that listens, a tear that glistens on the temple and leaves a trail of crystal."

On his part, the reporter of *Le Monde et la Vie* wrote:

Conchita was there in front of my eyes, in the corner of a circle of flashlights and cameras, lights focused on her: Her head, which I could see well during almost all the ecstasy, stayed motionless, tilted back in the way that so many photographs show. And her face appeared to gleam, extremely beautiful and transparent, evoking everyone's admiration.

Father Luna's testimony is exceptionally valuable:

I finally found myself on the hill, a little more than two meters from Conchita, who was already in ecstasy and whom I could see and hear perfectly. I was impressed by the more than human beauty of her face. She was speaking without blinking, under torrents of light projected on her from the cameramen and flashlights. I was overwhelmed on seeing her cry, as up until then, I had never seen this. From her eyes flowed tears that joined in a stream, filling the concavity of her ear (the only one visible to me at the time), falling on the ground like water as from a faucet…

I hear her speak with a voice that was gasping and breathless: "No! No!… Not yet!… Pardon, pardon!" Later I saw her, with her right hand raised, lift herself up unsupported, some 70 centimeters, to again fall to her knees on the ground with a chilling crunch. Later she said, as if repeating it and asking a question, "Priests?… bishops?… July 2?"

I saw her bless herself slowly and majestically. And suddenly she put her hands to her face, trying to protect her eyes from the bright lights. The ecstasy was over. There is one missing element in Father Luna's report, which the French reporters give us:

Conchita remained immobile some 12 to 13 minutes in conversation with her mysterious interlocuter. Suddenly, still in ecstasy, she got to her feet holding in her right hand a crucifix (that she later said had been touched by the Angel). She again fell on her knees and brought the crucifix to her lips with an extraordinary expression of love. It was at this moment, according to what her mother told me, that one of the police guards, with a changed look on his face, blessed himself solemnly, as to say: "I believe."

Then Conchita, without paying any attention to what was happening around her, without changing in the least the expression on her face or the fixedness of her glance, held out the crucifix so it could be kissed by three Frenchmen: an old priest at her side, the father of a family who had lived in Spain for some time, and a religion teacher from Mauleon.

After blessing herself with the crucifix with extraordinary reverence, she lowered her head, and smiling, without any sign of fatigue, got up. With difficulty, the six police guards managed to protect her from the crowd.

The guards' task was difficult. Everyone wanted to see Conchita up close, to touch her if possible, to ask her questions, especially when it was heard that she had received a message. In a letter previously quoted, Mr. Aniano Fontaneda wrote to Father Ramon Andreu:

"The crucifix she held out to be kissed in the ecstasy belonged to me. I had left it at her house when I went to the cuadro...On returning, she was holding out this crucifix for everyone to kiss at the door of her house. She continued until they finished kissing it; then she gave it back to me. After that, people came to ask me for it, since they wanted to kiss it. When I left Conchita's house, I had the same experience by Ceferino's tavern with the people from Catalonia, Argentina and Madrid. At every step, I had to take out the crucifix, until a woman from Segovia, Fuencisla Fernandez-Pacheco took charge of doing it.

"Among the few people who succeeded in getting into Conchita's house after the ecstasy, was the correspondent from *Le Monde et la Vie*. All that he could pry from the visionary about the message she had received was the vague statement: "It was very sorrowful." To find out its exact words, he would have to wait until the following morning. But not everyone could wait. Such was the case with Mr. Fontaneda:

"Conchita was going to reveal the Angel's message on the following day, Saturday, in the morning after she received Communion; but I couldn't wait. We left there at two in the morning, without having eaten and with only two Coca Colas that they had given me at Ceferino's place.

"By night, almost all was peaceful and quiet in the village. The need for rest and sleep had overtaken everyone, and now all that remained were the stars in the firmament above, keeping their sentinel-like watch. What mysterious designs were suspended over the earth?

Conchita reaffirmed what Our Lady said, "As my message of October 18 has not been complied with and has not been made known to the world, I am advising you that this is the last one. Before, the cup was filling up. Now it is flowing over. Many cardinals, many bishops and many priests are on the road to perdition and are taking souls with them. Less and less importance is being given to the Eucharist. You should turn the wrath of God away from yourselves by your efforts. If you ask His forgiveness with sincere hearts, He will pardon you. I, your mother, through the intercession of Saint Michael the Archangel, ask you to amend your lives. You are now receiving the last warnings. I love you very much and do not want your condemnation. Pray to Us with sincerity and We will grant your requests. You should make more sacrifices. Think about the passion of Jesus."

The last apparition for Conchita was on November 13, 1965, at the Pines. Conchita described this last conversation as happy, but Our Lady gently chastised her: *"Conchita, why don't you go often to visit my Son in the Most Blessed Sacrament?"*[15]

CHAPTER 6

What Some Notable People Have Said About the Warning

"For the stars of the heavens and their constellations will not give their light; the sun will be dark at its rising and the moon shall not shed its light. I will punish the world for its evil, and the wicked for their iniquity."

(ISAIAH 13:10-11).

Blessed Anna Maria Taigi (1769-1837)

Blessed Anna Maria Taigi spoke of a great Chastisement which would come to the world, preceded by an Illumination of Conscience in which everyone would see themselves as God sees them. She indicated that this Illumination of Conscience would result in the saving of many souls because many would repent as a result of this *"Warning,"* this miracle of *"self- illumination."*

Beatified in 1920, and a model for women and mothers, Anna Maria Taigi was not only a prophetess, but one of the most extraordinary mystics in the history of the Church. From the time she was twenty years old until she died at the age of sixty-three, she was accompanied by a mysterious light in which she saw past, present, and future events, some relating to struggles among nations, some relating to individual souls. Her body is incorrupt in Rome. Cardinals and bishops sought her counsel.

Blessed Anna Maria gazed into that light only when she felt an interior impulse, a sort of direction from Our Lord and the Holy Spirit. When she looked into the light she was asked to offer some special suffering for a special need of the Church or an individual.

In that light, Anna Maria saw a great Chastisement coming upon the world in the future, but at the same time a great blessing. She spoke about the Illumination of the Consciences of men, just as though suddenly every man was given the same kind of light that accompanied her, in which they would see themselves as God sees them.

Saint Faustina Kowalska, Divine Mercy —
And Her Illumination of Conscience — The Ultimate Divine Mercy

Saint Faustina Kowalska (1905-1938), of Krakow, Poland, experienced on a personal basis a *"judgment"* where she was allowed to see her sins as God sees them. She wrote about this spiritual experience: "Once I was summoned to the judgment (seat) of God. I stood alone before the Lord. Jesus appeared such as we know Him during His Passion. After a moment, His wounds disappeared except for five, those in His hands, His feet and His side. **Suddenly I saw the complete condition of my soul as God sees it. I could clearly see all that is displeasing to God. I did not know that even the smallest transgressions will have to be accounted for. What a moment! Who can describe it? To stand before the Thrice Holy God!"**

"Jesus asked me, 'Who are you?'"

"I answered, 'I am Your servant, Lord.'"

"You are guilty of one day of fire in Purgatory."

"I wanted to throw myself immediately into the flames of Purgatory, but Jesus stopped me and said, 'Which do you prefer, suffer now for one day in Purgatory or for a short while on earth?'"

"I replied, 'Jesus, I want to suffer in Purgatory, and I want to suffer also the greatest pains on earth, even if it were until the end of the world. Jesus said: 'One (of the two) is enough; you will go back to earth, and there you will suffer much, but not for long; you will accomplish My will and My desires, and a faithful servant of Mine will help you to do this. Now, rest your head on My bosom, on My heart, and draw from it strength and power for these sufferings, because you will find neither relief nor help nor comfort anywhere else. Know that you will have much, much to suffer, but don't let this frighten you; I am with you' (**Diary 36**).

Jesus spoke to Saint Faustina of a cross in the sky in the last days in great detail: "Before I come as the just judge, I am coming first as the King of Mercy. Before the day of justice arrives, there will be given to people a sign in the heavens of this sort: All light in the heavens will be extinguished, and there will be great darkness over the whole earth. Then the sign of the cross will be seen in the sky, and from the openings where the hands and the feet of the Savior were nailed will come forth great lights which will light up the earth for a period of time. This will take place shortly before the last day" (**Diary 83**).

I am reliving these moments with Our Lady. With great longing, I am waiting for the Lord's coming. Great are my desires. I desire that all humankind come to know the Lord. I would like to prepare all nations for the coming of the Word Incarnate. O Jesus, make the fount of Your mercy gush forth more abundantly, for humankind is seriously ill and thus has more need than ever of Your compassion. You are a bottomless sea of mercy for us sinners; and the greater the misery, the more right we have to Your mercy. You are a fount which makes all creatures happy by Your infinite mercy (**Diary 793**).

O human souls, where are you going to hide on the day of God's anger? Take refuge now in the fount of God's mercy. O what a great multitude of souls I see! They worshiped the Divine Mercy and will be singing the hymn of praise for all eternity (**Diary 848**).

Jesus looked at me and said, "Souls perish in spite of My bitter Passion. I am giving them the last hope of salvation; that is, the Feast of My Mercy. If they will not adore My mercy, they will perish for all eternity. Secretary of My mercy, write, tell souls about this great mercy of Mine, because the awful day, the day of My justice is near" **(Diary 965).**[16]

Saint Faustina's writings were silenced by the Church for over twenty years. The Diary of Saint Faustina, called *Divine Mercy in My Soul,* is considered a spiritual classic today. Saint John Paul II initiated the reinvestigation of her life and writings while he was Archbishop of Krakow. She was canonized as the first saint of the new millennium on April 30, 2000, by Saint John Paul II, on the Feast of Divine Mercy before a crowd of 200,000 people in Saint Peter's Square.

Janie Garza, Visionary & Stigmatist
Comments on the Illumination of Conscience

Janie is a wife, mother, and grandmother, living in the state of Texas. Janie has been receiving messages from Heaven since the early 1990's, and Signs of the Times is the publisher.

May 13, 1994—The Illumination of the Soul Given to Janie Garza by St. Joseph

St. Joseph: "My little one, I, St. Joseph, know that you have been struggling with the seriousness of the messages that you have received from

Most Holy Mary and St. Michael. I am here to help you to understand these messages. You see, my little one, the people of God have ignored His warnings. The world does not understand the darkness that surrounds them.

"Many people continue to live in sin, and forget that the day is coming when they will be allowed to see the state of their souls. What a terrible time this will be for many, many souls. Many will die, for they will not be able to withstand knowing the truth about the condition of their souls.

Janie: "St. Joseph, could you explain why many people will die when they see their souls? I don't understand this, please help me to understand.

St. Joseph: "My little one, the soul is where all truth lies and no one can see or know your soul except the Eternal One. He alone knows all souls, and He alone will judge all souls. No one knows the truth except the Holy Trinity. If people knew the truth, they would choose not to sin, for the truth would enlighten their hearts to know how much sin separates them from the truth. The Truth is the Eternal Father.

"You cannot live in sin and say you know the truth, for you cannot have two masters. You must choose to live in darkness or to live in the light. For those who believe that they live in the light but continue to break every commandment given by God, to these souls, I, St. Joseph, say that these souls will not be able to see the state of their souls and live.

Janie: "This is hard for me to know. Are you saying that people who do not live God's Commandments will die when they see their souls?

St. Joseph: Yes, my little one, that's how it will be for many unless they repent and decide for conversion. There is still time for repentance, but time is growing shorter with each day that goes by.

September 9, 1995 – The Illumination of the Soul Given to Janie Garza by Jesus

Jesus: "Our humble servant, the illumination that will take place will be for a short period. During this time My Father will allow all of humanity to see the state of their souls as My Father sees their souls. This will be a time of great grace when many souls will repent and return to My Father. Those souls that die will die from great shock to see the state of the darkness which exists in their souls."

March 19, 1996 – The Illumination of the Soul Given to Janie Garza by Saint Joseph

St. Joseph: "The time is coming when God will allow all His children to look deep into their souls and see their sins as God sees their sinful hearts. God will send an illumination throughout the world. This will be a time of great grace and conversion to many souls. Shortly after this great illumination of souls, God will send a great miracle for the world to see. After this great sign, the world will know peace. There will be great joy for all the faithful people of God. His children will be happy. There will be love in families everywhere. People will benefit from their labor, and they will build their homes and live to enjoy them. They will see their children's children, and all will live long lives."

Janie: "Beloved St. Joseph, what should we do to prepare for this?"

St. Joseph: "Pray, my little one, pray. Remain faithful to all that the Holy Spirit directs you to do. Act in everything that Most Holy Mary is calling you to. Be a strong messenger of living her messages of peace, prayer, Holy Mass, fasting, conversion and reading Holy Scripture. Do this as a family. Do not reject God's Most Holy Name, so that He will not reject you. Decide to be a holy family, to pray together, to love, and to forgive one another. This is a time of decision for all of God's children.

"Live as God's people, leading good, simple and just lives. Open your hearts to God's love and mercy. Every family must consecrate themselves to the Sacred Heart of Jesus, to the Immaculate Heart of Mary, and to my intercession and protection, that we may lead you closer to God. We will prepare you for the things to come. Live as children of the Lord, and you will live through all these troubled times."

Edmund Campion, S.J., (1540-1581)

British Edmund Campion S.J. martyr at Tyburn, England, referred to an event as "the day of change when the terrible judge should reveal all men's consciences."

María Esperanza, Venezuela, (1928-2004)

Servant of God, Maria Esperanza of Caracas, Venezuela, whose cause for canonization was opened in January 2010, called The Warning, "a great day of light when the consciences of the world will be shaken, and the hour of decision for man, and the light of the new dawn of Jesus."

"Little children, I am your Mother, and I come to seek you so that you may prepare yourselves to be able to bring my message of reconciliation. There is coming the great moment of a great day of light. The consciences of this beloved people must be violently shaken so that they may 'put their house in order' and offer to Jesus the just reparation for the daily infidelities that are committed on the part of sinners.

Madeleine Aumont, Dozule, France: (1924-2016), The Cross in the Sky

In the 33rd apparition on July, 4, 1975, as reported by Madeleine, Jesus said: "But, fear nothing, for here will rise in the sky the sign of the Son of Man (which Madeleine saw shining from east to west). I tell you, it is by this Cross set over the world that nations will be saved."

Heede, Germany (1937-1940)

Our Lady and Jesus allegedly appeared to four young girls over several years. Jesus gave a message about the Warning that said, "It will be terrible, a minor judgement. I will make Myself known to men. Every soul shall recognize Me as their God."

Pope Pius IX, (1792-1878, Pope from 1846-1878)

Another voice weighing in mystically concerning a worldwide event of great magnitude was Pius IX when he said:

"Since the whole world is against God and His Church, it is evident that He has reserved the victory over His enemies to Himself. This will be more obvious when it is considered that the root of all our present evils is to be found in the fact that those with talents and vigor crave earthly pleasures, and they not only desert God, but repudiate Him altogether. Thus, it appears they cannot be brought back in any other way except through an act that cannot be ascribed to any secondary agency, and thus will be forced to look to the supernatural.

"There will come a great sign which will fill the world with awe. This will occur only after the triumph of a revolution during which the Church will undergo ordeals that are beyond description."

Saint Teresa of Calcutta (1910-1997)

Saint Teresa of Calcutta believed what was said at Garabandal, and was public in affirming it. St. Teresa believed strongly in the authenticity of Garabandal. Saint Teresa visited with Conchita and Jacinta, and extended her blessings and prayers to them. Saint Teresa believed when she first heard of them in 1971, and when in New York City she would meet with Conchita. Saint Teresa visited with Conchita in New York just a short time before her death. The story of Conchita and Mother Teresa's relationship is well documented, with photos of the two in each other's presence. Jacinta, another visionary living in southern California, was once asked to visit Mother Teresa at one of her missionary houses in Tijuana, Mexico. On July 19, 1992, Jacinta traveled several hours to Tijuanna to visit Mother Teresa and was joyfully presented to the religious community of nuns as, "Here is Jacinta of Garabandal, Garabandal is authentic." Mother Teresa died five years later on September 5, 1997, at the age of 87.

Father Walter Ciszek, S.J. (1904-1984)

Father Walter Ciszek, S.J. was a believer in the apparitions at Garabandal. Father Ciszek was a Polish American priest who spent 15 years in confinement and hard labor at the infamous Lubyanka prison in Russia. In total, he spent 23 years in the Russian gulag system after being accused of being a Vatican spy while clandestinely administering the sacraments to the Russian people, who were denied religious rights after the Bolshevik Revolution. Other accounts say he spent 4-5 years in Lubyanka, fifteen years at hard labor in a Siberian gulag, and 3-4 years as a civilian living in the Siberian region. Once released from Russia, he lived at Fordham University in New York City and became familiar with Garabandal, and wholeheartedly believed in the authenticity of the messages. His memoir *With God in Russia* (1964), and his spiritual memoir, *He Leadeth Me-An Extraordinary Testimony of Faith* (1973), are spiritual treasures known intimately among the Jesuits worldwide.

Pope Paul VI (1897-1978)

"The maturity of conscience, most difficult to evaluate today, is the discernment between evil and good. Humanity has performed so many evil deeds that its conscience is now darkened by sin. We will need a terrible warning, and many will refuse to listen — a terrible warning. Most people will not heed it, but it will be essential to replace moral order. Many have lived using their freedom for every kind of pleasure, and they are under the gaze of our God; but this judgment will be direct — at the same time, with His tenderness — and they will be forced to recognize their sin and to separate their sin from their goodness. This time, sins of the world will be revealed."

Pope Paul VI (Pope from 1963-1978) called the struggle of good and evil going on in the world *"apocalyptic."* Pope Paul quoted Luke 18:8: *"When the Son of Man returns will He find faith on earth?"* and said the *"smoke of Satan had entered the sanctuary."* As the Blessed Mother said at Cana instructing the servants, *"Do whatever He tells you"* (John 2:5). Not taking away from the authority of Jesus in the least, she glorifies His Sacred Heart. She is a co-redeemer in His salvation plan for mankind, and what better vessel than

His mother, who came into the world without the stain of sin through the Immaculate Conception.

Christina Gallagher, Achill Island, County Mayo, Ireland (1953 -)

"There will come a sign, which everyone in the world, in an interior way, will experience — and it is not far away. Everyone will experience an inner awareness and they will know that this is from God, and they will see themselves as they really are in the sight of God. It is up to each one of us to help as many people as we can by our prayers, so that when this supernatural sign comes, they will change, and will be able to respond to that sign and be saved by God."

Elizabeth Kindelmann, Hungary (1913-1985), *Flame of Love*

Elizabeth Kindlemann is the locutionist behind the *Flame of Love* messages and devotion. She was a laywoman, and Third Order Carmelite from Budapest. Cardinal Peter Erdo gave his Imprimatur on June 6, 2009 to her original spiritual diary. She said, "The renewal of the earth will take place through the power and imploring force of the Blessed Virgin Mary." Her message also said, "Due to the lack of faith, earth is entering into darkness, but earth will experience a great jolt of faith," Our Lady told Elizabeth Kindelmann, "In that dark night, Heaven and earth will be illuminated by the Flame of Love that I offer to souls….It is so great that I cannot keep it any longer within me. It leaps out to you with explosive power. When it pours out, my love will destroy the Satanic hatred that contaminates the world. The greatest number of souls will be set free. Nothing like this has existed before. This is my greatest miracle that I will do for all."[17]

Saint John Paul II (1920-2005)

Those who knew Saint John Paul's history, know he had a strong Marian devotion since his days in the seminary. When author Albrecht Weber of Austria sent Pope John Paul II a book he wrote on Garabandal, Saint John Paul II personally wrote an inscription of encouragement in the book to him for all of his work promoting Garabandal. This story is elsewhere in this book.

CHAPTER 7

Saint Pio's (1887-1968) Belief in Garabandal from the Beginning

Saint Pio was one of the few priests in the history of the Church to receive the stigmata from Our Lord. Blessed with many spiritual gifts from an early age, Saint Pio believed in Garabandal.

The following is the story as told by Father Eusebio Garcia de Pesquera in his classic work on Garabandal called, *She Went in Haste to the Mountain*. Father Pesquera recounts the interest of Saint Pio when he sent an unsigned letter on March 3, 1962, to all four of the visionaries:

Felix Lopez, a former student of the Seminario Mayor de Derio (Bilbao), who later became the school teacher in Garabandal, was meeting with people in Conchita's kitchen when the issue of a letter arose. The girls received a letter they didn't understand, and asked him to translate it. It was in Italian, and Felix, after reading it said, "By its style it could well be Padre Pio."

The letter had come to Conchita without a signature, or a return address, but with an Italian stamp, and said this:

My Dear Children,

"At nine o'clock in the morning, the Holy Virgin told me to say to you: O blessed young girls of San Sebastian de Garabandal! I promise that I will be with you until the end of the centuries and you will be with me during the end of the world and later, united with me in the glory of paradise.

"I am sending you a copy of the holy rosary of Fatima which the Virgin told me to send to you. The rosary was composed by the Virgin and should be propagated for the salvation of sinners and preservation of humanity from the terrible punishments which the good God is threatening it.

"I give you only one counsel: Pray and make others pray, because the world is following the path to perdition. They do not believe in you or your conversations with the Lady in white **but they will believe when it will be too late.**"

Conchita asked Felix if he knew Padre Pio's address, and on receiving the affirmative answer asked him to help her compose a letter to answer it and express her appreciation. Writing a letter in response, she left it on the kitchen table unfolded. After a while, Conchita went into ecstasy and recited the Rosary. Returning to her normal state, the teacher said to her, "Did you ask the Blessed Virgin if the letter was from Padre Pio?" "Yes, and she gave me a secret answer to send him."

Conchita retrieved the handwritten letter. In front of everybody, she put it in the envelope which had been addressed by the teacher to Padre Pio, and she sealed it.

On February 9, 1975, *Needles* magazine asked Conchita the following question concerning the letter of Padre Pio.

Q. Conchita, do you remember anything about the letter?

A. I remember receiving in the mail a letter addressed to myself and the other three girls, Jacinta, Loli, and Mary Cruz. I wondered about the things that were in the letter and, as it was not signed, I tucked it in my pocket until I saw the Blessed Mother that day. When she appeared I showed her the letter and asked her who sent it to us. The Blessed Mother said it was from Padre Pio. Since I did not know who Padre Pio was, I questioned her no further.

After the apparition, I told people about the letter, and there was a seminarian priest who told me about Padre Pio and where he was from. Then I wrote a letter to Padre Pio saying that when he visits my country, I would like to see him. He responded with a short letter saying, "do you think I can go up the chimney?" I was only twelve years old at the time. I did not understand about the cloisters.

In January, 1966, Conchita was called to Rome by Cardinal Ottaviani, then head of the Sacred Congregation for the Doctrine of the Faith (CDF). Conchita and her mother went as asked. While there, she met with Pope Paul VI where five other people were present. Testimony of this meeting is based upon Professor Medi, then head of the European Association of Atomic Energy, and subsequently, the Vatican ambassador to Spain. Since Conchita had to wait a day to meet Cardinal Ottaviani, Professor Medi suggested they visit Padre Pio in San Giovanni Rotondo. In the 1975 interview are her words about the event:

"We all agreed and drove in Professor Medi's rented car to the monastery. We arrived around nine o'clock in the evening and we were told we could not see Padre Pio until the next morning at his five o'clock Mass.

Before Mass, Father Luna and the professor went into the sacristy. Professor Medi told me what happened there. He said that Father Luna told Padre Pio that the princess from Spain was there to see him. Padre Pio told Father Luna, "I don't feel very well and won't be able to see her till later in the day." Then Professor Medi said, "There's another lady that wants to see you. Conchita wants to see you." Padre Pio asked, "Conchita of Garabandal?" The professor answered, "Yes." Padre Pio then said, "Come at eight o'clock this morning."

When we arrived, we were brought into a small room, a cell which had one bed, a chair, and a table. I asked Padre Pio if this was his room and whether he slept here or not, he replied, "Oh no, you cannot see my room, this is a rich room." At the time I did not realize what a holy man Padre Pio was, as I know him to be now. I was very young at the time. I was only sixteen.

Q. Who was in the room with you?

A. "Only my mother, Father Luna, and a priest from the monastery who spoke Spanish and was taking many pictures. I don't remember the princess and the professor being in the room."

Q. Can you tell us what was said during your visit with Padre Pio?

A. "I remember only a little. I do remember the priest that was taking the pictures asked permission from Padre Pio and Padre Pio replied, "You have been taking pictures since you came in." I remember the crucifix kissed by Our Lady, and I said to Padre Pio, "this is the cross kissed by the Blessed Mother, would you bless it?" He then took the crucifix blessed by Our Lady and placed it in the palm of his left hand, over the stigmata. Then he took my hand and placed it in his palm, closing his fingers over my hand, and with his right hand he blessed my hand and the cross. He did the same for my mother when she asked him. "Would you please bless this rosary which was kissed by the Virgin?" I was kneeling in front of him the whole time I was there. He started holding my hand with the cross while he was talking to me."

The priest who took the pictures of Conchita with Padre Pio was Father Alessio Parente, now deceased. He was in the United States promoting Padre Pio's Cause for Canonization and visited Conchita at her home In New York City.

A young man by the name of Joachim Bouflet, Ph.D., went to Saint Pio for confession in July of 1968 (2 months before Saint Pio's death on September 23, 1968). Saint Pio told him, "Pray to the Madonna. Consecrate yourself to the Virgin of Carmel." "Yes, Padre, I pray to Our Lady of Mount Carmel. For that matter, I would like to become a Carmelite. Pio didn't comment on this but repeated with insistence, "Consecrate yourself to the Virgin of Carmel who appeared at Garabandal."

Bouflet: "So it's true?"

Padre Pio: "Certo e vero!" ("Yes, it's true!"). Joachim Bouflet went onto a career as a well-known writer in Europe on Marian apparitions and the Catholic culture.

Conchita mentioned that Saint Pio, during her visit with him in 1966, said to her:

"The great wonder of God (the Miracle) must be paid for with too much blood (demaciado de sangre) throughout Europe."[18]

After Saint Pio's Death

It was prophesied that Padre Pio was to see the Miracle. However, when Saint Pio died, Conchita was confused how he was going to see the Miracle. She expected Saint Pio to see it in his lifetime, thus the prophecy had not come true in her mind. One month after Saint Pio died in September 1968, Conchita received a telegram from Lourdes, France. The telegram requested Conchita go there to receive a letter addressed to her by Saint Pio. A priest by the name of Father Alfred Combe, a devoted friend of Garabandal, and a man by the name of Bernard l'Huiller from France were in the village at the time and agreed to drive Conchita and her mother to Lourdes. In a hurried state, Conchita forgot her passport and was unable to get into France. After a six-hour delay at the border, the party was granted special permission to enter France.

At Lourdes, they met with Saint Pio's confreres from Italy, including Father Bernardino Cennamo, OFM, from another monastery in Italy, who was well known at San Giovanni Rotondo. Saint Pio had dictated a note to Father Pellegrino, a close confidante and handler in his failing years, that he was instructed to give to Conchita. It read:

> For Conchita,
> I pray that the Blessed Virgin will comfort you and guide you always towards sanctity, and I bless you with all my heart.
>
> Signed, Father Pellegrino.

Father Cennamo told Conchita that he did not believe in the apparitions of Garabandal until Saint Pio told him to give Conchita the veil that was to cover his face after his death. The note and the letter were given to Conchita. Then she asked Father Cennamo, "How is it that the Virgin told me Padre Pio was supposed to see the Miracle, and he has died?" He answered," He saw the Miracle before he died. He told me so himself."

In the 1975 *Needles* magazine, Conchita sheds more light on the Lourdes incident.

> "...I had the veil in front of me as I was writing (to a friend in Madrid) when suddenly the whole room filled with a fragrance. I had heard of the fragrances of Padre Pio, but never paid much attention. The room smelled of perfume so strongly that I started to cry. It was the first time that I experienced this. All this happened after he was dead."[19]

The scent of perfume or roses is common in many Marian apparitions and places where the Blessed Mother is engaged. The stories about such occurrences are legion. She has said to mystics, "It is a sign of my maternal presence." Such is what Conchita experienced with this event. The scent is a signal grace to the individual.

Father Joseph Brennan, O.C.S., an early writer on Garabandal, summarized the prophetic statements made by saints, blessed and popes. He put it this way: *"They foretell a time of unprecedented and terrible confusion and suffering unlike anything that has ever been experienced in human history. It will affect every area of human life."*

In what would be the last issue for *Garabandal Journal* and Barry Hanratty's last issue before he died, some of the following narrative is from B. Hanratty, and other material from the author.

"A great Miracle, the greatest that Jesus will have ever performed for the world according to Conchita, has been predicted at Garabandal and it has been anticipated and hoped for with eager longing by believers in the events for many years. While there is nothing wrong with longing for the Miracle, we must not lose sight of the fact that the world, because of its flagrant disregard for God's commandments, must pass through two terrible trials before the healing rays of the Miracle will shine upon it.

The first of these trials has been named the Tribulation and will amount to an all-out attempt by Russia and its allies to turn the world into a confederacy of communist states. There will be bloodshed and great turmoil, and a persecution of the Church that will be, in the words of the Blessed Pius IX, *"beyond description."*

Since this Russian-led aggression will begin in Europe, will the United States help defend western European NATO countries as they have done in two world wars? But just when all seems lost, it has been foretold at Garabandal, the Warning will occur.

When Will the Warning Happen?

The Warning will happen after the Tribulation has run its course, since Jacinta has said that the Warning is what will put an end to it. Here is a good place for a word of caution. If we hear dates of the Warning or Miracle happening on a predicted date, we should be cautious and discerning. Stories of this kind have been circulating for decades, and **to date none have been correct.**

Something in the Sky

If we can't see how something like this can be so devasting without causing physical harm, the testimony of the great mystic, Saint Catherine of Genoa (1447-1510) may be of some assistance: "When I had the vision in which I saw how much the shadow of the smallest act against God matters, I don't know why I didn't die. I do not wonder that hell is so horrible, seeing that it is made for sin. But horrible as it is, I don't think that it's really proportionate to the horror of sin. I think rather that even there God shows mercy, so terrible does even the shadow of a venial sin seem to me. In comparison with this, what will mortal sin be? And so many mortal sins? I think if anyone saw them, even though he were immortal he would become mortal from grief. If the glimpse I had of it, which was only an instant, had lasted any longer, my body would have dissolved though it had been of the hardest diamond. As it was, all my blood was frozen in my body and I thought I must pass from this life. Those who understand how much an offense to God matters, cannot realize any other suffering of any other hell except the offense itself. All other pains that can be endured in this life are comforts in comparison with it…Give me any other penance, but not that of seeing I have offended You…Show me rather the devils with all their terrors and torments. I consider them as nothing in comparison with the sight of the least offence against You."

Conchita told a group of French youths at Garabandal in 1970, that we will not only see our sins of commission, but those of omission, the times we have failed in being charitable toward our neighbor, and the times we have been remiss in our duty to worship God as He deserves. It was revealed to the holy French priest Pere Lamy that one of the three causes of World War I was the violation of the Sabbath. Deliberately missing Mass on Sundays and Holy Days of Obligation is either a grave (mortal) sin of commission or omission and deserves special attention, since the Mass is so important to our Catholic Faith. In the Sudan, where Catholics live at the poverty level, they walk for two days to go to Mass, while the majority of Catholics in affluent western countries don't even bother to go at all. Another widespread failing is the non-observance of Sunday as the Lord's Day and a day of rest. Several years ago, a priest came to the United States from his native India and was shocked at how American Catholics did not observe the Lord's Day. In India, that day is devoted to God and includes spiritual reading and prayer.

Is the Warning Going to Happen in Our Times?

The primary reason for the Warning is: *To correct the conscience of the world* and prepare it for the Great Miracle. The second reason is to put a stop to the global advancement of atheistic Communism. This statement is especially meaningful today in light of the current state of the world and the direction in which it is going. If the Warning had happened thirty years ago, it could not have dealt with the increase in the heinous evils of today.

On Calvary, Jesus reconciled us with God the Father once and for all, but as our Savior, He *continually* saves us, especially by holding back the wrath of His Father through the Holy Sacrifice of the Mass. Saint Pio once said, "The world could get by without the sun in the sky, but never, never without the Holy Mass." For us today, Jesus must save us from the relentless onslaught of secularism, and this is where the correction of the world's conscience is relevant regarding any number of issues: widespread corruption and immorality, indecency, contraception, abortion, euthanasia, etc.

The widespread practice of abortion must come to an end before there can ever be a lasting peace. At Garabandal, in Conchita's last apparition on November 13, 1965, Our Lady spoke to her about abortion without using the word and said it was one of the things that was causing the cup (of iniquity) to overflow.

Conchita once told Father Marcelino Andreu that, "When you see the Warning, that will open up the end of time."

Signs

Are there any signs to alert us of the proximity of the Warning? When Barry Hanratty interviewed Mari Loli in 1982,[20] he asked her if people would be fighting with one another before the Warning. She remained silent to my question, which said enough since Loli was an honest person and would not say she didn't know if she did. And while she didn't answer me on this matter, she must have said something about it to Father Joseph Pelletier, who interviewed her several times in the early 1970's. He told Garabandal devoted souls that before the Warning there was going to be a civil war in the streets. Jacinta has also mentioned this civil unrest. Whether it will be related in some way to the persecution of the Church, we don't know, but according to the above, civil discord will precede the Warning.

Another sign is the outbreak of the Tribulation which, according to the German author Albrecht Weber and his book, *Garabandal -Der Zeigenfinger Gottes* (Garabandal—The Finger of God) who had a conversation with Conchita after her last apparition at Garabandal on November 13, 1965, **"It will begin after the Pope returns to Rome from a trip to Moscow."**

Preparation

Can we be prepared for the Warning? In our present society, sin is everywhere, and while we may not be active participants, we've grown so accustomed to it that we are no longer shocked. Pope Paul VI said, *"We have lost the sense of sin."*

But there is one thing we should all strive for: to be in the state of grace. If that be so, we should survive the Warning. Conchita also said that Catholics will endure the Warning better than others. I think one of the **main reasons** is that we have the Sacrament of Penance or Reconciliation. I am not certain of this, but it seems to me that sins that have been confessed and absolved by a priest in confession should not be seen in the Warning. Saint Faustina once asked Jesus which of her sins offended Him the most, and He was unable to answer her because they had all been forgiven — *and forgotten.* A **second** recommendation in anticipation of the Warning would be frequent confession. A **third** is to avoid near occasion of sin such as bad TV programs or internet websites (with pornography).

Leading a good life by keeping the Ten Commandments and the precepts of the Church should see us through. And Conchita did say that no one would die as a result of the Warning itself unless it be from shock, and that those who do not despair will draw great good from it."[21]

What did Garabandal Say About a Third World War?

There is a popular misinterpretation about Conchita addressing the issue of whether or not she said there would be another world war. At the time of the Cuban Missile Crisis, with the world on edge, with Soviet war ships on the way to Cuba, Conchita was asked, "Will there be war?" She replied, "In 1962, when they were also speaking of the threat of a war I asked the Virgin, "Will there be a war?" She **only** answered me, "God does not want war for His children."[22] This was also confirmed when again she was asked this question on November 17th, 1966.

The devoted who have said there will not be another world war are incorrect, and not factoring in the context of the times nor the answer. The world has seen multiple dozens of wars (albeit not what would be considered a world war) as of this date. The Cuban Missile Crisis was from October 16-29, 1962, and that was the context of the question and the response. This was not intended by Our Lady to be an indefinite extension to the present day. Its context was the threat in 1962, not perpetuity.

Summary of the Warning

- The Warning is an illumination of conscience.
- The Warning is a judgment in miniature.
- The Warning is a correction of conscience.
- The Warning is a life review.
- The Warning is where you will see all the good and evil you have done. Sins of omission and commission will be shown to you similar to a film of your life.
- During the Warning Jesus comes as the King of Mercy.
- The Warning will be the greatest act of mercy since Jesus' passion, death and resurrection.
- During the Warning, Jesus comes not as our just judge, but as our merciful Savior in search of His lost sheep.
- The Warning will be experienced by every man, woman and child on earth; there will be no exceptions.
- The Warning will be approximately 15 minutes in actual time, but it will feel much longer.
- During the Warning, there will be noise of some sort.
- The Warning will be like **two heavenly bodies colliding**; noise, and light. These bodies are flaming objects with a tail of flames. It will not be explained by science. However, skeptics will try to show fraud and a scientific response, but that will not be true.
- The Warning will come with a sign appearing out of the east.
- During the Warning, a great light from Jesus will pierce every soul in the world at the very same time.
- During the Warning, it will feel like all time is standing still.
- During the Warning, it will be like fire, but we will feel it bodily and interiorly. It is from Heaven.
- Confession lines will be packed after the Warning. Priests will have a difficult time finding rest.
- The Warning will be preparation for the Miracle, followed by a Permanent Sign. It will be like a play with three acts.

- During the Warning, many of those who do not live God's Commandments will find the event very difficult.
- The time of the Warning, will be a time of great grace, when many will repent and return to the Father.

The Reasons for the Warning

- Jesus comes as our merciful Savior to reach out to His lost children.
- Evil can no longer be as it was.
- To warn the people who are of this world. That is, those who have chosen to live together outside of marriage. Those who kill His little innocent ones. Those who have chosen to destroy the union of man and woman in marriage and have chosen, man to man, woman to woman in marriage.
- The reign of Satan is coming to an end. Jesus will not continue to allow mankind to destroy His creation.
- Mankind has become so cold and evil that it is only by purification that humanity can survive.
- Jesus is coming with the Warning not as a punishment, but rather an opportunity for our souls to be renewed, in order for us to be with Him, our Lord and Savior, in the Kingdom.
- The evil culture, this false worship and denial of Jesus, is causing the world to face great chastisement.
- To correct His disobedient children.
- The heart of the family is being diminished and humanity cannot survive.
- Actions for which there is no justification: abortion, man diminishing God's Commandments, His chosen sons (priests) steering away from truly teaching their flocks and diminishing His messages from the pulpit.
- To prepare the world for the time of Jesus' visitation.
- The truth will come out when the fullness of His mercy is poured out; out of great love for His people.
- To soften hardened hearts.
- All mankind will know that Jesus is the True Messiah.

- The Warning will be a time of judgment to awaken our souls to prepare each one of us for our final judgment.
- Those who choose to idolize money and power will come to see that their ways are not His ways and our ways will become simplified.
- The division in His Church will soon be brought to light. It will be a time of healing and reconciliation.
- There will be a great awakening of His chosen sons.
- His Church, the true Church, will be brought to light. It will have a profound impact on the unification of Christians.[23]

CHAPTER 8

The Great Miracle

He said to them, "It is not for you to know times or seasons which the Father has fixed by His own authority"

ACTS 1:7

Conchita, I bless you, and with me, the whole church will bless you.

POPE PAUL VI

"Listen to me, you devout sons of mine, and blossom like a rosebush on a stream bank. Bloom like a sweet-smelling lily, and send your fragrance into the air like incense. Sing the Lord's praise and thank Him for all that He has done…. All that the Lord has done is very good: all that He commands is sooner or later done. No one should ask why things are as they are;
these questions will be answered at the right time: whatever He commands is promptly done; there are no limits to His power to save….
He sees the whole of time, from the beginning to end, and nothing takes Him by surprise. No one should ask why things are as they are; everything in creation has its purpose."

SIRACH 39:13-21

A Great Miracle has been foretold by Our Lady of Mount Carmel at Garabandal which will take place near the village. A similar miracle, also predicted in advance, happened at Fatima in 1917, in what has come to be known as The Miracle of the Sun. The sun spun in the sky and hurtled toward earth on October 13, 1917. Some 70,000 spectators witnessed it. Marvelous as that may sound, even more amazing, the miracle of Garabandal will be experienced by many more people. People will undoubtedly journey there from across the world to behold its glory, to be healed, converted, and comforted.

The *"Illumination of Conscience"* will prepare us to see and hear God's glory together at Garabandal, where His people will be gathered once again, just as they were on Mount Sinai, where the protective covering of the Shekinah Glory — the cloud or pillar of smoke by day and a fire by night — offered a protective shield and guidance for the people of God. The Warning will alert the entire population of the world to the impending event of the Miracle, and open hearts to the message and the action of God that will be revealed there.

Although the news about Fatima in 1917 took decades to spread throughout the world due to a lack of communication technology, when the Great Miracle bursts forth at Garabandal, television, social media, websites, cell phones, the internet, radio, newspapers and the countless witnesses viewing the Miracle will spread the story rapidly to the farthest corners of the planet in a matter of minutes.

The Miracle of Garabandal is different from any event at any other apparition site in the history of the world. We are told by other visionaries that a Permanent Sign of some sort will be left at valid apparition sites around the world. Whether it is the same sign at different sites would be speculative on anyone's part, although the similarity of language is obvious. To connect them as the same event may be valid or not. Each apparition site has to stand on its own to be authentic after a thorough investigation by the Church. The validity of one does not determine the validity of another, even if there are similarities. Using the data from one apparition to support another because they have similar elements has not been a factor in how the Church weighs the authenticity of the one being investigated. It is unquestionable there are similar elements prophesied in the apparitions at Fatima, Medjugorje, Rwanda, and Garabandal among others, but what happens at one cannot justify the other. Each with rigorous scrutiny must prove valid on its own.

Understanding the heart and mind of God, and what the Lord is doing in our day, enables one to absorb more freely without constraint what Heaven is doing now at this point in history. It appears we are seeing the confluence of world-wide phenomena culminating in events people are barely able to comprehend. As Saint Thomas Aquinas wrote in Summa Theologica, *"Grace does not destroy nature, but fulfills its potential."*

Mari Loli said that the Blessed Mother told her, "A time would come, when it would look like the Church was finished, when priests would have difficulty saying Mass and talking about holy things. There would come a time when the Church would give the impression of being on the point of perishing. It would pass through a terrible test." When she asked Our Lady how this would happen, Our Lady called it "Communism."

Saint Michael the Archangel

Much has been written on St. Michael's role at Garabandal. St. Michael was the forerunner of Mary and was her messenger to Conchita on several occasions. Might his appearance also have significance for the Jewish people? St. Michael is named three times in the Old Testament, each time as a guardian of Israel or as its Prince. Daniel 10:20 reads: "He said then, 'Do you know why I have come to you? It is to tell you what is written in the Book of Truth. I must go back to fight against the prince of Persia: when I have done with him, the prince of Javan will come next. In all this there is no one to lend me support except Michael your prince.'"

Daniel 12:1-4 describes St. Michael again and his role in the latter times, "At that time shall arise Michael, the great prince who has charge of your people. And there shall be a time of trouble, such as never has been since there was a nation till that time; but at that time your people shall be delivered, every one whose name shall be found written in the book. And many of those who sleep in the dust of the earth shall awake, some to everlasting life, and some to shame and everlasting contempt. And those who are wise shall shine like the brightness of the firmament; and those who turn many to righteousness, like the stars forever and ever. But you, Daniel shut up the words, and seal the book, until the time of the end. Many shall run back and forth, and evil shall increase."

Daniel 10:13 speaks of the apparition of St. Michael, "The prince of the kingdom of Persia has been resisting me for twenty-one days, but Michael, one of the leading princes, came to my assistance." His power is great as he is "one of the leading princes." Although the Church applies this passage to itself, it is not possible to exclude "those who are Israelites," as they were the first to have Michael as their prince.

As Isaiah and others clearly pointed to the birth of a Messiah, Garabandal is pointing to something the world has never seen before. Those with a knowledge of Isaiah before the birth of Christ, were able to see the fulfillment of his prophesies. Jesus quoted Isaiah more than any other prophet for good reason — Isaiah was clear on who Jesus was, and what His mission would be.

Only at the Lord's death did it all make sense. All things were fulfilled to the letter, exactly as it had been written by many in the Hebrew Scriptures with the birth of the Savior. The messages of Garabandal will make more sense after the events — and the events will validate what the Blessed Mother said in the early 1960's. It will be similar to what Isaiah prophesied about the coming of the Messiah, which happened exactly as was written, not as many learned and skeptical imagined. As the law givers in the times of Jesus, the Sadducees and Pharisees did not recognize Him, so it is today with many of the leading prelates who pay little attention to what is happening in our time.

The Blessed Mother is the prophetess of our age appointed by the Most Holy Trinity interceding for mankind. This is similar to how Queen Esther interceded to the Persian King Ahasuerus to save her people from destruction. Esther prayed and fasted for three days before meeting with the king. Approaching the king unannounced could have cost Queen Esther her life, yet she had the confidence and boldness to intercede for her people. As Queen Esther intervened to save her people, so the Blessed Mother today never ceases to be an advocate for all mankind. She acts as any mother would. Queen Esther is a precursor to the Blessed Mother's role of interceding to the Most Holy Trinity for all mankind.

At Garabandal, Mary has revealed enough about the Miracle for us to prepare for this occurrence. Conchita has been forbidden by the Blessed Virgin to disclose it until eight days before it is to happen, and will then announce it to the whole world. At the time of this writing Conchita is 74 years old. This long waiting period distinguishes Garabandal from Fatima, where the predicted miracle of the sun happened during the course of those apparitions. No promise of healing was made at Fatima, but it was made for those present for the day of the Great Miracle in the village in Garabandal.

Millions will be able to see the Great Miracle on that day, for Garabandal is settled in a mountain range forming a broad natural amphitheater. It is well able to accommodate the vast multitude that will journey to that remote place, if world circumstances permit. A great assembly will converge on the village from everywhere, and all who manage to reach its hills will behold supernatural bliss beyond human measure. For those fortunate enough to personally see the Miracle, it will be a source of affirmation of their faith, and ineffable joy.

The Miracle Will Be Eucharistic and Marian

It should be remembered that Conchita received the Eucharist miraculously placed on her tongue by St. Michael. Could this be the precursor to a bigger and more widespread event?

We are told the Miracle will be Eucharistic and Marian. What this **precisely** could mean is unknown. The emphasis on devotion to the Most Holy Eucharist is so strong at Garabandal that a Eucharistic theme for the Miracle would be in perfect consonance with everything that happened in the village during the apparitions. We must be ready to receive an unmistakable proof from God, through the Miracle, that the Holy Eucharist is the center of our life in the Church, and that Jesus is truly present to us in the Eucharist.

On June 14, 1979, on the Solemnity of Corpus Christi, Father Gobbi of the Marian Movement of Priests received a message (Message number 176), had **his only prayer cenacle from Garabandal, which is titled, *Jesus in the Eucharist.*** This is important because the principal messages of Garabandal were about the supremacy of the Eucharist and the priesthood in the life of the Church. A direct message from Garabandal to the Marian Movement of Priests from Mary, is another compliment for Garabandal. The message reads in part,

> "(b)…The Triumph of my Immaculate Heart cannot take place except in the triumph of my Son Jesus, who will reign once again in the hearts, the souls and the lives of each person and nation: in all humanity.
>
> (c) But as Jesus is truly in Heaven, so also is He truly present on earth in the Eucharist with His Body, His Blood, His Soul and His Divinity.
>
> (d) His glorious reign will shine forth above all the triumph of His Eucharist Person, because the Eucharist will once again be the heart and center of the whole life of the Church.
>
> (e) **Jesus in the Eucharist** will become the summit of all your prayer, which should be a prayer of adoration, of thanksgiving, of praise and propitiation.
>
> (f) **Jesus in the Eucharist** will once again be the center of all liturgical action, which will unfold itself as a hymn to the Most Holy

Trinity, through the continual priestly action of Christ which will be carried out in the Eucharistic Mystery.

(g) **Jesus in the Eucharist** will once again be the center of your ecclesial gatherings, because the Church is His temple, His house that has been built above all that His Divine presence may shine forth in your midst.

(h) Beloved sons, in these present times the darkness has alas obscured even the tabernacle; around it there is much emptiness, so much indifference, so much negligence. Every day, doubts, denials and sacrileges increase.

The Eucharistic Heart of Jesus is wounded anew by His own, in His own house, in the very place where He has taken up His Divine dwelling in your midst.

(i) Become again perfect adorers and fervent ministers of **Jesus in the Eucharist** who, through you, makes Himself again present, immolates Himself anew and gives Himself to souls."

If Garabandal could be simplified to its most essential and core elements of the messages it would be how important **living a Eucharistic life** is to the individual. Understanding how Heaven views the **importance of the priesthood** is one and the same: no priesthood, no Consecration at Mass. This is precisely the subject of the message that Father Gobbi received at Garabandal, coinciding with what was said by Our Lady years prior to his 1979 message. As St. Thomas Aquinas said, the Eucharist is *the source and summit of the faith.*

On December 8, 1980, the Blessed Mother on the Solemnity of the Immaculate Conception, in a message titled *Great Mercy*, said to Father Gobbi,

(b) "How numerous today are the snares of my Adversary who appears to be reaching the peak of his great offensive! In every way and by the most subtle means, he seeks to seduce you, if only he can succeed in striking your soul, in wounding you with sin, so as to draw you away from Jesus, who is your only Savior.

(c) The whole of humanity is defiled with this invisible venom, and now needs to be healed by the merciful love of Jesus. He will manifest Himself to you in an extraordinary manner, through the intervention of your Immaculate Mother.

(e) **At the hour when all will seem lost, all will be saved through the merciful love of the Father, which will be made visible through the manifestation of the Eucharistic Heart of Jesus."**

Whether or not this message of Our Lady to the Marian Movement of Priests is related to the Miracle of Garabandal is unknown. However, it appears the world and the Church are at a moment of absolute desperation for their very survival. The Miracle will be ecclesial, that is, it will support the truth that all graces flow through the Body of Christ which is the Church. It will make clear that all men and women are called not only to follow Jesus personally, but also to enter His Church and to submit to its discipline, teaching, and sacraments. For this reason, the Miracle will coincide with a great Church event.

The Miracle will be Marian. It will demonstrate and reveal the glory and mission of the Mother of God, so that all Christians will embrace her role in the mystical Body of Christ, and pay her the honor that the Holy Trinity gives her. The world will begin to give the Immaculate Heart of Mary the honor and devotion due her. Through this great Miracle, many will begin to love "Holy Mary, Mother of God."

The Conversion of Russia, "All Will Love Our Hearts"

The Miracle is for the conversion of the whole world. This assertion was made by Our Lord Himself to Conchita at Garabandal. The Lord answered her question about Russia's conversion by assuring her that *"The Miracle was not only for the conversion of Russia,"* but *"for the conversion of the whole world,"* and *"**thus, all will love Our Hearts**"* (the Hearts of Jesus and Mary).

It seems by His words that somehow the Miracle will show us all how closely **the Hearts of Jesus and Mary are united,** as a symbol of the peace-giving love that should unite our hearts. Perhaps the Two Hearts on the reverse side of the Miraculous Medal were a prophecy as well as a lesson, foretelling an age where all hearts will be reconciled as are the hearts of Jesus and Mary. Reconciliation of hearts is central to conversion, and all authentic Marian appearances concern themselves with this.

The Great Miracle: The Diary of Conchita Gonzalez and Mari Loli

Below is a concise synopsis of the Great Miracle of Garabandal from Conchita and Mari Loli.

Conchita said, "The Blessed Virgin advised me of a great Miracle, saying that God, Our Lord, would perform it through her intercession. Just as the Chastisement will be very, very great, in keeping with the needs of the world.

"The Blessed Virgin has told me the date of the Miracle and what it will consist of. I am supposed to announce it eight days in advance, so the people will come. The Pope will see it from wherever he is, and Padre Pio also [as noted earlier he is reliably reported to have seen the Miracle before he died]. The sick who are present at the Miracle will be cured and the sinners will be converted.

"The Miracle will conclude with an event in the Church and with the feast of a saint who is a martyr of the Eucharist, and it will take place at eight-thirty on a Thursday evening (Spanish time). It will be visible not only to all those who are in the village but to those in the surrounding mountains. There won't be the slightest doubt that it comes from God and that it is for the good of mankind.

"There will be no doubt in the mind of anyone who sees this great Miracle which God, Our Lord, will perform through the intercession of the Blessed Virgin. And how as we await this great day of the Miracle, let us see if the world changes and the chastisement is averted."

Mari Loli Mazon

"The Miracle will take place within one year after the Warning." It has been reported over the years that Mari Loli told some priests that the Warning would be in an even numbered year. Again, this gets back to what could be considered anecdotal versus the integrity of the original messages. Time will tell, but sticking to the original message is safer and more prudent analyzing what the Blessed Mother said over a four year and four month period from 1961-65.

Elements of The Great Miracle at the Nine Pines in Garabandal

*Peace, I leave you; My peace I give to you. Not as the world gives do
I give it to you. Do not let your hearts be troubled or afraid.*

JOHN 14:27

Below are the major points from the visionaries about elements of the Miracle.

1. It will coincide with **an event in the Church**.

    On October 1, 1961, Our Lady of Mount Carmel at Garabandal told something very important to Conchita. It had to do with a future "**major Church event**" where there would be the "**reunification of the Christians**." To have a reunification implicitly means there was a "split" of some sort. Two of the greatest "splits" in Christendom are the division of the Eastern Rite from the Western Rite in 1054, and the Protestant Reformation in 1517, which is considered to have begun when Martin Luther posted his 95 theses on the door at the castle church in Wittenberg, Germany. There may be lesser ones, but these two would be considered the most significant.

Author's note:

What is interesting is that it doesn't say whether it will be a positive or a negative event. The reunification in the Church according to Catholic Magisterial doctrine would be considered a positive event, while a schism would be negative. However, the proper translation of *an event in the Church* is addressed in this book under that subhead title.

This prophecy is seldom mentioned, or has been forgotten by people that speak of a major Church event as part of the Garabandal story. Whatever it is, it will be for the Church Universal, and not a local event. It could possibly be the declaration of the Fifth Marian Dogma of Co-Redemptrix, Mediatrix, Advocate. If the Warning and Miracle itself are the events to bring unity back between the Eastern and Western rites, something must happen that precipitates the desire of the East and the West for the reunification.

On July 16, 1054, (July 16 is the Feast of Our Lady of Mount Carmel), the Church in Constantinople and the Roman Church split over several issues that have lasted to this very day. As we near one thousand years of separation, is there an event to unite them again? Could the Warning and the Great Miracle be the catalyst? What could trigger the East and the West operating in unity again, or as has often been said, "the Church breathing again with two lungs." Saint John Paul II said early in his pontificate that a goal of his was to unite East and West again. As a Polish priest, bishop, and cardinal who lived his life in eastern Poland bordering the church in Ukraine, Russia, Belarus, Lithuania, and at the time Czechoslovakia, he would have had an intimate knowledge of Eastern culture, Church structure, and religious norms. Towards the end of his pontificate, he said he failed in the attempt to accomplish this reunification.

Could the reunification of the Church imply something so profound as the Protestant and Catholic Church under one roof? Speculation abounds as to what this may mean. The event is described as ecclesial, which means it is a Church event. A negative Church event due to the final Synod documents may cause an official schism. Whatever the event is, it will be significant, and could only be accomplished through the work of God.

2. It will be **THE** greatest miracle ever performed by Jesus for the world. It is supernatural and has never been seen before and will not be explained by science.
3. Padre Pio will see the Miracle. (He did see it before he died).
4. The reigning pope will see the Great Miracle from wherever he is.
5. Before the Miracle something will happen that will cause people to stop believing in Garabandal.
6. The Miracle will occur on a Thursday evening, at 8:30 pm Spanish time.
7. The Miracle will happen between the dates of the 8th and 16th (inclusive) of March, April, May, or June.

Author's note:

Much of the literature mentions March, April, or May, but Conchita on television in Ireland as a young woman said, "March, April, May, or June." Another time she said March, April, May, and another time April, May or June. The two consistent months are April and May for her known statements. In addition, many people say April, but that is an anecdotal story from people who have followed Garabandal for decades. It is not in the early statements of the seers. Whether or not the secret was leaked is suspect in light of the divine protection of Conchita and Mari Loli with this information. The story that it would be in the month of April is from Maria Saraco, a friend devoted to Garabandal. Maria Saraco was originally from Massachusetts, then Pasadena, California. She said she was told by Mari Loli that the Miracle was in April. Again, with the passage of time, more information tends to emerge.

Author's note:

March in the Church is the month of Saint Joseph.

April is the month of the Holy Eucharist.

May is the month of Our Lady.

June is the month of the Sacred Heart of Jesus and the Immaculate Heart of Mary.

8. According to Mari Loli, the Miracle will take place **within one year after the Warning** (this does not mean that it has to happen in the same calendar year, but it may).
9. It will be on the feast day of a young martyr of the Eucharist.
10. It will last about fifteen minutes.
11. It will be seen in the sky.
12. It will be possible to photograph and televise, but not touch it.
13. All those in the village and in the surrounding mountains will see it.
14. The sick who are present will be cured.
15. Sinners and non-believers will be converted. The incredulous will believe.
16. Russia will be converted after the Miracle.
17. Conchita, who knows the date of the Great Miracle, will announce it to the world **eight days in advance**.
18. Conchita said about this great supernatural event:

    Before the Miracle, there will be many reported "apparitions" throughout the world. (She said this in December 1962).

- A Bishop of Santander will come along who will not believe at first, but will receive a sign and allow priests to go to Garabandal for the Miracle.
- Before the Miracle, many will stop believing in Garabandal. On the day after the Miracle, the body of Father Luis Andreu, S.J. will be removed from his grave and found incorrupt.

Based upon compiled data over my lifetime, I think the Great Miracle will be so extraordinary, it may be as great as the miracles the Hebrews experienced leaving Egypt after 400 years of captivity. The Miracle will be an undeniable act of God. Mankind will know the Miracle is directly from the hand of God, and not of human origin. The parting of the Red Sea by Moses was a significant event by any standard of miracles in the Bible, but that was a local event where a finite number of people witnessed it. Not to diminish the parting of the Red Sea by any means, but this will be a global-phenomenon of grace for the entire world, and for a world in desperate need of it.

The Miracle Will be Much Greater Than What Happened at Fatima

What has been said about the magnitude of the Great Miracle is hard to digest. However, two knowledgeable sources about the events, provide their thoughts. When asked, Barry Hanratty's response was, **"Yes, the greatest miracle that Jesus has ever performed for the world."**[24] Conchita said, **"The Miracle here will be much greater, more tremendous than Fatima. The miracle at Fatima is nothing in comparison. It will cause such an impression that none of those who see it will be able to leave with doubts. It would be well if all the world were here, since that way there surely would be no chastisement, since everyone would believe."**[25]

Conchita Will Announce the Miracle Eight Days Before

There has been considerable discussion of whether an eight-day notice will be enough time for people to make plans and get to Garabandal on the day of the Miracle. Since the Warning precedes the Miracle by an unknown number of months, and we know the Miracle is in the months of March, April, May or June, it is thought there will be time to make plans, or else

Heaven would not have planned it this way. If March passes, then it leaves each passing month(s) as a possibility, and so forth. Having an updated passport will be necessary, as well as flight preparations, lodging to the best of one's ability, medicines if necessary, etc. Being prepared for travel will be essential to move prudently if the Miracle is announced by Conchita.

With the present means of communication and travel, eight days are sufficient for people around the world to gather at Garabandal. The day of the Miracle may be the last opportunity given to us by God for repentance, and may be also Our Lady's last effort to save the world from punishment already threatened unless there is an amendment of life. Conchita once said, "The Blessed Mother will not allow me to reveal the nature of the Miracle, although I already know it. But before the Miracle takes place, Our Mother has said that all mankind will receive a Warning from Heaven first."

The more details of the Garabandal story are read and digested, the more it is difficult to process all of the mystical phenomena that happened from 1961-1965. When millions recount the same stories of a miraculous Warning, their witness will validate the legitimacy of the apparitions and messages to the most hardened skeptic. People will fall on their knees in repentance when the promised Miracle is seen from the natural amphitheater of the tranquil Cantabrian Mountains, looking down upon the nine pines. That in itself is part of a much bigger story that is being scripted by Heaven. The sins of man are so scandalous, and solutions so elusive, it will take an event such as this to reorient man to God's design for living.

After the Miracle

A permanent, visible supernatural sign will remain at the nine pines until the end of time. It will be possible to televise, film and photograph this wonder, but not touch it. It has been likened to a column of smoke or a ray of sunlight, but is not either one.

Conchita was told by the Blessed Virgin that a sign would remain at the nine pines. It would appear as a thing not of this world, but it would originate from God. It would be miraculous, and permanent.

A Gift of Unfathomable Mercy

What is it in an individual that makes him or her open to all of the Blessed Mother's phenomena? After decades of observation, I think it is that the people who gravitate to her messages are open to what God is willing to freely give, and they simply say — YES in a spirit of child-like faith. Since Mary as a young girl from Nazareth gave her YES, her fiat to the angel Gabriel that she would be the Mother of God, then God was able to accomplish His will for the salvation and redemption of the world. By saying YES, the Lord can work in our life. When there is surrender, there is growth. Only when our ego submits to the will of Heaven, is there growth. As Jesus said, *"Unless a grain of wheat falls into the ground and dies, it remains alone; but if it dies, it bears fruit"* (John 12:24). Scripture provides all we need for salvation, if we live it. However, Our Lady is a sumptuous feast of modern-day epistles. To grasp the totality of the messages and their impact we must be humble, and accept that we do not know the magnificent things Heaven will do on our behalf because of the love it has for all people.

The prophesied events at Garabandal will change history like possibly no other event since the Incarnation of Jesus. Msgr. Eugenio Beitia Aldazabal (deceased 1985) who was the Bishop of Santander, Spain from 1962-1965 when the apparitions took place, after reading a letter that Conchita gave to him, the Bishop said, **"if these girls are not insane, this event alone (most likely the Miracle) is comparable to the death of Christ."**

As predicted, there has been confusion and controversy in regard to the spread of the message of Garabandal. Jesus told Conchita: "Do not worry yourself whether people believe or do not believe... I shall do everything. But I will also give you suffering. I will be with whoever suffers for Me.... You will have much to suffer for few people will believe you." The suffering of Conchita and the other visionaries, as well as the lack of belief in the apparitions, were foretold by Our Lady.

We are now in a period of waiting and expectation in regard to the prophesied events of Garabandal. During this time let us all in faith, while living and spreading the messages, pray and make sacrifices and place everything in the hands of Our Lord. Let us keep up our courage and remember there is nothing that so enlarges the capacity of the Heart for

God as suffering and putting our trust in Him. He is the King of love, mercy, and peace. One who finds God, finds peace.

Isaiah writes how the Lord uses signs: *"I come to gather nations of every language; they shall come and see my glory.* ***I will set a sign among them;*** *from them I will send fugitives to the nations…, to the distant coastlands that have never heard of my fame, or seen my glory; and they shall proclaim my glory among the nations. They shall bring all your brethren from all the nations as an offering to the Lord…."* This is clearly talking about the coming of a Messiah and the signs that He would make available to all the nations.

Isaiah continues what it would be like. *"As the new heavens and a new earth which I will make shall endure before me, says the Lord, so shall your name and your race endure. From one new moon to another, and from one Sabbath to another, all mankind shall come to worship before me, says the Lord"* (Is. 66:18-23).

CHAPTER 9

Our Lady — Appointed by the Trinity

*"'Jesus said to her,' Did I not tell you that if you would believe
you would see the glory of God"*

JOHN 11:40

(to Lazarus's sister Martha before He raised Lazarus from the dead).

W hen all is lost, a child goes to its mother. It is with the mother that the
child finds the solace, gentleness, forgiveness, and understanding
that only a mother can give. Mankind has cried out many times in history
to the Blessed Mother, and it has been through her direct intervention that
history has been altered on many occasions.

At the moment, we are a morally rudderless world, and it will be again
through the Blessed Mother that life-changing events will get us back on
course. Events like Lepanto (1571) and the Siege of Vienna (1683) are just
two instances where Heaven saved the Christian world from disasters.
Sister Lucia of Fatima once used the emotive phrase, that the world was in
a state of **"diabolical disorientation."** Heaven is going toe to toe with the
enemy, and "the gates of Hell will not prevail against the Church" (Matthew
16:18). The battle has already been won. That is the promise of Scripture.
The chosen instrument for that task by the Most Holy Trinity is the Blessed
Virgin Mary — the Daughter of the Father, the Mother of the Son, and the
Spouse of the Holy Spirit.

Consistent Themes

*"Amen, I say to you, unless you become like a little child, you will not enter
the Kingdom of Heaven. Whoever humbles himself like this child is the
greatest in the Kingdom of Heaven."*

MATTHEW 18:3-4

There are important links between La Salette, France; Fatima, Portugal; Akita, Japan; and Medjugorje, Bosnia, and other apparition sites to Garabandal. Similar themes include:

- the importance and power of the Rosary and of the priesthood,
- messages and secrets given to young innocent children,
- the emphasis on the Eucharist,
- the presence of angels,
- emphasis is placed on the sacraments,
- secrets given which will be revealed at later dates,
- the urgent call for prayer and penance,
- the emergence of a main visionary among the children,
- visions of coming calamities unless there is repentance.

Garabandal is yet another instance where the Blessed Mother points to the absolute basic fundamental tenets of the faith.

A Fatima Garabandal Connection[26]

"All true apparitions of Our Lady have their own uniqueness. Lourdes has its grotto, Fatima its *cova* and Garabandal its *calleja*. But while the locations and characteristics of each manifestation change, the messages which the Blessed Virgin comes to deliver are similar and always include requests for prayer and penance.

"When Our Lady appeared at Fatima in 1917, she did something she had not done before: she addressed messages specifically to the entire world. While she appeared again after Fatima at Beauraing (1932-33) and Banneux (1933), she did not speak to the world at either of those places. At Garabandal again we find this universal appeal. Although Fatima and Garabandal are separate events, there is continuity in the revelations and similarities in features of the events not found among the other visits of Our Lady during the Marian Age.

An Angel Leads the Way

"At both Fatima and Garabandal an angel appeared first to prepare the way for the Blessed Virgin. At Garabandal it was Saint Michael the Archangel and at Fatima the Angel of Portugal. At both Fatima and Garabandal, the visionaries received Communion from the angel, the only two apparitions of Our Lady where this occurred.

"Both Fatima and Garabandal had a visionary named Jacinta.

"At Fatima in August of 1917, to prevent the young seers from going to the site of the apparitions, they were detained in jail by civil authorities. At Garabandal in July of 1961, Conchita, who was thought to be the ringleader and the one influencing the others, was taken to Santander where she was detained for several days.

"At Fatima, the seers saw a vision of hell. At Garabandal, the seers saw visions of hell on earth in the tribulation and Chastisement.

"At both Fatima and Garabandal a great miracle was/is to serve as the seal of authenticity for the events. At Fatima, Our Lady said she would perform a miracle so all would believe. At Garabandal she said, as a result of the Miracle, "all will believe."

Rosary and Scapular

"The Virgin appeared at Fatima as Our Lady of the Rosary, thereby giving great emphasis to that powerful and important Marian prayer. At Garabandal, the Rosary theme continued with the visionaries being commanded by the Virgin to pray it during almost every apparition. Our Lady herself taught them the mysteries and how to pray it well.

"In the sixth apparition at Fatima on October 13, 1917, during the visions of the Miracle of the Sun, Our Lady appeared as Our Lady of Mount Carmel with the scapular on her wrist. On July 2, 1961, the Virgin appeared at Garabandal as Our Lady of Mount Carmel with a large brown scapular draped over her right arm.

Russia

At both Fatima and Garabandal, Russia was mentioned. At Fatima, Our Lady warned that if people did not change, Russia would spread her errors throughout the world. At Garabandal she said that if people do not change, Russia would rule the world. At Fatima, the Virgin said that as a result of the Collegial Consecration (still a red-hot issue which some believe has been done, while others do not), Russia would be converted. At Garabandal, Conchita was told by Our Lord in a locution that Russia would be converted as a result of the great Miracle.

The following excerpt is taken from *The Immaculate Heart—The True Story of Fatima* by Fr. John De Marchi, I.C.M., published in 1952:

"Though no attempt has been made in this volume to describe the fulfillment of Our Lady's promise to return to the Cova da Iria a seventh time, it can be said with certainty that the apparition did take place. It occurred June 18, 1921, Lucia's last day in Aljustrel before leaving for the convent school at Vilar. That evening, having left her home and paying a last visit to the Cova da Iria, she is said to have seen Our Lady standing at a spot now occupied by the lower steps of the Basilica. I wrote to Sister Lucia about this, but have not yet received a reply. I have, however, been assured by a priest very close to Lucia that she has confirmed this happened.

At Garabandal, Saint Michael first appeared to the visionaries in the evening (8:30 pm) of June 18, 1961, exactly 40 years (a biblical number) to the day, and even the same time of day from the last vision at Fatima."[27]

Vatican II—Fatima, Garabandal & Times of Change, Notables Comment

Most of humanity will have no interest in Garabandal prior to the prophesied events, but few, if any, will be able to ignore it after the Illumination of Conscience. Garabandal is an extension of Heaven's plan for the salvation of mankind — and to prepare the world for it. It had been expected that Saint Pope John XXIII would reveal the Third Secret of Fatima in 1960, but he did not, to the disappointment of the faithful. Is it a coincidence that just a year later the Blessed Mother came to Garabandal?

Vatican II was opened by Pope John XXIII on October 11, 1962 and was closed by Pope Paul VI on December 8, 1965. There have been thousands of books and an unknown number of articles written on Vatican II, and what has happened to the Church since the Council. There isn't a view that has not been expressed. One thing at this point is certain. Vatican II has had a profound impact on Catholic thought and practices world-wide. Well over 100,000 priests left the priesthood as they no longer wanted to be a part of a Church where they felt reverence and custom were severed. They felt orthodoxy was being challenged, and the Church was being hijacked by liberals, taking the Church in a direction the orthodox never wanted. There was a battle among the progressives and conservatives, largely not in public view during the Council, over the direction of the Church. Many feel the Synod on Synodality expected to end in October 2024, is operating in the same divisive manner.

The core of the messages at Garabandal were about the sanctity and the supremacy of the priesthood and the Eucharist, both immutable concepts in Roman Catholic practice. Both of these were challenged at Vatican II, if not in the documents, then in practice after the Council. Is this the reason for the very important bookends of messages, *"The cup is filling up,"* to *"The cup is flowing over,"* as the Blessed Mother stated early on in her messages.

Much of the information below deals with Fatima, the Third Secret, evil at the summit of the Church, apostasy, the culture, and the Church in general. The messages of Garabandal are eerily similar to Fatima as they pertain to the direction of the Church going forward from 1961 to the present day.

Cardinal Karol Wojtyla, two years before he became Pope John Paul II, said the following on November 9, 1976 at the Eucharistic Congress in Philadelphia, Pennsylvania:

> "We are standing in the face of the greatest historical confrontation humanity has gone through. I do not think that wide circles of the American society or wide circles of Christian community realize this fully. We are now facing the final confrontation between the Church and the anti-Church, of the Gospel and the anti-Gospel.

This confrontation lies within the plans of divine providence. It is a trial which the whole Church... must take up."

In November of 1980 in Fulda, Germany in one of Pope John Paul II's early visits from Rome speaking to a small group of Catholics as reported in the October, 1981, issue of *Stimme des Glaubens*, (Voice of Faith), the Holy Father was asked, "What about the Third Secret of Fatima? Should it not have already been published by 1960?" Pope John Paul II responded, "Given the seriousness of the contents, my predecessors in the Petrine Office diplomatically preferred to postpone publication so as not to encourage the world power of Communism to make certain moves.

"On the other hand, it should be sufficient for all Christians to know this: if there is a message in which it is written that the oceans will flood whole areas of the earth, and that from one moment to the next millions of people will perish, truly the publication of such a message is no longer something desired..."

The Pope grasped a Rosary and said: "Here is the remedy against evil. Pray, pray, and ask for nothing more. Leave everything else to the Mother of God."

What is going to happen to the Church? Pope John Paul II answered, "We must prepare ourselves to suffer great trials before long, such as will demand of us a disposition to give up even life, and a total dedication to Christ and for Christ...With your prayer and my prayer it is possible to mitigate this tribulation, but it is no longer possible to avert it, because **only by this can the Church be effectively renewed.** How many times has the renewal of the Church sprung from blood? This time, too, it will not be otherwise. We must be strong and prepared, and trust in Christ and His Mother, and be very, very, assiduous in praying the Rosary."[28]

Some of the quotes below are from material that has no known source, but were sent to me by a friend from material he had gathered on Garabandal over time. From this accumulation of information over the years, he has sent many of the quotes from Vatican officials and others. Under the quote, sources are provided where available.

Pope John Paul II again addressed the issue of Fatima, Russia, and the obstacle of Communism for world peace when he said in 1993, "I have come to understand that the only solution to all the problems of the world, the deliverance from war, the deliverance from atheism, and the defection from God, is the conversion of Russia. The conversion of Russia is the content and meaning of the message of Fatima. Not until then will the triumph of Mary come."

July 21, 1983: During an interview with Abbe' Alfred Combe from France, Bishop Joao Perieira Venancio, Bishop of Leiria-Fatima declared, "This message given by the Most Holy Virgin in Garabandal is the same that she gave in Fatima, but it is updated for our time."[29]

November 14, 1984: Cardinal Joseph Ratzinger, who had intimate knowledge of revelations at Akita, Japan and the Third Secret of Fatima (since he knew the contents of both messages) said, "The Third Secret is a radical call for conversion; the absolute importance of history; the dangers threatening the faith and the life of the Christian, and therefore of the world. And then the importance of the '**novissimi**' (the last events at the end of time). But the things contained in the Third Secret correspond to what has been announced in Scripture and are confirmed by many other Marian apparitions."

Pope Paul VI on October 13, 1977 said,

> "The tail of the devil is functioning in the disintegration of the Catholic world. The darkness of Satan has entered and spread throughout the Catholic Church, even to its summit. Apostasy, the loss of faith, is spreading throughout the world into the highest levels within the Church."[30]

> "In 1975 Cardinal Alfredo Ottaviani, former Head of the Holy Office and Head of the Congregation for the Doctrine of the Faith, personally spoke with Sister Lucia of Fatima in May 1955. Cardinal Ottaviani had read the Third Secret of Fatima, and also spoken with Conchita Gonzalez of Garabandal in January 1966 at the Vatican stated that, 'he believed in the supernatural character of Garabandal.' Cdl. Ottaviani also said, 'We must pray a great deal, so that the Church may acknowledge Garabandal.'"[31]

> "An inopportune revelation of the text would only have further exasperated the two tendencies which continue to tear the Church apart: a traditionalism which would believe itself to be assisted by the Fatima prophecies, and a progressivism which would have lashed out against these apparitions, which in such a scandalous manner would seem to put the brakes on the conciliar Church's forward progress ... Pope Paul VI judged it opportune and prudent

to delay the revelation of the text until better times. Pope John XXIII declared that the text did not refer to his pontificate ... And the following popes did not consider that the moment had come to lift the veil of mystery, in circumstances where the Church has still not overcome the frightening impact of twenty post-conciliar years, during which the crisis of the Faith has installed itself at every level."[32]

"Sister Lucia of Fatima never gave one positive quote regarding the Second Vatican Council. If Sister Lucia had said something positive about Vatican II, then we would have heard about it. Her silence on this point means something... it means a lot."[33]

"Can you see now the reason why Our Lady ordered the Third Secret to be revealed in 1960 before Vatican II? After the Third Secret was buried, Sister Lucia was silenced. Our Lady then came to Garabandal in order to give us the contents of the same Message in a 'brief updated form.'"[34]

"Referring to the situation of the Church today, the Holy Father (Pope Paul VI) states that he has the feeling that, from some fissure (crack) the smoke of Satan has entered the temple of God ...It was believed that after the Council would come a day of sunshine in the history of the Church. But instead, there has come a day of clouds and storms and of darkness." ..."

"Today the Church is experiencing a moment of anxiety. Some practice self-criticism, one would even say auto-demolition [self-destruction]. It is like an acute and complex interior upheaval, which no one would have expected after the Council."[35]

"How did this happen? The Pope confides his thoughts to those present: that there has been the intervention of an adverse (adversarial) power. His name is the devil, this mysterious being which is also alluded to in the Letter of St. Peter."[36]

Antonia Gonzalez, Conchita's aunt, stated, "I have also heard them say that if we do not amend our lives, Russia will rule the world. Yes, they said all that, in front of me, during their ecstasy. And also that some big Chastisement would come. Conchita often repeated it. She also talked about the cardinals — that they would go against the Pope. All this is coming true, little by little."[37] "In the Third Secret it is foretold, among other things, that the great apostasy in the Church begins at the top."[38]

Cardinal Joseph Ratzinger told a personal friend, a German priest and former professor of theology in Brazil (Father Ingo Döllinger), that Our Lady warned that there would be an evil council in the Church that would cause great scandal. Not long after the June 26, 2000 publication of the Third Secret of Fatima by the Congregation for the Doctrine of the Faith, Cardinal Joseph Ratzinger told Fr. Döllinger during an in-person conversation that there is still a part of the Third Secret that they have not published! "There is more than what we published," Ratzinger said. He also told Döllinger that the published part of the Secret is authentic and that the unpublished part of the Secret speaks about **"a bad council and a bad Mass" that was to come in the near future.**

"What we have published is not the whole secret. We were instructed to do so." — Gottfried Kiniger's recorded conversation with Father Ingo Döllinger.[39]

Mother Angelica said to her national television audience on May 16, 2001: "As for the Secret, I happen to be one of those individuals who thinks we didn't get the whole thing... Because I think it's scary ...."[40]

On July 15, 1946, Catholic historian Professor William Thomas Walsh interviewed Sister Lucia at her convent of the Dorothean Sisters at Vilar, Portugal. This interview clearly demonstrates that Our Lady's request for the consecration of Russia will only be fulfilled when the Pope, together with the world's Catholic bishops, consecrates Russia specifically.

"Sister Lucia made it plain that Our Lady did not ask for the consecration of the world to Her Immaculate Heart. What She (Our Lady) demanded specifically was the consecration of Russia. Sister Lucia stated more than once and with deliberate emphasis: 'What Our Lady wants is that the Pope and all the bishops in the world shall consecrate Russia to Her Immaculate Heart on one special day. If this is done, she will convert Russia and there will be peace. If it is not done, the errors of Russia will spread through every country in the world."

Professor Walsh asked, "Does this mean, in your opinion, that every country (including the United States of America and the Vatican City State), without exception, will be overcome by Communism?"

Sister Lucia replied, "Yes." (this was her precise answer).[41]

On October 25, 2011, Fr. Gabriel Amorth was interviewed by José María Zavala. During the interview, Fr. Amorth related—as he has done elsewhere—that he did not believe the consecration of the world by Pope

John Paul II in 1984 was sufficient to satisfy the requirements set forth by Our Lady. Fr. Gabriel Amorth, the famous Roman exorcist, personally knew Saint Pio (Padre) for twenty-six years, and it is from this towering figure of 20th century Catholic sanctity, that he claims to have learned the contents of the Third Secret of Fatima. Saint Pio also confirmed the apparitions of Our Lady in Garabandal. The interview follows:

Zavala: "Forgive me for insisting on the Third Secret of Fatima: Did Padre Pio relate it, then, to the loss of faith within the Church?"

(Fr. Gabriele furrows his brow and sticks out his chin. He seems very affected.)

Amorth: "Indeed," "One day Padre Pio said to me very sorrowfully: 'You know, Gabriele? It is Satan who has been introduced into the bosom of the Church and within a very short time will come to rule a false Church.'"

Zavala: "Oh my God! Some kind of antichrist! When did he prophesy this to you?"

Amorth: "It must have been about 1960, since I was already a priest then."

Zavala: "Was that why John XXIII had such a panic about publishing the Third Secret of Fatima, so that the people wouldn't think that he was the anti-pope or whatever it was …?"

A slight but knowing smile curls the lips of Father Amorth.

Zavala: "Did Padre Pio say anything else to you about future catastrophes: earthquakes, floods, wars, epidemics, hunger …? Did he allude to the same plagues prophesied in the Holy Scriptures?"

Amorth: "Nothing of the sort mattered to him, however terrifying they proved to be, except for the great apostasy within the Church. This was the issue that really tormented him and for which he prayed and offered a great part of his suffering, crucified out of love."

Zavala: "The Third Secret of Fatima?"

Amorth: "Exactly."

Zavala: "Is there any way to avoid something so terrible, Fr. Gabriele?"

Amorth: "There is hope, but it's useless if it's not accompanied by works. Let us begin by consecrating Russia to the Immaculate Heart of Mary, let us recite the Holy Rosary, let us all do prayer and penance…"[42]

Interview on October 19, 1982 — Mari Loli

Q: "Do you remember what the Blessed Mother said about the Communist tribulation that is to precede the Warning?

A: It would look like the Communists have taken over the whole world and it would be very hard to practice the religion, for priests to say Mass or for the people to open the doors of the churches.

Q: Is that what you meant when you said that it would seem as though the Church had disappeared?

A: Yes.

Q: It would be because of the persecution and not because the people would stop practicing their religion?

A: Yes, but I guess a lot of people will stop. Whoever practices it will have to go into hiding.

Q: Will this only be in Europe or do you think it will be here in the United States as well?

A: I don't know because for me at that time, Europe was the whole world. I just assumed it was that way. The Blessed Mother didn't specify in what place. To me it looked like it was everywhere.

Q: Approximately 67% of the earth's land is now dominated by Communism. Do you think that's sufficient to fulfill Our Lady's prophecy?

A: I really don't know. It sounded to me like it would be more than that.

Q: In other words you think it will be worse than now?

A: That's what I thought from what she said but I really don't know exactly. To me it looked more like it was every place out there, the places I saw in my mind. In a lot of countries in Europe you can still practice your religion.

Q: So, the situation in the world is not bad enough for the Warning to happen?

A: The Warning is not going to happen yet so it's probably going to get worse.

Q: You said that it would be very difficult for priests to say Mass. Was this something that the Blessed Mother told you or was it something that you thought yourself because of the Communist tribulation?

A: From what I remember, it was something she said.

Q: And the Virgin said that it would seem as though the Church had disappeared?

A: Yes.

Q: Did the Blessed Mother ever say anything about the Holy Father having to leave Rome at the time of the Warning?

A: No, but what it looked like to me — maybe at this time I was confusing in my mind what I was seeing and what the Blessed Mother was saying to me because it's been so many years — but what it looked like to me was that the Pope couldn't be in Rome either, you know what I mean, out in the open. He was being persecuted, too, and had to hide just like everybody else.

Q: Will people be fighting with one another when the Warning comes?

A: (No answer)"[43]

In the conclusion to his study of the Third Secret, Fatima scholar, Frère Michel sums up his findings as follows:

"Having reached the end of our inquiry, we are able to discern, with near certainty, the essential elements of Our Lady's final secret: **While 'in Portugal, the dogma of the Faith will always be preserved,' in many nations, perhaps in almost the entire world, the Faith will be lost.** The pastors of the Church will fail gravely in the duties of their office. Through their fault, consecrated souls and the Faithful in great number will let themselves be seduced by pernicious errors spread everywhere. This will be the time of the decisive battle between the Blessed Virgin and the devil. A wave of diabolical disorientation will be hurled over the world. **Satan will introduce himself even to the highest summit of the Church.** He will blind the minds and harden the hearts of pastors. And God will deliver them to themselves as a chastisement for their refusal to obey the requests of the Immaculate Heart of Mary. This will be the great apostasy predicted for the 'last times'; 'the False Lamb' and 'False Prophet' will betray the Church to the profit of 'the Beast,' according to the prophecy of the Apocalypse."[44]

July 13, 1998 – On the 81st Anniversary of the Third Secret of Fatima, during a famous radio interview on *Coast to Coast AM with Art Bell*, Father Malachi Martin said:

> "The Secret was meant for the people, not for the pope, not for the bishops, not for the Holy Office. It was meant to be published, in 1960, by explicit order, by the mandate of Heaven. John XXIII, God bless him and rest his soul, decided not to. He had his own reasons. We think, with all due respect and veneration etc., that he made a very bad mistake. And indeed, there was a second appearance of Our Lady, this time in Spain, in Garabandal. And the message was very dire."

In the End Comes the Triumph of the Immaculate Heart as Prophesied at Fatima

Very early in the messages given by the Blessed Mother to Father Stefano Gobbi, reported in *To the Priests Our Lady's Beloved Sons* (December 19, 1973, number 29), was a message entitled, **The Triumph of My Immaculate Heart**. The Marian Movement of Priests gave a message of great hope to the faithful and her direct intervention at some point. It reads:

"(e) I have chosen you and prepared you for the triumph of my Immaculate Heart in the world, and these are the years when I will bring my plan to completion.

(f) It will cause amazement even to the angels of God, a joy to the saints in Heaven, a consolation and great comfort for all the just on earth, mercy and salvation for a great number of my straying children, a severe and definitive condemnation of Satan and his many followers.

(g) **In fact, at the very moment when Satan will be enthroned as the lord of the world and will think himself the sure victor, I myself will snatch the prey from his hands, in a trice he will find himself empty-handed, and in the end the victory will be exclusively my Son's and mine. This will be the Triumph of my Immaculate Heart in the world."**

The word trice means "in an instant, a very short time, a burst, or moment." Garabandal will burst on the world at some point in the future to a very unknowledgeable population that has no familiarity with the subject. After the event, it will consume their interest for some time to find out what just happened and to learn what happens next. They will also find out it had all been prophesied far earlier, but they remained ignorant of it.

Mother Angelica's View on Garabandal

Mother Angelica was one of the people who, without reservation, believed in what happened in Garabandal. Mother Angelica was crippled as a young woman using a floor buffer machine, and as a result, had worn metal braces on both her legs for forty-two years. She experienced a miraculous healing. Of all places in the world where she could have chosen to give thanks in gratitude, she went to Garabandal. When healed, she once joked, she forgot what to do with her arms when walking, so she decided to just swing them! In the year 2000, Mother Angelica (before her illness which made her bedridden) was a guest in my home for several days, and we spoke of Garabandal. She was a speaker at the International Week of Prayer and Fasting (IWOPF.org) at the Basilica of the Shrine of the Immaculate Conception, in Washington, D.C. During that stay with us, she told me of her affection for Garabandal. My wife and I have organized and sponsored the event since October 7 (Feast of the Rosary), 1990, and she told me her most popular show in history was when she interviewed Joey Lomangino on EWTN. It was Rita Rizzo (who became Mother Angelica), an Italian woman who had a difficult youth, speaking to an Italian man from New York, and the spiritual and cultural connection was obvious.

Mother's holy boldness was well known. She told me that she was going to ask Conchita to give her an extra day's notice on the announcement of the Miracle so she could get her camera crew there before the crowds descended. Flights and lodging would surely become more difficult for the Great Miracle prophesied to happen there. Only Conchita would ever know if Mother did ask for a day jump before the eight-day notice for the rest of the world. Anyone who ever knew Mother would believe this story.

Young Rita had grown up around stigmatist and mystic Rhoda Wise (1888-1948), in Canton, Ohio. As a young girl Rhoda had made an indelible impression on her that lasted her whole life. She had seen the fruit of Rhoda's spirituality that then became ingrained in her. EWTN's growth exploded in the mid 1990's, when Mother started to bring on more guests like Joey who would openly speak of the mystical and supernatural. EWTN had been a force before then, but in the mid 1990's, many of her guests were people who spoke of things that were traditionally not mentioned by the more established Catholic media. Mother had a spiritual openness to what the Holy Spirit was doing in the world, and she was fearless operating in that dimension. This is what makes people saints.

The Fatima Prophecy Continues to Unfold

In January, 1951, three years after Cardinal Mindszenty (1892-1975) of Hungary was arrested for organizing resistance against atheistic Communism, he briefly escaped and sought refuge in the American Embassy. He lived in the embassy until 1971. Soviet influence had been there previously, but Soviet tanks rolled through the streets in 1956. Since the end of World War II, Stalin had dramatically expanded his empire through the skillful application of force and deception. He now had dominion over 21 countries — fifteen union republics and six European satellites. The borders of his real estate stretched from the North Pole to the 35th parallel and enclosed twelve seas belonging to three oceans (Artic, Atlantic, and Pacific), 27,000 lakes, and 150,000 rivers with a total length of 2 million miles. Counting the Communist revolution in China that had largely been initiated and organized by Soviet advisers, and was now about to succeed, the rulers in the Kremlin would oversee more than a third of the world's population.[45] Still today, Communism and Russia continue to be a scourge on humanity. Communism is still the central threat to the world according to the Garabandal messages.

The Fatima message was clear and direct: Russia would spread her errors throughout the world if Our Lady's messages were not heeded. When the Blessed Mother appeared in May of 1917 at Fatima, Portugal, it was six months before the Bolshevik Revolution happened. In just a few short years, there had been enormous damage by an atheistic godless pagan ideology that spread to the world, causing incalculable damage. Countries throughout the world toppled one at a time under the hammer and sickle of Russia.

Bella Dodd (1904-1969), a leading member of the American Communist Party, writes in her autobiography titled, *School of Darkness (1954),* how the Communists had deeply penetrated the seminaries of the world and placed young men in them to infiltrate the Church. Over time, she states that many became influential, with several even becoming Cardinals. In 1952, she was received back into the Church at Saint Patrick's Cathedral in New York City (she had been raised Catholic), under the guidance of Archbishop Fulton J. Sheen. This was also the era when Stalin was firing on all cylinders, exporting his cultural poison through an organized and well-funded effort around the world. Stalin was specifically focused on Spain at the time prior to, and during the Spanish Civil War of 1936-39. Due to the war, Stalin felt Spain was a fruit ripe for the picking, and resources were sent to the Spanish Communists. Russia was specifically mentioned at Fatima, and Russia again was specifically mentioned at Garabandal. Heaven sees the future and warns against impending danger on a continual basis, and if the message is unheeded, it is to man's peril.

Right out of the Communist play book, year after year, and decade after decade is an agenda to create class warfare in its many forms. Russia under the Tsarist regime as early as 1881 had a pogrom in the Ukrainian town of Yelisavetgrad. A pogrom or organized persecution against the Jews was a way to create a new order of control, creating a common enemy of the masses to vent anger and frustration. Pitting people against people with a common enemy had been a tactic Stalin learned well from his predecessors, and then perfected for global export in the 1930's. After assuming leadership of Russia upon Lenin's death in 1924, Stalin had then amassed total control over Russia and its Republics by the 1930's. This then became the unified and powerful USSR Empire, spanning eleven time zones.

In 1950, President Truman approved one of the most important U.S. government documents of that time: National Council Report 68, or NSC 68. This was a fifty-eight-page, top secret report of the National Security Council (declassified in 1975), which set forth the strategy of containment and became a significant weapon in the Cold War. By 1950, the Soviet Union had detonated an atomic bomb, installed a Communist government in China, and expanded its reign over a third of the world. The NSC report described the challenges facing the United States in cataclysmic terms. *"The issues that face us are momentous,"* the document stated, *"involving the fulfillment of destruction not only of this Republic, but of civilization itself."*

The Communists, much like the progressives, liberals, socialists, and Communists in the United States today, scattered throughout leadership have applied the principles of class warfare to control the population. They have also weaponized liberal clergy under a mantle of social justice to bring in their agenda, saying it is the merciful gospel message of Jesus Christ. Their method has been to never stop pushing. Yuri Andropov, when Premier of the Soviet Union, continued

to give the American population the Communist message like cocaine daily, until they become addicts. When a high-level Soviet defector left the Communist propaganda campaigns after a thirty-year career, he said, "A drop makes a hole in a stone not by force, but by constant dripping. This is how disinformation works: drop, by drop, by drop. It would take time, but whenever you could not use a drill, the best way was to make a hole."[46] This has been the tactic of liberal governments in the West to indoctrinate the masses with idolatrous doctrine, thereby destroying people's souls. The Communists' primary focus was infiltrating and taking over the teacher unions of the world, and then the students would be ripe for the plucking, as they were just decades later. It was a brilliant strategy that worked to perfection. A long-time march on perversion has overtaken school systems at the administrative level, and they are now the masters of educational curricula in the school rooms throughout the West.

CHAPTER 10

The Old Testament and Garabandal

The Permanent Sign—A Sign that Will Fill the World with Awe

The Permanent Sign is what the Blessed Virgin promised will remain at Garabandal after the miracle at "the pines," a grove of nine pines outside the village, at the top of a rocky lane leading up the hill. A permanent sign will remain forever as a result of **the Great Miracle**. It will be of supernatural origin and something that has never been seen before on earth. Conchita has written: "A sign of the Miracle, which will be possible to film or televise, will **remain forever at the pines**." No one, however, will be able to touch it. It will remind us forever of the great Miracle, which will center on that very spot. Anyone who wishes will be able to go to Garabandal after the Miracle and see the sign.

The sign to call His people to Himself will focus our attention on the truth that God has visibly intervened on this mountain, just as He did on Mount Sinai, Mount Carmel, Mount Zion, and Calvary. Patriarchs of old set up altars and monuments to commemorate forever their experience of God at a certain place, which became forever sacred by His coming. At Garabandal, the Lord Himself will set His own sign in the pines for a perpetual memorial of His saving act for today's world.

The sign will call us all to holiness. The Israelites were continually reminded by the fiery cloud (called the Shekinah Glory) hovering over the meeting tent, that God was with them, leading them to holiness, and to the Promised Land. The sign will be with us like that cloud of God's glory. It will remind us that the Lord is leading us to holiness and Heaven and that He will not tolerate idolatry among His people.

Father Joseph Brennan, O.C.S., an early writer on Garabandal, summarized the prophetic statements made by saints, blessed and popes, this way: "They foretell a time of unprecedented and terrible confusion and suffering unlike anything that has ever been experienced in human history. It will affect every area of human life."

When one looks today at the confusion surrounding us from every sphere of human endeavor, the global interconnectivity of the world economy, the breakdown of every social indice possible, one would not have to be a visionary to see how things would unravel even more rapidly with a global systemic financial or negative geopolitical event. Like never before in human history, a significant event in one country will have profound implications for many other countries.

When one studies the Old and the New Testament, there is an understanding of what God is asking of us, and we are given a more complete picture of the identity of God. There is a completeness and fullness in the New that was prophesied in the Old. Jesus said, "I did not come to abolish the law, but to fulfill it" (Matthew 5:17). What messages might the New bring to the Old? Romans 9:4-5 speaks about the privileges of Israel. It reads, "They were adopted as sons, they were given the glory and the covenants; the Law and the ritual were drawn up for them, and the promises were made to them. They are descended from the patriarchs and from their flesh and blood came Christ who is above all, God forever blessed!" In Romans 11:26, St. Paul also foretells that "all Israel should be saved, as it is written: there shall come out of Zion he that shall deliver, and shall turn away godlessness from Jacob." The apparitions and messages of Garabandal are overflowing with Old Testament signs and symbolisms as part of Heaven's plan for the conversion of the world and a new Era of Peace, a New Jerusalem, New Times — A Second Pentecost, which Heaven has promised.

Is the Permanent Sign a Message to the Jews?

Conchita was told by the Blessed Virgin that a sign would remain at the Pines forever. It would appear as a thing not of this world, but it would originate from God. It would be miraculous, a permanent miracle. Is it comparable to a pillar of smoke, but also to rays of sunlight, insofar as it can be seen, but not touched? It will be made up of an unknown substance, but is not specifically the Shekinah Glory because we are told it has never been seen in the world before.

However, we have been told it will be like it. All the Hebrews who followed Moses out of Egypt saw the "pillar of cloud by day and of fire by night" (Exodus 13:21), saving them from the Egyptians (Exodus 14:24), accompanying the Torah at Mount Sinai (Exodus 19: 16-18, 34 :5), remaining present among

His people, serving as their guide "wherever they halted on their journey," (Exodus 40:36), "marking out their encampments" (Deuteronomy 1:33). The prophets announced it would come back, "a cloud and smoke by day, and the shining of a flaming fire by night" (Isaiah 4:5). "It shall come to pass that I will pour out my spirit upon everyone … and I will show wonders in the heavens and on Earth, blood, fire, and pillars of smoke" (Joel 2: 30).

The luminous cloud has always been a choice subject of rabbinic thought and of Christian mystical theology. All Jews know what the pillar meant: a manifestation of God dwelling among His chosen people, tabernacling amongst them, guiding them, shedding light upon them, speaking to them. The nations of Israel knew this (Numbers 14: 14). It is the Shekinah, the most sacred and mysterious sign of the deity. The Shekinah Glory is Heaven itself. It is God's physical presence that was with the Ark of the Covenant in the desert. A cloud by day, a fire by night.

The mysterious cloud invaded the Temple of Solomon (I Kings 8:10). Nehemiah celebrated the Lord "leading Thy people on their journey, hidden by day in a pillar of cloud, by night in a pillar of fire, to light the path they must tread" (Nehemiah 9:12,19). The Psalms mention the Shekinah five times: as the guide of God's people (Psalms 77:17-21 and 78:14), overcoming the idolaters (Psalms 97:2-7), as protector (Psalms 105:39), as carrying His word: "His voice came to them from the pillar of cloud; so they heard the decrees, the law He gave them" (Psalm 99:7). **The prophets announced it would come back,** "a cloud and smoke by day, and the shining of a flaming fire by night" (Isaiah 4:5).

Conchita has said that the Permanent Sign will be **like** a pillar of smoke above the pines. **On November 18, 1961, a column of smoke by day and fire by night was seen by a number of people between the nine pines.** Ramon Gonzalez, a shepherd about twenty years old, was tending his sheep and noticed a small fire about 50 centimeters in diameter. Again, in the autumn of 1962, this same fire was seen by a number of people for a period of several months, all of whom provided written testimony. It was seen again on November 25, 1965, by four French witnesses. The column was seen at night, clear and luminous. The significance of this is hard to explain to the uninformed. This is just one event of the four years of mystical phenomena that surround Garabandal.

Mary Appears at Garabandal Under a Biblical Name— Our Lady of Mount Carmel

For the first time in the history of Marian apparitions, as announced by St. Michael the Archangel, the Blessed Mother appeared under a title which refers to a biblical holy place—Mount Carmel. The three holy mountains of the ancient people of Israel were Mount Carmel, Mount Sinai (or Horeb), and Mount Zion (or Jerusalem). Mount Carmel is the mountain made holy by Elijah the prophet. It is the mountain which Mary had often seen from where she lived. Moreover, of all religious orders, the Carmelites are by far the closest to Judaism. For this reason, Elijah is considered by Carmelite friars and sisters as their founder and model. They celebrate his feast on July 20th each year.

I am a Jewess in Heaven

Conchita described Our Lady in her diary as a beautiful Jewish woman with dark and wavy hair, a perfect nose, full lips, and a rather dark complexion. In other apparitions, Mary appears as a beautiful girl with the features of other girls of the country where she appears. Mari Loli asked her one day if she was Jewish, and her answer was yes, and she said she was a Jewess in Heaven. It was the first time in the history of apparitions that the Blessed Virgin identified herself as such, saying that even in Heaven, she belonged to the Jewish people. This statement was confirmed by the late Garabandal writer, Father Laffineur.

The Likely Reaction from the Rabbis

For observant Jews and Rabbis, a thorough knowledge of the Scriptures is a large measure of their religious life. In Israel, whatever their beliefs, all citizens have studied the Hebrew Scriptures as a text, if only as classical literature. Whether or not they consider it as divinely inspired, believe, and obey it, most still know it. If one were to indiscriminately open the Bible, we would see in many stories how the Lord is using signs and/or wonders as a marker for an event, something to look for to validate what He is saying. The Warning, the Miracle and the Permanent Sign are such events, where something has been foretold, and then it happens.

Jews know it has been prophetically announced that, "your sons and your daughters will prophesy" (Song of Songs 3:6; Joel 2:28; and Acts 2:17-21). They will be interested, especially the Sephardim, the Spanish Jews. Their interest will be extreme and lasting, because the Miracle will be a sign for them. They know if the Permanent Sign is a pillar of smoke by day and a fire by night, or something like it, this will be prophetic sign of enormous significance.

Saint Bernard of Clairvaux and Saint Thomas Aquinas

Historians consider that the first schism in the history of the people of God was between the Gentiles and the church of the Jews. This schism was caused by the refusal of the Synagogue to accept Jesus of Nazareth as the Messiah. In the Roman Basilica of Santa Sabina (early Fifth Century), portentous figures of the Church from the Gentiles and of the Church from the Synagogue stand side by side as true believers. Saint Bernard (1090-1153), mystic, monk, and Doctor of the Church, and Saint Thomas Aquinas (1226-1274), theologian and Doctor of the Church, wrote that the Church would allow the Synagogue to enter into the fullness of her redemption. Saint Bernard wrote that the Synagogue has not, in the eyes of God, forsaken her birthright over her sister the Church. **Saint Thomas in his commentary on the Song of Songs, taught the future reintegration of Israel would usher in the third era of the Church.** His authority is immense, and this view opens up great vistas. Will the Warning and the Great Miracle bring the Jewish pople into the Catholic faith?[47]

It is not merely that there will be a realization, that part of Israel hardened itself (Romans 11: 7-24), but it may potentially come as a consequence of what will happen at Garabandal.

Mysterious Phenomena

*"For ask now of the days that are past, which were before you, since the day that God created man upon the earth, and ask from one end of Heaven to the other, **whether such a great thing as this has ever happened or was ever heard of. Did any people ever hear the voice of God speaking out of the midst of the fire, as you have heard, and still live?***

Know therefore this day, and lay it to your heart, that the Lord is God
in Heaven above and on the earth beneath; there is no other."

DEUTERONOMY 4:32-33, 39

The visions that the girls in Garabandal experienced were preceded by three interior calls (llamadas), each becoming stronger than the last. After the third call, they ran to the sunken lane where the visions first began and, crashing to their knees on the jagged rocks, entered into a heavenly rapture. Their heads were thrown back, the pupils of their eyes dilated and their faces imbued with an angelic countenance. At the time of the apparitions they were all oblivious to their surroundings.

With their heads and bodies in unnatural positions or even contorted states, the girls could march arm in arm up the steep rocky path so rapidly it looked like their feet never touched the ground. Some describing it as gliding, defying all physical and natural law. They could stop so fast it was as if there was no progression of motion to a halt, but to an immediate standstill. After these occurrences of extreme movement over a long period of time, there was never a sign of shortness of breath, perspiration or disheveled clothing on any of the visionaries. They could fall on their back in ecstasy and rise supernaturally with no help from anyone.

Sarai (later she became Sarah) being told at 90 she would conceive and have a son Isaac (while Abraham was 100), the parting of the Red Sea, the ten plagues of Egypt, and the day the sun stood still upon Joshua's request to Yahweh, are all examples of the supernatural. The sun never set on the day of battle so Joshua could fight in prolonged daylight for his people (Joshua 10:13-14). Jesus walking on water, Jesus turning water to wine, and many other miracles, will all be insignificant in scope compared to what is to happen. Over the last several generations, the world has become more secularized, and the Divine and supernatural have been stripped from education and faith formation, but we must not think it isn't real and very possible in our time.

The unnatural occurrences that happened in Garabandal, and those prophesied for the future, have disturbed some people who are detractors of Garabandal. If one were to open Scripture, one would find the supernatural that is the story of God's very nature. In the gospel of Mark 5:12, it is written, "Now many signs and wonders were done among the people by the hands of the apostles." The Book of Acts writes that signs and wonders accompanied the life of Jesus and the apostles wherever they went (Acts: 2:43). To deny the supernatural is to deny the Majesty of God and how He wishes to move and act. God is the supernatural, and to deny its existence is to deny Him. The sun hurtling towards earth at Fatima, where 70,000 people that were in attendance saw it, is not a natural occurrence, yet it happened.

Another remarkable event of Garabandal emphasized the importance of the Eucharist. An angel appeared bearing a golden chalice. The angel asked the children to think of the One whom they were going to receive. He taught them to recite the Confiteor (prayer of Confession or Repentance), after which he gave them Holy Communion. He also taught them to say the Anima Christi in thanksgiving. These direct interventions occurred regularly whenever the priest from the neighboring village of Cosio was unable to come to Garabandal.

Another area of the supernatural was the young visionaries' ability to read hearts. There are several mystical phenomena that have similar outcomes, but with nuances. There is the reading of souls, the reading of hearts, a word of knowledge, or a word of wisdom. These are clearly unique spiritual gifts that are manifested to select souls. They are primarily given to people to edify another soul, and bring the person to a deeper spiritual union with God. The gifts mean different things in the spiritual realm. The young girls displayed gifts that were only supernaturally given on many occasions with the pilgrims visiting Garabandal.

In the natural realm many could call these gifts, instincts, premonitions, guessing, or a gut intuition. These can be based on one's experiences, education, observation, cultural background, or intelligence. With natural gifts acquired over time, decisions could be provided to an individual for a specific situation. For instance, a good Christian psychologist or psychiatrist treating an individual in need of mental care is often not a direct spiritual gift. Such as a medical doctor treating a patient with a rare disease where no one else can break through for a cure is based upon the natural gifts and experience of the doctor. The reading of hearts and souls is a supernatural gift given to a person where no one has an answer unless it is divinely inspired can only come from God. There were instances of this behavior at Garabandal at different times. It was Our Lady who told the young girls about a circumstance or individual. A divinely inspired statement to catapult the person to correct a sin is a spiritual gift. The shock value alone would have merit if there is a sincere desire for repentance and amendment of life of the individual. Many know this was fairly common in the life of Saint Pio (Padre) of San Giovanni Rotondo, Italy, throughout his life. The stories are legion around him where he would say things to people in the confessional that had not been confessed, yet he would then tell them their sins so there could be change often in their own language. This is what started Joey Lomangino on his odyssey of faith promoting Garabandal for a lifetime. The gift is specifically for an individual at a specific point in time to improve another's spiritual state. The Warning and Miracle will be much larger events impacting the entire world, designed to shock the world back to what God desires for all of us. It is the Ultimate Act of Mercy for a lost world. It explains the **"Why."**

CHAPTER 11

The Sanctity of Marriage and the Priesthood Were Major Issues at the Apparitions

The Holy Spirit is dynamic and moves where there is impending trouble coming to mankind. The Blessed Mother sees these troubles in advance, and provides remedies to the situation by asking for amendment of life to avert the disasters in front of us. Nowhere have we seen the downfall of our civilization as clearly as with the disintegration of morals and those failing to maintain fidelity in marriage. The negative repercussions of divorce that are now backed up with strong empirical data, are generational and incalculable.

Very often, wedding rings were given to the young girls to give to the Blessed Mother so she could kiss them. This was done so often, no one kept count. In very large crowds and often in a sea of people, and late at night, the correct ring would be given back to their rightful owner even if the spouses were separated. The girls would often appear to be looking straight up to Heaven, yet returned rosaries, rings, and holy objects to their rightful owners. At one point, Mari Loli had ten wedding rings on her fingers. Over time, there would be miraculous stories told by people who had objects kissed by the Blessed Mother.

"On October 18, 1961, a man from the village, Cecilio Gonzalez, had stayed quietly at home with his wife, while the visionaries had gone to the pine trees to communicate their message. A number of people had left their wedding rings on the kitchen table, hoping that one of the visionaries would present them to the Virgin to be kissed. Late at night, Mari Cruz suddenly arrived in ecstasy, grasped the bunch of rings and began distributing them without the slightest hesitation or mistake to the people who had come to the house with her or had stayed there. Cecilio did not say whether these rings had in fact been kissed, but Our Lady kissed a great many at a time."[48]

Our Lady and The Priesthood at Garabandal Sanchez, Ventura y Pascual, F. The Apparitions of Garabandal The entire article below is from: Our Lady and The Priesthood, Garabandal Journal, July/ August 2018, B. Hanratty, P. 8-12.

In all her appearances during the Marian era beginning with Rue da Bac (Miraculous Medal) in 1830 to Beauraing in 1933, Our Lady did not make the priesthood a subject of her visits, since it was not necessary. Most people understood the essential role of the priest in the Catholic Faith. At Garabandal, the Blessed Virgin did focus attention on the priesthood. Conchita said that Our Lady spoke of priests in almost every apparition. Why she did this would become clear in the following years.

In October of 1965, the Second Vatican Council had its final session. Four months previously, Our Lady, in her second message at Garabandal on June 18, 1965, said, "Many cardinals, many bishops and many priests are on the road to perdition and taking many souls with them." Was this a warning for some clergy planning to make drastic changes in the Church? Perhaps, but if that were the case, they paid no attention. Under the guise of the "spirit of Vatican II," radical changes were introduced to replace the Church's traditional rituals and devotions; even dogmas of faith and morals were fair game for revision and dissent. Another target was the priesthood. In a false ecumenism, for the Catholic Church to be united with Protestant churches who have no priests, the role of the priest must be down-graded to a "sacramentary minister" alongside music ministers, youth ministers, hospitality ministers, etc., in the "new model of Church." This would result in many priests agonizing over an "identity crisis."[49]

Our Lady's Response Ahead of Time

In a remote village like Garabandal, young girls thought that a priest, as a man of God, was beyond reproach. So when the Blessed Virgin told the visionaries to pray for the priests, they were surprised. Our Lady explained why they must do this. In a 1978 interview with Fr. Francis Benac, S.J., Mari Loli said: "One of the things which Our Lady asked of me most frequently was to pray for priests and make sacrifices for them."

In order to emphasize the importance of priests to the seers, the Blessed Virgin told them that, "If you ever see a priest and an angel, greet the priest first and then the angel."[50] As a result of this, the visionaries held the priests in the highest esteem, admired and loved them, and wanted them to come up to the village as often as possible.

This was also the wish of Our Lady, and she interacted through the seers in different ways with the priests who came to the village. Sometimes she gave the seers messages for them, which the girls forgot after telling them to the priest. The visionaries had the ability of recognizing priests even if they were wearing civilian clothes, but they could only do this at the time of apparitions. Our Lady respected the requests of the priests. She once gently chided a Dominican priest for wearing civilian clothes. The Virgin made the seers laugh, telling them how ugly his clothes were in comparison to his beautiful habit. After the ecstasy, Conchita told the priest why they laughed.

The Blessed Virgin provided proof for priests to believe in the truth of the apparitions. On one occasion, she relieved the anxieties of a priest in a striking way. It occurred in the first year of the apparitions in the early days of September, 1961.

Father Ramon Andreu was in Ceferino's tavern and store in Garabandal when a priest in a foul mood entered brusquely, and aggressively made his way toward him.

"Listen, are you Father Andreu?"

"At your service."

"Well, I'm here to tell you that I don't like any of this!"

"No one can know better than you what you don't like. Nevertheless, I appreciate the information. Have you been here long?"

"Ten minutes."

"Hombre! I've been here four weeks and still haven't come to see everything clearly and you — in ten minutes!"

This was a priest from Asturias, who was strong and built like a truck driver. To get out from under this, since he said right away that he was getting very irritated, Father Andreu called over to Dr. Ortiz of Santander, who was passing by, and said to him, "Listen, Dr. Ortiz, this priest here is very interested in this and since you are an intellectual, you can explain some things to him."

Dr. Ortiz took the priest with him. Ten minutes later the priest returned. This time, his attitude was completely different. He was pallid, trembling, not at all the same man he had been before.

"Father Andreu, it's for real! I'm convinced!"

"Listen, let's go slow. Ten minutes ago, you didn't like it at all. And now you are already a convert? Don't you think you're in a bit of a hurry?"

"Judge for yourself what has happened to me. I was walking over there with Dr. Ortiz when we came upon one of the girls named Jacinta, in ecstasy. She came up to me and made the sign of the cross over me; and there was a little man at my side, and she made the sign of the cross over him too. And then she gave me a cross to kiss, and she also gave it to the little man. Then she made the sign of the cross over me again, and did the same to the little man. During this I thought, 'If it is true that it is the Virgin who is appearing, then let the ecstasy end.' At that very instant, the girl lowered her head and looked at me entirely normal!" This left me breathless, and I said to her:

"Aren't you seeing the Virgin?"

"No, senor."

"Why is that?"

"Because she has gone away!"

And so it actually was, as soon as it became evident, that the little man was a parish priest from one of the villages. For some time, he had been tormented by doubts about his priestly ordination: whether or not he had a clear and explicit will to be ordained; and whether as a consequence, his ordination was valid or not; and thus, whether he had been exercising his priestly function validly. Only God could know what the man had been suffering because of these scruples. When he heard talk of Garabandal and of the marvels that were happening there, he thought that he might be able to find a way out of his dark tunnel.

As soon as he could, the doubting priest went to the celebrated village. But before arriving there, he disguised himself carefully. At that time, it was very unusual for a priest or religious to take off his cassock or his habit without serious reason. He had so carefully disguised himself that Father Andreu said, "There was no way to suspect even remotely the presence of the priest there; his outfit was the strangest that could be imagined."

It was a consoling response to the priest's interior doubts that the girl was so definitely repeating to him everything that she had done previously to the priest who was at his side. But that was not enough. What more could be asked for to bring peace to his scrupulous conscience! After the first joy, spiritual confusion returned and he thought: "I cannot leave like this; I need more proof."

He found a place in a stable to pass the night, hoping to see if, on the following day, he would obtain the absolutely convincing proof that he needed so much. The new day came and the poor man did not have to wait for nightfall as would ordinarily be the case. Already in the morning there was an important ecstasy; many people were gathering for the celestial visit and the little man naturally was in the front row.

When the girl in ecstasy began to hold out the crucifix to be kissed, the people rapidly formed a line along her path so the girl could do it more easily. The little man positioned himself like everyone else in the middle of the line, and from there observed with what celestial grace the visionary offered the crucifix, and with what feeling those lined up were kissing it, one after the other. But he did not content himself with observing; his mind was working, and he formed this idea: "If I am truly a priest, instead of giving me the crucifix to kiss like the others, let the girl come and make the sign of the cross over me with it."

Then the girl went up to the police chief who was so well disposed to the cause of Garabandal. She stopped in front of him and smiled, and without looking at him — actually she looked at no one, since during the ecstasy her face was turned sharply upwards — she slowly made the sign of the cross over him. Then she continued her way down the line, presenting the crucifix to be kissed. She came in front of the little man and made the sign of the cross over him! The answer seemed very clear, but…

The man was hard to satisfy. He did not hesitate to think: "This isn't enough since she made the sign of the cross over the police chief too, and the police chief isn't a priest. If instead of this she had given the crucifix to everyone without exception to kiss, and if on me, only on me, she had made the sign of the cross three times, then there definitely would have been no doubt."

He had not finished thinking this when the girl stopped in her tracks and made her way back to the beginning of the line, to once more begin holding out the crucifix to be kissed. She came again in front of the police chief, and she must have heard something from the Vision, since she was heard to ask, "What?" Following a brief pause, she smiled, and gave the crucifix for him to kiss like the others. When she arrived in front of the little man again, we can imagine his emotions. The girl was very carefully making the sign of the cross over him repeatedly—until it was done three times! And something more: she said to him clearly, "Yes."

That was too much; the poor man tried to hide his tears while the girl continued down the line, and he went to the church as soon as he could. There in the sacristy, he opened up the sack that he had brought with him; he put on his priest's cassock with more feeling than ever before, and then fell on his knees in front of the tabernacle, without being able to express to the Lord and His Mother all his feeling of love and gratitude. When he left the church, he was truly another person, much more interiorly than exteriorly.

In showing her predilection for priests at Garabandal, there were times when the Blessed Virgin, through the visionaries, pursued them. The following episode occurred during a nighttime ecstasy in 1961.

At 10:30 at night they gathered in front of the Ceferino's ancient house. Then Conchita arrived in ecstasy, drew near, and began to hold out the crucifix to be kissed. The two men kept themselves away from her, and in order to hide better, went up the outside stairway of the ancient house next door.

The girl, however—with her head tilted far back, without seeing either them or the stairway—miraculously climbed the stairs and held out the crucifix for them to kiss. The first man was visibly shaken and turned away, but the girl managed to make the sign of the cross on him twice with the crucifix. She insisted again that he kiss it and once again the man refused. A third time the girl made the sign of the cross over him with a most gentle expression on her face. Only then did the man relent and put his lips to the crucifix! Almost the same thing happened with his companion.

"The Virgin told me to make sacrifices for the sanctity of priests, so that they may lead many souls to Christ; that the world gets worse each day and needs holy priests to make many people return to the right way. Previously, the Virgin told me to pray especially for the priests who want to give up the priesthood—so that they may continue to be priests."

Conchita majestically descended the stairs and went toward the captain of the Civil Guard to give him the cross to kiss. Unexpectedly she turned and again walked toward the two men and held the crucifix in front of them. Once again, they refused to kiss it! The onlookers were both indignant and scandalized. The girl suddenly came out of the trance, and everyone could see the most obstinate of the two trembling as if he were in pain. He went to hide in a corner, where some of the young boys followed him.

"Father X, what happened?

"Leave me alone, leave me alone."

In the end he confessed: "You saw how I refused the crucifix that the girl offered me. Well, after finally kissing it, I mentally asked God for proof. 'My Lord, if all that is happening here is truly supernatural, let the girl come another time and let her ecstasy stop immediately; that way I'll be able to believe.' You saw what happened. Don't ask me anything more."

Those two men were priests; one of them appears to have been a pastor of Turon, the big mining center in Asturias.[51]

Having heard Our Lady say what she wants in priests, Conchita was able to put together the following:

"The first thing that the Virgin wants from a priest is his own sanctification.

He should fulfill his vows for the love of God, and lead many souls by example and prayer, for in these times it is difficult to do it any other way.

That a priest sacrifice himself for love of souls in Christ!

That at times he retire in silence to hear the God Who speaks to him constantly."

"That he meditate frequently on the passion of Jesus, so that his life may be more united to Christ the Priest, and thus invite souls to penance, sacrifice....

To speak of Mary, who is the most secure way to lead us to Christ.

And also, to speak about and make people believe that if there is a Heaven, there is also a hell. I think that this is what Heaven (Our Lord and Our Lady) is asking from priests."[52]

Garabandal's focus on the priesthood could not have been more dramatically emphasized than by the events involving Jesuit Father Luis Maria Andreu.

On August 8, 1961, while observing the girls in ecstasy at the Pines, Fr. Luis also saw Our Lady and a preview of the great Miracle to come, something the visionaries themselves did not see. His story has been well-publicized, so there is no need to give a complete description here. Suffice it to say that he was the only other person besides the visionaries to have seen Our Lady at Garabandal and one of only two people we know of to have seen the great Miracle in preview (the other being St. Pio) and the only person to have seen it where it will actually occur in time.

In the early morning of August 9, 1961, while being driven by car back to his place of residence following his vision at the Pines, 38-year-old Jesuit Father Luis Maria Andreu, with no health problems other than hay fever, quietly and peacefully passed from this life to the next. Rafael Fontaneda, who was in the same car along with his wife, daughter and chauffeur, could find no other explanation for Fr. Luis's mysterious death than to say that "he died of joy," and recorded for posterity these memorable words uttered by Fr. Luis during his final hour on earth: "I feel overwhelmed with joy. How lucky to have a mother like that in Heaven! We shouldn't be afraid of the supernatural. The children have given us an example of the attitude we should take to the Blessed Virgin. I haven't the slightest doubt that this business of the children is true. Why has she chosen us? Today is the happiest day of my life." Then died on the spot.[53]

A Mystical Communion, The Little Miracle

On June 22, 1962, the angel told Conchita that God would perform a "special miracle." The angel instructed her to reveal the message fifteen days in advance. The people would be allowed to see the Sacred Host appear on Conchita's tongue at the moment she received Communion, in order that they might believe. Conchita's diary entry for June 30, 1962, stated: "While I was in the pines I heard a voice which said that the Miracle would take place on the eighteenth of July." She was unable to receive Communion on the 18th, but did receive the mystical Communion at 1:40 am on July 19th, 1962. This occurred in front of numerous witnesses and was filmed.

Several "Angelic Communions" were recorded on film, showing the movement of the girls' lips, tongue, and throat. However, since these hosts were only visible to the girls, many skeptics doubted that they were actually receiving Holy Communion. We know the promised Miracle is Eucharistic in some form. Father Andreu died of joy from seeing the Miracle. Did he also see a precursor to the Eucharistic Miracle like Conchita received by the angel? When questioned about where the Hosts came from, the angel told them that the Hosts were taken from the tabernacle of the church. The Hosts can only be consecrated by a priest.

Hundreds of witnesses were present to see Conchita receive the mystical communion. The event was recorded on movie film by an amateur photographer, Don Alejandro, a businessman from Barcelona. This film was later submitted to the Bishop of Santander. Conchita left her home in ecstasy, went around a corner and fell to her knees. As the crowd mingled near her, she put out her tongue, and a Host mystically appeared on it.[54]

Witnesses said that Conchita knelt and put out her tongue to receive the Host. At first, nothing was visible. In a few moments, a white Host, thicker than usual, appeared on her tongue. It remained there for a few moments before being consumed. The Eucharist miraculously was placed on Conchita's tongue by St. Michael the Archangel and was called by her the *"Little Miracle."* It became visible for all to see. This calls our attention to the reality of the Real Presence of Our Lord in the Holy Eucharist. Does this portend to a larger Miracle that centers on some aspect of the Eucharist, or something much more profound?

Martyrs of the Eucharist — One Stands Out in the Spirit of Garabandal, Blessed Imelda Lambertini

The Miracle will happen on the feast day of a young martyr of the Eucharist. It may be a female or male, and age is never mentioned specifically, as it just says "**young.**" In the history of the Roman Catholic Church, the list must be nearly endless in the historical anthology of martyrs for potential candidates. Also, with a statement of *little known,* it is like finding a needle in a haystack.

Many have thought the Miracle may happen on the feast day of Saint Hermenegild of Spain, whose feast day is April 13. He is a martyr who fought heresy, and died in the year 585. Others have thought a good candidate, and validly so, is Saint Pancras (died circa 304 or 305AD), a martyr at the age of fourteen with a feast day on May 12th. Another name spoken of is Saint Tarcisius, (366-384) who lived in Rome under Emperor Valerian known for his extreme persecution of the new Christian sect converting in Rome. Tarcisius volunteered to take the Eucharist to prisoners who were condemned to death because, he said, no one would suspect him as a boy so young - so the bishop agreed to let him do it. He was beaten to death while carrying the Eucharist because he refused to give it to a mob. All of these young children are valid candidates for the prescription of the prophecy to be fulfilled.

However, there is one little girl who falls in line with a mystical reception of the Eucharist, and the events of the spirit of Garabandal like no other, and her name is seldom mentioned. Her name is Blessed Imelda Lambertini. She was born in Bologna, Italy in 1322. Imelda begged to receive the Eucharist at the age of nine and was denied because of her age even after making an inquiry to her bishop. A bold and unusual request for a little girl. She was told she could not receive Communion until age 14. On May 12, 1333, on the vigil of the Ascension, she went to Mass and presented herself for Holy Communion at age 11. The priest ignored her completely. A radiant Host rose into the air and stopped in front of her, and she received the Eucharist. She instantly died of ecstasy and pure joy. She was beatified in 1826 and is the Patron Saint of First Communicants.[55]

Imelda died on May 12th, but her feast day is celebrated on May 13th. What is fascinating and rare by all accounts for mysticism in the Catholic Church, is the extremely infrequent mystical appearance and reception of the Consecrated Host given by an angel. It has happened in Church history, but it is still rare. In the case of Conchita, she mystically received a Host on her tongue from Saint Michael, and for Imelda, the Host mystically appeared on her tongue as well. Blessed Imelda, a little-known young martyr of the Eucharist, fits all the criteria and framework of the spirit of the apparitions at Garabandal, especially as it concerns the mystical communion Conchita received from an angel. Her body was found to be incorrupt. In **the old liturgical calendar in the Catholic Church, May 13th was the Feast Day of Our Lady of the Most Blessed Sacrament.** Today, it is generally celebrated as the Feast Day of Our Lady of Fatima, as May 13th was the day the Blessed Mother came to three young visionaries at Fatima.

CHAPTER 12

Significant Witnesses

There are significant witnesses to the phenomena of the apparitions and whose lives were dramatically changed by the events of Garabandal. They are Joey Lomangino, Father Luis Andreu, S.J., and his brother Father Ramon Andreu, S.J., from Spain.

Joey Lomangino

Joey Lomangino was born on October 5, 1930, in Brooklyn, New York. In June, 1947, when Joey was sixteen years old, tragedy struck the Lomangino family. Joey was inflating a tire on one of his father's ice and coal trucks, when suddenly the tire exploded in his face. The tire struck him between the eyes, severing his olfactory and optic nerves and causing total loss of his sight and smell. The following years were difficult. However, with patience and perseverance, Joey completed his education and formed a sanitation business (recycling) with his three brothers.

While on vacation in Italy in 1961, Joey met Saint Pio. This meeting altered his life dramatically, and it became his life mission to promote Garabandal. Joey recalls that he was not a very religious man at the time. However, the meeting with Saint Pio began the process of conversion in his life.

Joey returned to Italy in 1963 to meet Saint Pio again. It was during this visit that Saint Pio encouraged him to go to confession. Joey states that as he blessed himself to begin his confession, Saint Pio interrupted him and began to list in perfect English all of the sins that Joey had committed during his entire life! This overwhelming experience was just the beginning of what was to follow. A few days later, Joey was kneeling and waiting for Saint Pio to begin Mass. As Saint Pio walked by, Joey experienced what he thought to be an explosion in his head. At that moment, Joey instantly regained his sense of smell. He was immediately aware of the scent of roses. Doctors described the miracle as, "A light bulb suspended in the center of the room, without wires attached, and was still capable of lighting." During this visit, Joey asked Saint Pio if Our Lady was appearing at Garabandal. His reply was "Yes." Joey also inquired if he should go there. The answer was "Yes, why not?" So began a series of events that would earn Joey the title of "Blind Apostle of Garabandal." He visited Garabandal many times, and developed a close relationship with the visionaries, and especially Conchita as she eventually lived in New York City not far from Joey.

On March 19, 1964, Conchita received an interior message from Our Lady at the pines. She was told that Joey Lomangino would see again on the day of the great Miracle. Conchita also was told that Joey would establish a "House of Charity" in New York that would bring great glory to God. Joey traveled the world giving his witness to Saint Pio and the messages of Garabandal.

Joey Lomangino Dies, A Cause of Confusion for Many

Joey died at the age of 84 on June 18, 2014, on the fifty-third anniversary of Saint Michael the Archangel first appearing in Garabandal. Joey's death caused confusion. His death was a great disappointment and discouragement for many people who had been waiting and expecting Joey to receive his sight on the day of the Miracle. As a true prophecy is given, it will happen exactly as it was said, but not necessarily the way we perceive. It has been shown over millennia that a prophecy is never completely understood until time passes, which will prove it true or false. It is for this reason the Church usually waits until the death of the visionary to make a final judgment on an apparition's authenticity. Time is the ultimate test. The only explanation at this point is that we may see a miracle in a way no one ever imagined.

On December 6, 1962, Conchita had a ninety-minute ecstasy at 5:30 pm when she mentioned there would be two things that would happen prior to the Miracle. First she said, ***"Something will happen that will cause many people to stop believing in the apparitions of Garabandal. Second, the doubts and desertions will not be due to the excessive delay in the Miracle happening."*** There is no doubt many people stopped believing in Garabandal after Joey died, as well as during all of the years that have passed since the apparitions began.

There has been material written that speculates Joey left his prayer life, and did not receive his sight due to his disobedience. However, to point a finger in any one direction of why something happens or does not happen in the spiritual realm is disingenuous, and dangerous. It is just not that simple an explanation for an instance like this. If Joey were alive today, he would be ninety-four, and all of the criteria for the events to happen have not been met as of yet. Here one could be guilty of the sin of presumption or when we take things for granted, or thinking we will know the outcome of a situation. We are living a mystery, and Garabandal is indeed a mystery.

There are several areas of concern and confusion for the prophecies and why certain people have already and could still, fall away in believing. We have seen a significant falling-away of Garabandal when Joey Lomangino died in 2014. The prophecy was that his sight would be restored at the time of the Miracle, yet he died blind. Another thing could be the prophecy of a pope going to Moscow, and then the events not happening. This too would deflate the faithful. These areas of rational concern are addressed throughout this book. **However, Conchita said, "It would not be because of the delay of the Miracle that people would fall away." There must be reasons for her to say this.**

Whether or not the prophecies of Garabandal are examples like Jonah going through Nineveh calling for repentance, or the Lord would destroy the city, and then it didn't happen, because the people repented, no one knows. Chastisement is always conditional on mankind's response to Heaven's request. In the time of Jonah, the king called for a fast and the people put on sackcloth and ashes, and the Lord spared the people (Jonah 3). Jonah was mortified his prophecy did not come true, so he went and hid in shame. The prophecy was not as clean and neat as Jonah perceived it — and seldom has it ever been in history. There were conditions, and God saved the people because of their mortification and repentance. However, there can be no restoration without repentance.

Father Luis, A Vital Person in the Garabandal Events

Fr. Luis Maria Andreu played a vital role at Garabandal. What is possibly his most important function in that event is one which, until now, has been the least stressed. That function is to be a direct witness to the truth of the apparitions by having shared in one of the visions himself.

In referring to these apparitions, writers have spoken of "the girls," almost always failing to mention Fr. Luis as one of those who saw Our Lady. Father Luis saw Our Lady as truly as the visionaries did. It is not necessary that he see her 10, or 20, or 100 times. If he truly saw her but once, this suffices to make him an integral part of the apparitions. This is a most important point. We have Fr. Luis' word that Our Lady appeared at Garabandal, just as we have the word of the girls.

Our Lady, at the very start of the apparitions, predicted that there would come a day when the girls would contradict each other and even come to deny that she had appeared to them. We still have the word of Fr. Luis that Our Lady appeared at Garabandal. That is undoubtedly why Fr. Luis did not see Our Lady privately, while alone and separated from the girls. He was with the four of them and shared the same apparition with them. This caused him to repeat many times during the few hours which he lived after this apparition: "What a favor the Blessed Virgin has bestowed on me." The girls have given us an example of how we must conduct ourselves with the Blessed Virgin.

So, we cannot disassociate Fr. Luis from the four girls in their roles of seers or visionaries. He too is a seer or a visionary of Garabandal. If the girls did deny that Our Lady appeared to them at Garabandal (only for a short time), we still have the testimony of Fr. Luis that she appeared to him at Garabandal and that the four girls shared with him in that very same vision.

What is the value of Fr. Luis' testimony?

- It is the testimony of a mature adult, a man 36 years old.
- It is the testimony of a completely reliable person who was held in the highest regard by all who knew him.
- It is the testimony of a professional theologian with a critical and trained mind. Fr. Luis had indeed been a member of the Jesuit faculty of theology at Ona, Spain, and pursued studies at Innsbruck, Rome, Geneva and Paris.

As one who saw the Miracle in advance, Fr. Luis plays a third important role in relation to the Garabandal event. He is a witness to the authenticity of this particularly significant part of the Garabandal message. His role in this regard is to encourage us as we wait for the Miracle. This Miracle, which was promised by Our Lady and will be the crowning point of the Garabandal events, has already been seen by Father Luis and Saint Pio.

As we promote the message of Garabandal, let us not overlook the important role of this young Spanish priest whom God called to Himself so quickly and mysteriously, but not before having used him powerfully and effectively.[56]

Father Ramon Andreu, S.J.

Father Ramon is the brother of the deceased Father Luis Andreu, the priest who saw the great Miracle and later died of joy. Father Ramon received permission from his Jesuit superiors to visit Garabandal. Father Ramon also received authorization from the Apostolic Administrator of the diocese of Santander, Bishop Doroteo Fernandez. He was privileged to have witnessed more than 200 ecstasies. During his visits to the village, he kept a detailed record of everything he saw and heard. His notebooks represent some of the most valuable documentation of the events of Garabandal. The most startling event for Father Ramon was the revelation from the visionaries that they had conversed with his dead brother, Father Luis Andreu. Conchita's diary entries of August 15 and 16 1961, state the following:

> "A few days after Father Luis' death, the Blessed Virgin told us that we were going to talk to him at eight or nine o'clock in the evening. The Blessed Virgin appeared to us smiling, very, very much, as usual. She said to the four of us; 'Father Luis will come now and speak with you.' A moment later, he came and called us one by one. We didn't see him at all, but only heard his voice. It was exactly like the one he had on earth. When he had spoken for a while, giving us advice, he told us certain things for his brother, Father Ramon Maria Andreu. He taught us some words in French, German and in English and he also taught us to pray in Greek."

Father Ramon was told precise details of his brother's funeral and details of his personal life that were unknown to anyone but himself. On another occasion, Father Luis gave a message for his mother: "Be happy and content for I am in Heaven and I see you every day." This was a message of great joy for his mother, who entered the convent.

Father Ramon Andreu orginally went to Garabandal extremely cynical about the apparitions and was not in a good mental state when he first visited, as stated in his own words. Father Ramon said, "At the time when I felt myself the most alone in my life, I was in fact totally known, even to my most hidden thoughts; all of my thoughts had been very easily known to the girls by means of the mysterious person they claimed to see."[57]

After Mari Loli and Conchita told him that the Blessed Mother spoke about him to them, his attitude changed. Our Lady conveyed to Conchita what Father Ramon was going through, and told him exactly what he was thinking while visiting the village. Conchita told Father Ramon that Our Lady spoke of him for about fifteen minutes. He immediatley changed his attitude and became a central figure over the years and what happened there.[58] Father Ramon at one point was stationed in Southern California, and maintained a close friendship with Jacinta's family, and remained her spiritual director until his death at the age of 81. He died in the University of Southern California hospital.

During July of 1962, Conchita, Mari Loli, and Jacinta were shown a vision of the impending Chastisement. Our Lady told the visionaries that, if we do not heed her warnings, and mankind does not change after the Warning and Miracle, God will send the Chastisement. In a note, Conchita stated: "The punishment is conditioned upon whether or not mankind heeds the messages of the Blessed Virgin Mary." Conchita said in her diary: "If the world changes, the Chastisement can be averted." In describing the vision of the Chastisement, Mari Loli said: "It would be worse than having fire on top of us—fire underneath us and fire all around us." She saw people throwing themselves into the sea, but instead of putting the fire out it seemed to make them burn more.

"It was so horrible that I asked the Most Holy Virgin to take all the young children with her before all this happened. But the Virgin told us that when it would come, they would all be adults...."

Mari Loli wrote a letter to a Mexican priest, Fr. Gustavo Morelos, which is in the possession of Mrs. Carmela (Maria) Saraco of California.

"During the night of terror, although we could still see the Blessed Virgin, we also saw a great multitude of people who were suffering very much and screaming with great anguish..."[59]

A recurring theme of the apparitions all of the young girls spoke about was that at the time of the Warning, Communism would have engulfed the earth to such a degree that it would make the Mass impossible. It is for this reason such great emphasis in this book is to show the evils of a Communist doctrine, not just in the world, but Spain specifically, around the time of the

Spanish Civil War. To date, Communism has not totally engulfed the world, but it is incrementally happening. When these events occurred from 1961-65, Communism was very different than it is today. Now the United Nations and other sovereign government bodies have a well-funded and organized agenda, to remove God from our culture — not yet breaking into homes to violently remove people, but legislatively and administratively.

The more gradual and sure approach is to remove all freedoms and liberties through a process of continually dumbing down the population through insipid entertainment until their senses are so dull, they don't even know they were taken over from within, similar to putting a frog in a pot of water and imperceptibly turning up the heat until the frog is scalded to death. This is happening today on a far wider basis than in the past, as we see even the West expelling God from society. Their first point of attack was the schools, and they have won for the time being. There has been a war on Christianity at the policy level over the last several generations. A slow strangulation of Christianity is taking place in the world. One must remember that for Communism to be effective, it will be implemented by enforced government public policy year after year, decade after decade, until people no longer know their rights, and their freedoms and liberties have been stripped. Marxism will work with existing law until they can go no further. After that runs its course, they will resort to all levels of corruption and violence to force their agenda by any means to achieve their stated goals — the overthrow of the existing social and political structures.

Aerial view of the village with the nine pines on the bottom right.

Fr. Valentin (arrow) was the first priest to see an ecstasy.

This tiny hamlet of San Sebastian de Garabandal with its cluster of nine pine trees overlooing the village, is located in the nortwest mountainous region of Spain.

FRANCE

PORTUGAL

Fatima ●

● Lourdes

Garabandal

● Madrid

SPAIN

A typical street scene in Garabandal.

The calleja was a rocky trail leading out from the village.

The village church.

Loli in her home.

Conchita in front of her home.

Finally he said: Good, we are
going to wait two or three days
to see what he will tell you
and whether you are going to
continue to see this figure that
you call an Angel....
Then I will go to the Bishop.

The typical village setting.

The statue of St. Michael in the village church.

"And look out! There are rocks and stones throughout those streets."

"The girls walked as if their feet had eyes."

It appeared to be the eye of God. That day we talked much with the Virgin. And she talked with us. We told her everything....

They play and converse like other children.

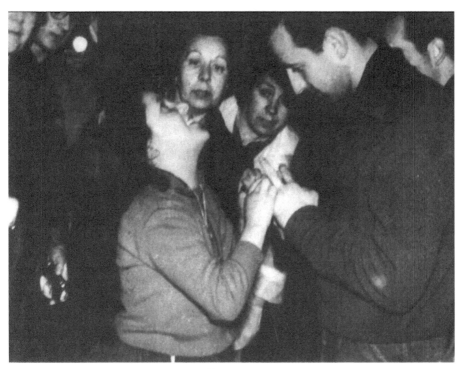

Loli returning a wedding ring kissed by the Virgin.

"Men, women, children, you know our message."
The Virgin wishes it accomplished, for the good of all peoples.

Left to right: Loli, Conchita, Mari Cruz, Jacinta.

Conchita holding up rosaries for the Virgin's kiss.

We would go outside (to the site of the apparition) after the second call. For if we would go after the first we would have to wait a long time, since from the first to the second there is a long wait.

Between calls... waiting for the rapture.

Conchita, Jacinta, Loli

Dr. Ortiz checking Conchita's pulse during a rapture.

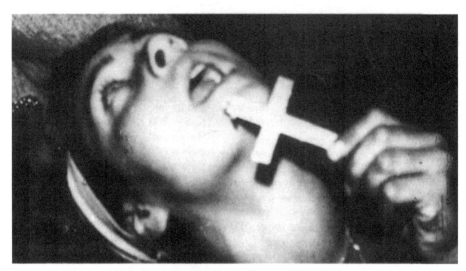

"I went to give the crucifix to be kissed."

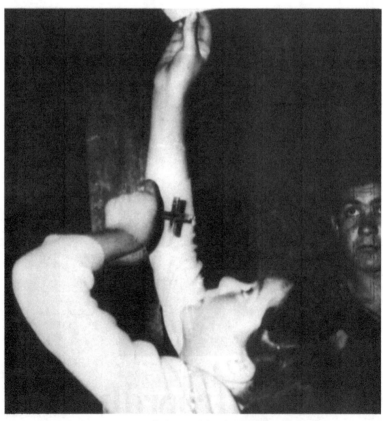

Jacinta presents religious articles for the Virgin to kiss.

Fr. Luis and brother Ramon.

"The girls demonstrated a special predilection for priests and religious."

It was exactly the same as when he spoke on earth. And after giving us advice, he also told us something for his brother Father Ramon. And he taught us words in French, and even to pray in Greek. He taught us words in German and in English too.

Father Luis (on right) with mother and his two priest brothers.

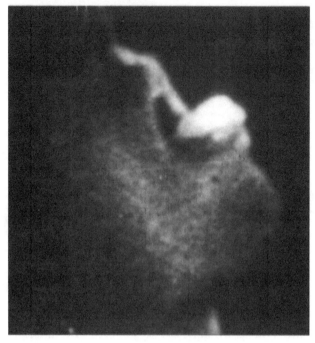

"A white body of the same size and shape as the hosts used for Communion."

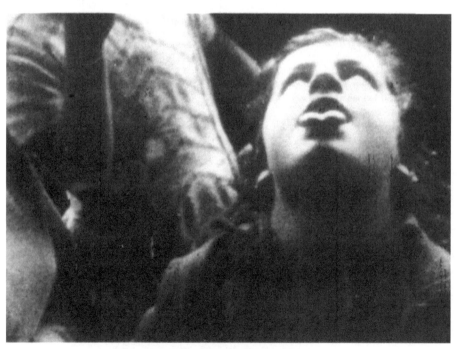

Loli receives Mystical Communion.

Fr. Laffineur and visionary.

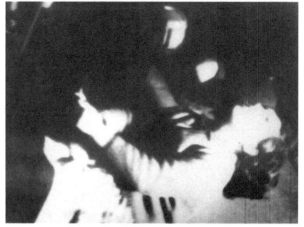

"The falls in the state of trance increased."

As many as 3,000 spectators a day came to see the ecstasies and participated in them.

Peace came to tormented consciences
as the seer presented the cross to be kissed.

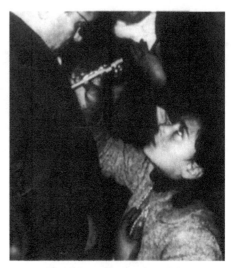

"Conchita made the sign of the
cross over all of them, one by one."

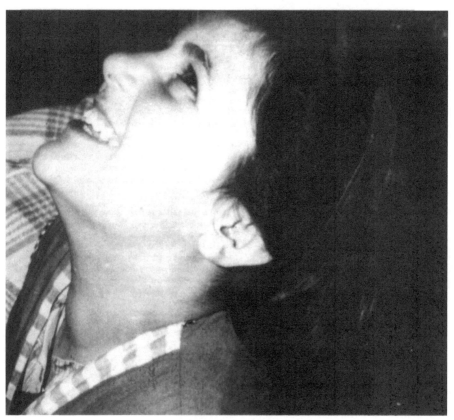

"Radiant and full of light."

"Joining her hands in the position for receiving Communion, Conchita went into ecstasy."

CHAPTER 13

Possible Data Points on the Timing of the Warning and Miracle

Austrian author Albrecht Weber is the key figure in the Garbandal story as it relates specifically to the story of the Moscow prophecy. He is the **sole source** of the Moscow prophecy story which he alleged took place in the kitchen of Conchita's home on November 14, 1965, the day after the last apparition of November 13 at Garabandal.

In 1993, Weber published a book in German called *Garabandal — Der Zeigefinger Gottes*, which in English is, *Garabandal — The Finger of God*. The book was sent to Pope John Paul II, and his then assistant Bishop Stanislaus Dziwisz who was later made Cardinal. In the year 2000, there was a revision of the book by Weber with the following written on page 19, and reprinted by Our Lady of Mount Carmel Garabandal Association, London, England, which then appeared in their newsletter in June of the same year. It reads:

> *"May God reward you for everything, especially for the deep love with which you are making the events connected with Garabandal more widely known. May the message of the Mother of God find an entrance into hearts before it is too late. As an expression of joy and gratitude, the Holy Father gives you his apostolic blessing."*
>
> Signed, Msgr. Stanislaus Dziwisz

Inscribed was a greeting by Pope John Paul II in his own handwriting. This is another instance of a well-known and authoritative figure in the Church (a reigning pope, no less) expressing belief in what happened at Garabandal.

There is an area of puzzlement on the Moscow prophecy. The following quote is attributed to Conchita by Albrecht Weber. It was not Conchita's mother who said this as many claim. It was said by Conchita in a conversation with Weber in her house on November 14, 1965. It says, ***"The pope will go to Moscow. As soon as he returns to the Vatican, hostilities will break out in different parts of Europe."***

It is true that Mr. Weber confirmed Conchita's statement several times; at least once to the recently deceased American editor of the Garabandal Journal, Barry Hanratty (1938–2022). Argentine author, Santiago Lanus, with a *Garabandal News Blog* researched this quote. Both were friends of Garabandal.[60]

However, the quote **does not appear** anywhere in Mr. Weber's book, *"Garabandal – Der Zeigefinger Gottes,"* (1993, revised 2000). People in possession of the second edition of the book, who have personally gone through the entire work seven (7) times have never found the word "Moscow" in the book.

An unanswerable question remains: **Why would Mr. Weber withhold such a significant piece of information from his own publication, and also with a revision of his book in 2000? This remains a puzzle, and actually quite bizarre.** Speculation could be a draft of the book was circulated to one of the visionaries, and they asked that this be withheld. However, this is unlikely.

Weber writes:

Author: "When should we expect the Warning?"

Conchita: "When Communism comes again everything will happen."

Author: "What do you mean by comes again?"

Conchita: "Yes, when it newly comes again" she replied.

Author: "Does that mean that Communism will go away before that?"

Conchita: "I don't know," she said in reply, "the Blessed Virgin simply said 'when Communism comes again."[61]

IF the pope does go to Moscow, and **nothing** happens **"as soon as he returns to the Vatican,"** and events do not unfold as people expect, it could be another reason some will see the prophecy unfulfilled, and become further disillusioned to Garabandal's authenticity. However, the war in Ukraine and Russia is getting more dangerous by the day — and anything is now possible.

However, there is recently another reason that could have a much broader implication for the faithful who believe what happened at Garabandal, which would deflate enthusiasm for **any** apparition. On April 15, 2023, a new body was created by the **International Pontifical Marian Academy** *'to discern the* *different cases of Marian apparitions as well as mystical phenomena linked to the figure of the Virgin Mary.*" Its goal for the future is to prevent alleged messages from generating confusion inside the Church. Father Stefano Cecchin, OFM, President of the Academy states, *"The apparitions which speak of the punishments from God are absolutely false."* This would mean under these new guidelines for authenticity, Fatima, Garabandal, La Salette, Tre Fontane, Akita, Medjugorje, and many others will fall into this category. Of all reasons that have the potential to quell excitement among people for Garabandal, these are serious considerations.

There are several possible scenarios why people may lose enthusiasm before the events. Conchita was asked about the timing of the Miracle, and her response was, ***"The Miracle will not delay in coming."* Conchita added an interesting observation: "Although it is taking time to come, it will not be late. God's time is always the appropriate time."** On another occasion, Conchita indicated people fall away not because of the timing of the Miracle, but for other reasons.

Pope Francis expressed interest in visiting Moscow as early as 2016, and said the same again on his way back to Rome after his five-day Greece and Cyprus trip in December, 2021. Patriarch Kirill of Moscow sent a representative soon after to the Vatican to work out details. However, no trip was announced. Pope Francis visited the Russian Embassy in Rome on February 25, 2022, at the beginning of the Russia-Ukraine war, making a plea for peace.

Patriarch Kirill and Pope Francis were on cordial speaking terms prior to the war in Ukraine. They previously met at the Havana, Cuba airport, on February 12, 2016, just months before Fidel Castro died. Their meeting lasted over two hours and was called extremely cordial. As the war continued in Ukraine, Kirill publicly sided with Vladimir Putin's position on the war and talks cooled between the Vatican and Moscow. However, Pope Francis has continued to be resolute, hoping to get an invitation from Putin and Patriarch Kirill to visit Moscow.

It is known that Putin disagrees with many of the more liberal positions of the World Economic Forum (WEF) and the progressive elites in the West, as well as their economic and social positions. Putin has stated on numerous occasions that he does not want to bring Russia into the orbit of western Central Bank control and LGBT social policies. Putin believes Ukraine under President V. Zelensky is captive to these immoral and economic programs, and is a puppet of the West. He also believes that Ukraine is a giant laundering center washing cash for the West, and the U.S. in particular. A trip to Moscow by Pope Francis could pose an embarrassment for Putin if peace terms are proposed that he is unwilling to accept. The term in diplomatic circles for resolution to a conflict is *an off ramp* for one of the parties involved in a war. Many feel the West has never given Putin an off ramp to save face. Pope Francis early on in the war said that the West and NATO nations provoked the war. If a meeting does take place, it could be called miraculous because the differences are so vast in the politics of the Church and state between the two countries.

On May 13, 2023, President V. Zelensky of Ukraine flew to Rome to meet with Pope Francis in a plea that the Pope would back his proposal for a peace plan. After a forty-minute meeting, few details were provided on a tangible solution to end the war. However, the press noted that the meeting did not go as Zelensky had hoped. May 13, 1917 was the first apparition of the Blessed Mother at Fatima, in which Russia was central to the messages. The Vatican surely had this Fatima date in mind, after months of Vatican officials working back channels for a resolution to the war. What will be the final resolve to end the war, or the role of Pope Francis brokering a deal is anyone's guess at this point. In June of 2023, the Vatican sent a delegation headed by Cardinal Zuppi to Kyiv (meeting was June 8th and 9th) and Moscow to seek a settlement both sides could accept. Patriarch Kirill did meet with the delegation June 29th and 30th in Moscow. Whether or not this was a meeting to pave the way for Pope Francis is unknown, as the Vatican has said little.

On July 24, 2023, it was reported by the Russian press that Pope Francis had asked to meet Patriarch Kirill on his way to Mongolia or on the return trip home as the plane refuels. The dates proposed were either August 31, or September 4 or 5. There was never news of this refueling request from Vatican sources, but only Russian.[62] The stopover did not happen and there was no meeting.

Mongolia is the 19th largest country in the world, about the size of Alaska. It is sparsely populated with only 2.8 million people, and has Russia to the north, and China to the south. There are approximately only 1,450 Catholics in all Mongolia. As a way for Pope France to get a meeting with Patriarch

Kirill, this trip was used as a pretense that Francis has wanted for some time. The on-going developments in a pope's visit to Moscow will surely continue.

Ukraine at the beginning of the war was a country with 44 million people, and with millions now either killed, wounded, or displaced to refugee status because of the war. At some point leaders will need to come to their senses and seek a proposal for peace and bury past conflicts, and move towards the future. With approximately 45% of the Ukrainian population declaring themselves Russian, especially in the east and south, this is a problem for which there doesn't seem to be a resolution at the moment.

An Unorthodox Situation

This aspect of the Garabandal story will continue to change and evolve until a pope does visit Moscow at some point. The war in Ukraine will continue to drive the narrative for an official visit. On March 13, 2023, the story was reported that President Volodymyr Zelensky of Ukraine ordered authorities to close the 980-year-old Ukrainian Orthodox Church (UOC) Pechersk Lavra Monastery complex, which is under the authority of the Russian Orthodox Church. Zelensky gave them three weeks to vacate the premises, after having a compound there for nearly 1,000 years. Zelensky asserts that the Church is undermining Ukrainian unity and collaborating with Moscow. This prompted Russian Orthodox Patriarch Kirill to ask Pope Francis and others with influence to stop the shuttering of the facility. Zelensky further said by doing this, *"It is one more step towards strengthening our spiritual independence."* The Russian Orthodox Church has a long-established presence in Ukraine, and Zelensky now wants to close Ukrainian Orthodox Churches because he feels the church is undermining Ukrainian influence. Millions of people in the Ukraine who identify as Russian will take a strong stand against this, further complicating internal politics. What this will look like in the future is unknown, as both sides see no common ground for peace. One thing is certain about the war: it is a very complex situation with a long and tumultuous history between the two countries.

Kirill has been an advocate of Russia's position in the war. If Kirill did not take the stance of Putin, then he would immediately be removed from his position as Patriarch of the Russian Orthodox Church.

It has been nearly 1,000 years since Eastern Orthodoxy split from Rome. It would be a significant event for reconciliation to take place. Events are now pointing to the fruition of the prophecies by just looking at the social upheaval in the world and nuclear conflict as an increasing possibility. We may know shortly if Weber is correct.

Was the Synod on Synodality Prophesied at Garabandal?

Another event that is interesting to note in the possible timing of the Warning is that it would be around the time of a synod. Synods are not new in the Church, nor are Councils or large meetings. A Spanish nun, Mother Nieves Garcia, who was the head of Conchita's boarding school in Spain, knew Conchita when she was first a student there at sixteen years old. Sister Garcia was told by Conchita the Warning would **occur shortly after a Synod of the Church,** and **it would precede the end times**. Conchita had allegedly told Mother Nieves that "**an important one**" (Synod) would be held before the events took place. The seers were told the secrets would happen in their lifetime. Conchita was born in 1949.

In a recorded interview with Santiago Lanús, Mother Nieves García stated that, during the apparitions, the Virgin told Conchita that, before the future events occur, a Synod will take place, an important Synod. Conchita told her aunt, "No, the Virgin didn't say Council, she said Synod, and I think a Synod is a small council" (The word mini was also used). It was said the Illumination would occur shortly after a Synod in the Church.[63]

Pope Francis initiated a program called **"The Synod on Synodality,"** which is a three-year process of listening and dialoguing at the parish level that began with a solemn opening in Rome on October 9, 2021. The Synod is being held in three stages: local, continental, and universal. In October 2023, the universal phase began with the sixteenth Ordinary General Assembly of the Synod of bishops, which brings together 300 bishops and laity to the Vatican. A second assembly will end in October 2024. In early 2023, Pope Francis took an unprecedented step of granting equal voting rights to both episcopal and non-episcopal members.

The reason it is an important synod is that it has relevance to every diocese and parish in the world, because there has never been one quite like it. The Synodal process will conclude in October, 2024. Pope Francis said about the Synod, "I invite the Church to reflect on the theme that is decisive for its life and mission. It is precisely this path of synodality which God expects of the Church of the third millennium. This journey which follows in the wake of the Church's renewal proposed by the Second Vatican Council, is both a gift and a task: by journeying together and reflecting together on the journey that has been made, the Church will be able to learn through her experience which processes can help her to live communion, to active participation to open herself to mission."

This is another issue of concern because many of the lay faithful are of the opinion that Pope Francis is using the Synodal process to make changes that will be more progressive than many like, taking the Church in a direction that conservatives feel will aid in the further destruction of orthodoxy and tradition. At the diocesan level, there are meetings mandated by bishops, with clergy participating in listening sessions with laity to discuss the direction of the Church. Conservatives are concerned that it will bring more of a liberal social justice agenda to these *"listening sessions"* throughout the world. The late Cardinal Pell of Australia said the pontificate of Pope Francis was "A catastrophe and the synod a toxic nightmare while the papacy is silent on grave moral matters." Other leading prelates have called the Synod **"a spiritual poison,"** and many feel that it is an attempt by progressives to alter moral doctrine that has been generally accepted as Roman Catholic Magisterial truth for millennia.

Cardinal Burke said, "Synodality and its adjective, synodal, have become slogans behind which a revolution is at work to change radically the Church's self-understanding, in accord with a contemporary ideology which denies much of what the Church has always taught and practiced." The danger to the Church with the orchestration of its doctrinal demise from within, is building a new Church that is accepting age old heresies that it is has traditionally never accepted.

Since Catholic orthodox people believe there has been a crusade of the Pope Francis pontificate on some of the traditions of the Church: Truths which have Scriptural foundations that cannot ever be altered. As the Synod was starting the process of *"listening sessions"* (which was phase one at the local level) Pope Francis said, **"there is no need to create another Church, but to create a different Church."**[64]

Cardinal Muller of Germany, and former head of the Congregation of the Doctrine of the Faith (CDF), before being removed from the position by Pope Francis, called the Synod "a hostile takeover of the Catholic Church. I pray all this will be a blessing and not harm the Church," and insisted the

Synod must not become a "political dance around the golden calf of the agnostic spirit of the age." He further spoke of false prophets including "even bishops who no longer believe in God as the origin and the end of man and the Savior of the world," and voiced his fears that the "Synod would focus on issues such as climate change rather than the Catholic faith. The Synod must not and cannot change Catholic doctrine, as no one on earth can change, add to, or take away from the Word of God." Regarding suggestions that the Synod might open the way for Church blessings of same-sex couples, he said, such an action would be "a direct contradiction of God's Word and will, a gravely sinful blasphemy." He added, that "not even a Pope or the bishops could approve such a radical change, "because they contradict Revelation and the clear confession of the Church."[65]

An argument could be made that the changes being promoted from within the Church rather than from outside the Church, are greater than the changes that happened as a result of the Protestant Reformation. The changes coming from the Reformation were largely from an outside element of dissent. The dissent at the moment is from an element with good standing inside the Church which makes things very volatile for the present structure, doctrine, practice, and administration of the Church. If radical changes to Tradition do happen in the Church with the blessing and acceptance of a substantial number of the hierarchy, this will be a big blow to the Church. As a result, the faithful can expect to see a great deal more open and hostile division among the hierarchy in the worldwide press. The prophecy of Akita, Japan spoke of, "cardinal opposing cardinal and bishop against bishop." This open opposition of confreres is new in the Church, or at least on this scale with such visibility with such emotional exchanges of leading voices in the Church.

The Influence of Pierre Teilhard de Chardin, S.J. and the Politics of Argentina on a Young Jorge Bergoglio (Pope Francis)

Many long-time observers of Vatican politics feel the key to understanding Pope Francis is to understand the theology of Pierre Teilhard de Chardin (1881-1955).

Growing up in Argentina only made it worse for the young Jorge Bergoglio to wrestle with all of the complexities of an orthodox Christian message in a country of continuous social, political, economic, and religious upheaval that exists to this very day. Argentina has been a boiling cauldron of instability for the formative years of a young man like Jorge Bergoglio that were greatly impacted by the politics in Argentina, and the incongruous thoughts of Chardin. For over one hundred years Argentina has been a patchwork quilt of turbulence in every sector of the country.

Teilhard had an enormous impact on Jesuit intellectual thought in the Twentieth Century, and Francis is a product of that in his formative years of training. Teilhard continually came into conflict with Rome over issues of orthodox doctrine during his life time. Those familiar with Teilhard and Father Jorge Bergoglio, S.J., see great similarities in their thinking and approach to faith, religion, and science. "In his book *The Myth of an Anti-Science Church: Galileo, Darwin, Teilhard, Hawking, Dawkins,* geneticist Gerard M. Verschuuren devotes an entire rather detailed chapter (pp. 77-121) to Teilhard as scientist and theologizer. He observes: 'His greatest stature was reached when he became almost an oracle and icon to many of what a twentieth-century Jesuit should be. Teilhard had become their role model. In spite of ecclesiastical admonitions regarding Teilhard the ideologue, his ideas kept spreading in the Society of Jesus. Not only has his way of thinking infiltrated or infected, according to some — thinking Jesuits, but it would also become a major element of thinking in other Catholic groups. Many Jesuits and other theologians have adopted Teilhard's evolutionary approach'" (118). Those who know both Chardin and Pope Francis feel that Pope Francis is an earnest disciple of Chardin.[66]

Many feel the abdication of Jesuit orthodoxy to the Magisterium of the Church can be directly linked to Teilhard's philosophy and practice. It is a profound element where the Jesuits lost their way as an Order of men. An Order who had previously done great good in the Church and world, to recent generations inflicting doctrinal harm and practice. Teilhard's impact on new recruits looking to enter the Society of Jesus was enormous, and many feel this is when the teaching of the Jesuits went off course, according to many orthodox priests and laity.

Is a Schism Coming to the Church?

Another area of grave concern is the German bishops progressing on the Synodal Path towards same-sex unions. On March 10, 2023, 176 out of 202 Catholic clergy and lay leaders throughout Germany voted in favor of the

Church sanctioning same- sex unions. There were only 14 in dissent and 12 abstaining from the vote. This is a mere seven percent challenging this heresy. The crucial number of at least 67 bishops voted in favor, which gave the two thirds majority they needed to go forward. Same-sex unions are now being planned for March 2026 to gain official recognition in the Church. Germans admit it is already taking place, but not with "official" recognition. In addition, the council of German lay leaders and clergy approved lay leaders to baptize and preach at Mass. Will Pope Francis step forward and condemn this action? Will it create a schism if it is not condemned? The answer to that question is yes. It will cause a rift wider than the Grand Canyon, where the faithful will finally say, "enough is enough." The challenge to this moral doctrine was previously unthinkable by the hierarchy, but northern Europe, and Germany in particular, have a history of challenging orthodoxy.

On the Feast of Corpus Christi June 8, 2023, German women pastoral workers dressed in priest vestments, processed the Blessed Sacrament in a monstrance throughout the streets of Ludenenscheid, Germany, openly defying Canon Law.

According to a news conference of June 20, 2023, topics open for discussion at the Synod on Synodality are women's diaconal ordination, married priests, welcoming remarried divorcees, people in polygamous marriages, and welcoming LGBTQ+ people. Cardinal Mario Grech, *Secretary General of the General Secretariat of the Synod of Bishops* says this discussion is born from the **"fruit of the listening process"** that has taken place thus far. The working document is called the *Instrumentum Laboris* (IL). Cardinal Grech denies the working document is already written.[67] Another possible phrase for this Synod could be the "Synod on Homosexuality." Welcoming LGBTQ+ people into the Church, and loving them as Christ loved all people is an admirable goal, but when Jesus met the adulterous woman, He said to her "Go and sin no more" (John 8:11). Same sex unions are mortal sin, and the Church cannot condone mortal sin. Pope Francis again asserts his views on the matter. On October 2, 2023 Pope Francis said to clergy, "decide for yourselves whether to bless same sex unions." Although this is not a tacit endorsement for the sacrament of marriage for same sex unions, however, it further erodes orthodoxy, that will in time usher in normalized acceptance as the door opens year after year.

Several members of the Synod representing the United States are Cardinals Blase Cupich (Chicago), Wilton Gregory (Washington, D.C), Robert McElroy (San Diego), Sean O'Malley (Boston), Archbishop Paul Etienne (Seattle), and Father James Martin, S.J. (New York).

Instrumentum Laboris is the summit of Freemasonic thinking and action to finally destroy the papacy — a goal they have had for hundreds of years. The more orthodox element in the Curia calls this "Bergoglioism" at its finest. This orthodox element, like Archbishop Vigano, Bishop Athanasius Schneider (Kasakhstan), and others, feel this is the penultimate accomplishment of a life-long dream to rid society of any moral structure administratively run by the Roman Catholic Church. Cut the head off, and the body will decay. Destroying the primacy of the papacy will accomplish this vison. The proclamation of a new Church under new guidelines will obliterate the papacy by means of local churches implementing a new structure of their own making.

Something like that has never happened to this degree in 2,000 years. For well over one thousand years before the Incarnation of Jesus, Mosaic Law outlawed such immoral issues that are being proposed in this Synod. These issues are anathema to Mosaic Law as well. The rise of local churches organizing as a democratic body assures this dream coming true. It will castrate any directive coming from Rome that has stood the test of time as objective truth based upon Scriptural precepts. These age-old precepts are now openly debated and in question as sound doctrine. Severing the relationship between the clergy and laity will separate the people from Rome, giving the laity greater voice to create their own morally acceptable doctrine.

This report could be the single instrument to cause schism in the Church. **Conchita once used the word "schism"** during an apparition that was overheard by her brother. There was no elaboration on that topic by Conchita. The point where the orthodox no longer submit to the authority of the papacy, due to doctrinal error being promulgated, may be upon us. Is this what Conchita heard when she spoke of the word "schism?"

The ideological divide is getting wider with each passing week on what many believe are the true intentions of Rome under the pontificate of Pope Francis. In an interview with Archbishop Carlo Maria Vigano, he stunned many when he said, "Bergoglio's logic is very evident: he wants to create the premises for a schism, which he denies and deplores in words, but which he has been preparing for some time. Bergoglio wants to separate, in one way or another, the good part of the faithful and clerics from the official Church. Bergoglio wants to create the premises for a schism, and separate the faithful clerics from the Church. His purpose is to create confrontation." Vigano also stated that, with the stacking of the College of Cardinals with extreme progressives, the likely candidate for pope at the next conclave would be a liberal in the image and likeness of Pope Francis, however, Vigano also said that there are often surprises in conclaves.[68]

In the Buenos Aires Cathedral, on March 5, 2023 Archbishop Fernandez, appointed by Pope Francis as head of the Dicastery for the Doctrine of the Faith (DDF), as part of his homily said,

"If we don't start learning to look at people in a different way, nothing changes.

"If we don't start looking at their beauty beyond their appearance, their intellect, their sexual orientation or whatever it may be. If I don't start looking beyond all, we cannot end up loving that person. The way that person presents himself, the way that person is, whether I like it or not, in that way that person is worth more than anything on earth. Each brother and sister is worth more than anything on earth.

"As you well know, during many centuries, the Church was going in a different direction. Without being fully aware, the Church developed a whole philosophy and morality full of classifications, to classify people, to label them, this is X, this is Y, this can receive communion, this one cannot receive communion, this one can be forgiven, this other cannot be forgiven. It is terrible that this has happened in the Church. But thank God that Pope Francis is helping us to be free from those patterns."[69] Archbishop Fernandez claims any opposition to Pope Francis' unique charism risks 'heresy and schism.' The Francis pontificate has now reversed who the culprits will be if there is an official schism. If one dissents (from a cardinal, bishop, or anyone else) from the directives of Pope Francis and his direction of creating a new church, it will be they he will label schismatic. To understand the mind of Pope Francis, one must critically examine the political turbulence of the Argentina that molded him into the man he is today.

The intentions of the Pope Francis pontificate seem to be obvious to many observers. Pope Benedict's official biographer, Peter Seewald, blasted Pope

Francis, accusing the pope of trying to "break out" of the Tradition of the Church, and leave the continuity of doctrinal traditions. Seewald said, "It could be observed that Pope Francis' course becomes more radicalized with increasing age, or shall we say: *unveiled*. Seewald particularly condemned Francis' appointment of Archbishop Victor Manuel Fernandez (appointed to cardinal by Pope Francis) as the new head of the Dicastery of the Doctrine of the Faith.[70]

"Serafín, Conchita's brother, affirms having heard his sister announce during an ecstasy, that the Warning will be brought about after the Church has been cruelly torn by "**something like a schism.**"[71]

Father Stefano Gobbi of the Marian Movement of Priests (MMP), in the book, *Our Lady Speaks to Her Beloved Sons,* addresses the issue of schism:

"The hour of its great trial has above all come for the Church, because it will be shaken by the lack of faith, obscured by apostasy, wounded by betrayal, abandoned by its children, divided by schisms, possessed and dominated by Freemasonry, turned into fertile soil, from which will spring up the wicked tree of the man of iniquity, the Antichrist, who will bring his kingdom into its interior" (Message number 486r, titled *The Great Trial).*

"My Secret Concerns the Church."

"In the Church, the great apostasy, which will spread throughout the whole world, will be brought to its completion; the schism will take place through a general alienation from the gospel and the true faith. There will enter into the Church the man of iniquity who opposes himself to Christ and who will bring into her interior the abomination of desolation, thus bringing to fulfillment the horrible sacrilege, of which the prophet Daniel has spoken" (Matthew 24:15). (MMP message number 539hi, titled *My Secret).*

The rift between the orthodox and progressives throughout the world is widening.

The Bishops of the Byzantine Catholic Patriarchate sent a letter to Rome in June, 2023 expressing extreme displeasure in the direction of the Synod with an LGBT Agenda they felt was set for global approval. They wrote,

"Dear Bishops of Asia and Australia,

The suicidal synodal LGBT agenda is to be approved worldwide this autumn. Cardinal Muller (Germany) described the synodal journey as *'doctrinally incompetent and canonically illegitimate.'* The synodal process changes the nature of the Church, turning it into a system of non-profit organizations. Just like the Soros non-profits, which lead every nation to self-destruction, so do these non-profits. Previously, such non-profits would have been condemned as treason in the country or heresy in the Church. These non-profits are part of the synodal journey in every parish, in every diocese, in every nation, on every continent."

The letter went on in some length about the real agenda of the synod is to distort doctrine. The former United States Nuncio, Archbishop Carlo Maria Vigano, is quoted saying, "The Deep Church is an offshoot of the Deep State, in a certain sense. For this reason, it should not surprise us that we are witnessing the demolition of Faith and Morals in the name of ecumenism and synodality, applying liberal errors in the theological sphere…" Vigano continued on the issue of Catholic clergy celebrating Pride Masses promoting the homosexual agenda, saying "all faithful Catholics must remove the servants of the Antichrist from the sacred precincts." He also called participating clergy in such events "homo-heretics."[72]

On October 13, 1973 the 56th Anniversary of the Great Miracle of the Sun at the Cova da Iria in Fatima. Our Lady delivered this message to *Sister* Agnes Katsuko *Sasagawa in Akita, Japan.*

"My dear daughter, listen well to what I have to say to you. You will inform your superior.

"As I told you, if men do not repent and better themselves, the Father will inflict a terrible punishment on all humanity. It will be a punishment greater than the deluge, such as one that has never been seen before. Fire will fall from the sky and will wipe out a great part of humanity, the good as well as the bad, sparing neither priests nor faithful. The survivors will find themselves so desolate that they will envy the dead. The only arms which will remain for you will be the Rosary and the Sign left by My Son. Each day recite the prayers of the Rosary. With the Rosary, pray for the Pope, the bishops and priests.

"The work of the devil will infiltrate even into the Church in such a way that one **will see cardinals opposing cardinals, bishops against bishops.**

The priests who venerate me will be scorned and opposed by their confreres … churches and altars sacked; the Church will be full of those who accept compromises and the demon will press many priests and consecrated souls to leave the service of the Lord.

"The demon will be especially implacable against souls consecrated to God. The thought of the loss of so many souls is the cause of my sadness. If sins increase in number and gravity, there will be no longer pardon for them. With courage, speak to your superior. He will know how to encourage each one of you to pray and to accomplish works of reparation. It is Bishop Ito, who directs your community."

And She smiled and then said:

> "You have still something to ask? Today is the last time that I will speak to you in living voice. From now on you will obey the one sent to you and your superior.
>
> "Pray very much the prayers of the Rosary. I alone am able still to save you from the calamities which approach. Those who place their confidence in me will be saved."[73]

Howard Dee, former Philippine ambassador to the Vatican, revealed in a 1998 interview with Inside the Vatican that "Bishop Ito was certain Akita was an extension of Fatima, and Cardinal Ratzinger personally confirmed to me that these two messages, of Fatima and Akita, are essentially the same. If the messages of **Fatima and Akita** are, as Cardinal Ratzinger admitted, 'essentially the same'- a great crisis of faith within the Church, accompanied by a worldwide chastisement — then it appears we must look to the Third Secret for the content that would make such a comparison apt. The Third Secret, then, as does the Akita prophecy, would make explicit Sister Lucia's own reference to a combined spiritual and material chastisement of the Church much worse than what had already transpired with World War II and the rise of world Communism."[74]

On August 13, 1962, The Pact of Metz (France) was an agreement signed by Cardinal Eugène Tisserant, representing the Holy See, and Metropolitan Nikodim (Rotov) [Archbishop of Yaroslavl], representing the Russian Orthodox Church. **As a result of this meeting, the Vatican agreed that it would not condemn Communism during the Second Vatican Council.**

This Vatican-Moscow Agreement silenced the Second Vatican Council regarding the evil of Communism. The Vatican did the exact opposite of the mandate of Heaven given by Our Lady on July 13, 1917.

In a public admonition to his spiritual sons amidst the Second Vatican Council, in 1963, Padre Pio said:

"Due to the rampant injustice and abuse of power, we have reached a compromise (The Vatican-Moscow Agreement or Pact of Metz) with atheistic materialism Communism, a denial of the rights of God. This is the punishment foretold at Fatima …. All the priests who support the possibility of a dialogue with the negators of God and with the Luciferian powers [Freemasonry] of the world are mad, have lost their faith, no longer believe in the Gospel! In so doing they betray the word of God, because Christ came to bring on earth perpetual covenant only to men of heart, but did not join with the men thirsty for power and dominion over the brothers …. The flock is dispersed when the shepherds ally with the enemies of the Truth of Christ. All the forms of power made deaf to the will of the authority of the heart of God are rapacious wolves that renew the passion of Christ and make the Madonna shed tears…."[75]

The prophecy of La Salette, France (1846), may be coming to its fruition. It said, "the Church would be in a state of eclipse and Rome would become the seat of the Antichrist." If one were to look at the eclectic and cumulative volume of prophecy at major apparition sites over the last 175 years, and those actually approved by the Church, data points to very significant changes coming to the Church, and the world. It is Our Lady of Guadalupe who is seen in the image as stepping on the head of the serpent, and that day may be soon upon us. Our Lady of Guadalupe will play an important role in the coming Triumph of the Immaculate Heart.

Do the Faithful Leave the Church, or Does the Church Leave the Faithful?

Our Lady at Garabandal said,

"Many cardinals, many bishops and many priests are on the road to perdition and are taking many souls with them. Less and less importance is being given to the Eucharist. You should turn the wrath of God away from yourselves by your efforts."

In 1956, Father Joseph Ratzinger first wrote about a 4th Century North African theologian by the name of Tyconius. The future Pope Benedict felt his writings had great relevance that pertain to the Church in our times, and especially to Fatima. Father Ratzinger's paper was titled, *Observations on Tyconius' Concept of the Church,* based upon Tyconius' *Commentary of the Apocalypse in the 4th Century.* As Pope Benedict XVI, he continued his fascination with Tyconius, whom he called a "great theologian." On April 22, 2009, at his General Assembly Audience, Pope Benedict saw the Christian North African's thoughts as having relevance to the present eschatological drama unfolding in the Church.

Pope Benedict wrote, "Tyconius understands that the great 'falling away' (the great apostasy) of the end times will **not be caused by unfaithful people leaving the Bride of Christ, but rather by the Bride of Christ pulling away from those within her who are unfaithful. In other words, for Tyconius, it is not the infidels who will 'fall away' but rather the true believers, who will withdraw from the evil within the Church.**"

How does Tyconius understand and interpret the meaning of 2 Thessalonians 2? The 'Tyconian' interpretation can absolutely happen!!![76]

In 1957, Sister Lucia of Fatima said, "Our Lady made me to understand that we are now living in the last times of the world." When asked about the content of the Third Secret on one occasion Sister Lucia replied, "It's in the Gospels and the Apocalypse (Chapters 8-13); read them." Chapter 13 deals with the False prophet and the Antichrist.[77]

Cardinal Luigi Ciappi placed the Third Secret in the context of 2 Thessalonians 2: "In the Third Secret it is foretold, among other things, that the great apostasy in the Church begins at the top."[78]

The apparitions at La Salette, France, in 1846, also address the Church being in a state of eclipse:

> "A certain precursor of Antichrist, together with his followers from many nations, will fight the real Christ, the only Savior of the world. He will endeavor to eliminate the adoration of God in order to be considered as God himself. Much blood will flow. Then the earth will be visited by all kinds of blows, from constant wars until the last war, which finally will be made by the ten kings of the Antichrist.
>
> "During the time of the arrival of Antichrist, the gospel will be preached everywhere, and all peoples and nations will then

recognize the Truth. **Rome will lose the faith and become the seat of Antichrist**. Yet the heathen Rome will disappear. See, here is the Beast with its subjects that claims to be the Savior of the world. Proudly it rises in the air to go straight to Heaven, but it will be strangled by the breath of the Archangel Michael and cast down. And the earth, which for the past three days was in continuous convulsions, opens her fiery jaws and swallows him with all his cohorts forever into its hellish abyss. Eventually will water and fire cleanse the earth and the works of human pride will be destroyed and all will be renewed. Then will all serve God and glorify Him.

"The just will have much to suffer; their prayers, works of penance and tears will ascend to heaven. All of God's people will cry for forgiveness and grace and beg my help and intercession. Then Jesus Christ will command His angels, by a special act of His Justice and Mercy, to deliver all His enemies to death. Then suddenly all persecutors of the Church of Jesus Christ and all evil doers will perish, and rest and peace between God and man will appear. Jesus Christ will be served, adored and glorified. Love of neighbor will begin to flourish all over. The new kings will be on the right hand of the Church which will grow strong, and which will be humble, pious, poor, zealous and followers of the virtues. All over, the Gospel will now be preached, people will make great progress in faith; there will be unity amongst the laborers of Jesus Christ, and people will live in the fear of God"[79] "The apostasy of the city of Rome from the vicar of Christ and its destruction by Antichrist may be thoughts so new to many Catholics, that I think it well to recite the text of theologians of greatest repute. First Malvenda, who writes expressly on the subject, states as the opinion of Ribera, Gaspar Melus, Biegas, Suarrez, Bellarmine and Bosius that Rome shall apostatize from the faith, drive away the Vicar of Christ and return to its ancient paganism. Then the Church shall be scattered, driven into the wilderness, and shall be for a time, as it was in the beginning, invisible and hidden in catacombs, in dens, in mountains, in lurking places; for a time it shall be swept, as it were from the face of the earth. Such is the universal testimony of the Fathers of the early Church."[80]

St. Francis of Assisi said,

"At the time of this tribulation a man, not canonically elected, will be raised to the Pontificate, who, by his cunning, will endeavor to draw many into error and death. (...) There will be such diversity of opinions and schisms among the people, the religious and the clergy, that, except those days were shortened, according to the words of the Gospel, even the elect would be led into error, were they not specially guided, amid such great confusion, by the immense mercy of God. (...)

"Those who preserve their fervor and adhere to virtue with love and zeal for the truth, will suffer injuries and persecutions as rebels and schismatics; for their persecutors, urged on by the evil spirits, will say they are rendering a great service to God by destroying such pestilent men from the face of the earth. (...)

"Some preachers will keep silence about the truth, and others will trample it under foot and deny it. Sanctity of life will be held in derision even by those who outwardly profess it, for in those days Jesus Christ will send them not a true Pastor, but a destroyer."[81] In the back of this book under the section titled, Gemstones, there is more narrative of this prophecy.

"The prophecies of the Apocalypse (book of Revelation) show that Satan will imitate the Church of Christ to deceive mankind; he will set up a church of Satan in opposition to the Church of Christ. Antichrist will assume the role of Messiah; his prophet will act the part of Pope; and there will be imitations of the Sacraments of the Church. There will also be lying wonders in imitation of the miracles wrought in the Church."[82]

"As the Church is the mystical body of Christ, so the evil world-powers constitute the body of Satan, of which he is the soul. As a dragon, Satan through the evil world-powers of that time will enter the Church, interfere with her liberty and perhaps by stealthy suggestions having long before directed the choosing of candidates for the episcopate will now endeavor by threats of force to hinder the election of the worthiest candidate for the papacy."[83]

"It is self-evident that the Catholic Church and the anti-Church currently co-exist in the same sacramental, liturgical and juridical space."[84]

"Before Christ's second coming the Church must pass through a final trial that will shake the faith of many believers. The persecution that accompanies her pilgrimage on earth will unveil the 'mystery of iniquity' in the form of a religious deception offering men an apparent solution to their problems at the price of apostasy from the truth. The supreme religious deception is that of the Antichrist, a pseudo-messianism by which man glorifies himself in place of God and of his Messiah come in the flesh."[85]

"Satan reigns now in all the highest command posts (…). Satan will enter the leading places of the Church. (…). The temptations will be terrible, the world will live in such confusion that the elect themselves will argue in doubt! There is no escape […] everyone will experience terrible moments of war, destruction and political, religious and cultural chaos. How many errors and how many heresies meander in every nation, in every convent."[86]

"Malachi personally confirmed to me in 1997 that the 'pope' who will lead the apostasy in the Church will be a heretic and an antipope."[87]

The Queen of Heaven will Not be Silenced

July 2, 1961 – Our Lady comes to San Sebastian de Garabandal (The Feast of the Visitation of the Blessed Mother).

Was it a coincidence that Our Lady appeared in Garabandal after the Third Secret of Fatima was hidden and not released as Our Lady asked?

July 4, 1961- The First Message of Garabandal is delivered by Our Lady. (5 months, 21 days before the Convocation of Second Vatican Council):

"We must make many sacrifices, perform much penance, and visit the Blessed Sacrament frequently. But first, we must lead good lives. If we do not, a chastisement will befall us. The cup is already filling up, and if we do not change, a very great chastisement will come upon us."

October 18, 1961 – Public Announcement of the First Message of Our Lady of Garabandal.

December 25, 1961 – Convocation of the Second Vatican Council by Pope John XXIII (Nativity of Our Lord Jesus Christ).

February 22, 1962 – Pope John XXIII publishes, *"Veterum Sapientia,"* an Apostolic Constitution emphasizing the importance of Latin in the liturgy and how it must never be discarded, during the Roman Synod preparing for Vatican II (Given in Rome on Feast of the Chair of St Peter). Did this document suggest that the Third Secret could have predicted modernizations or changes to the Mass?[88]

The Great Chastisement of Fire from Heaven will come if humanity does not turn from its evil ways after the Great Miracle. Three of the young girls of Garabandal were shown the Great Chastisement of Fire on the night of June 20, 1962 (the second Night of Screams), and they screamed for more than three hours as they watched.

There are strident feelings of orthodox clergy on the potential reforms of the Synodal Process under way. They may not all be spoken in public, for fear of running afoul with their bishop, but they all have an opinion. The divide and chaos over the direction of the Church will increase before the prophesied events happen at Garabandal, and the Synodal Report, when complete, will play a major part in this division.

For all of those watching the direction of the Church and the path it is on towards an increasingly progressive agenda, the word **schism** is increasingly being mentioned as a distinct possibility. In many ways, we already have a de facto schism, with many leaving the Catholic faith all together. The message at one church can be so different from another, the faithful are increasingly voting with their feet, their wallet, and their service to neighboring parishs or denominations.

Conchita had a brother named Serafin, who continued to live in Garabandal. In 1994, I visited him in his home. He told me that, at the time of the Miracle, it would be difficult to travel there. I asked why, and he remained silent.

Serafin was privy to a lot of information being Conchita's brother, and living in the same home while the apparitions took place. With moral doctrine being challenged, something striking was said that may be very relevant today in light of the changes in the Church.

The Proper Translation of "An Event in the Church?"

The following provides some insight into the issue of what an **EVENT** may mean in the Church.

"During the winter of 1963, he [Serafin] felt that, as the eldest brother, he should take a stand concerning Conchita. So one night while the family was in the kitchen of the house, he said to Conchita, 'You will have to tell us once and for all what this is all about; we can't go on like this. And don't be afraid of what will happen…I'm ready to take you away from the village and bring you anywhere you want. If you want to go to school, we can arrange that too…But we have to know the truth. All these things about the apparitions: Are they true, or are they something that you made up?' Conchita replied that it was true, that she had seen the Virgin, that it wasn't something that the girls made up, and that there was no reason to leave the village…"[89]

While at home, Conchita said to her brother, "Serafin? Come up a minute." The man told me he felt as if his heart missed a beat as he thought, "There it is! She has finally made up her mind. She must have thought about this all night long and is going to tell me that it has all been a fraud. "What do you want", he asked her on arriving upstairs?

"So that you can see that all this is true, the Virgin has told me to tell you this…"

And she talked to him about the Miracle, and explained what it would consist of. Later Conchita wrote it down briefly on the back of a holy card of the Child Jesus, which Serafin keeps concealed and which none of the family have seen. She told him that it would occur when a **definite event in the Church ("un determinado acontecimiento en la Iglesia" in the original Spanish) took place**, and she also explained it to him. This is how Serafin came to know date of the miracle. Later, Serafin and I discussed the following excerpt from a leaflet written by a friend of the family, Dr. Puncernau, "During one of my trips to the pastures, I was alone with Serafin and we were eating in the barn. After eating, I tried to draw him out since it was said that he knew from Conchita when the Warning would be. The only thing that I got definitely from him was that it would be **preceded by a special happening in the Church**. After many questions and answers, it seemed clear to me from his vague remarks that it would **be something like a schism. That is the way I understood it.**"

The description of **a great event in the Church** is an exaggerated, poor translation of the original spoken by Conchita. It is incorrect to translate the phrase as "a great event in the Church." The actual phrase was:

"un determinado acontecimiento en la Iglesia" can be translated:
"a particular event (occurrence) in the Church."
"a specific event (occurrence) in the Church."
"a definite event (occurrence) in the Church."[90]

"And what do you say about Dr. Puncernau's opinion?" I (Father Eusebio Garcia de Pesquera) asked Serafin.

"He is free to think what he wants. But I don't think I gave him reasons for such an opinion."

"But will this happening actually be a schism in the Church?"

"I have nothing to say."

"During that May of 1976, I (Father Eusebio Garcia de Pesquera) spoke also with Jacinta's mother, Maria. She told me that she had heard repeatedly from her daughter that **affairs were going to go very bad for the Church, that the Eucharist would constantly be given less importance, that many priests would become worse and worse, and that wickedness would spread everywhere.** It can be noticed that Dr. Puncernau does not speak of the Miracle, but of the Warning. Is this a mistake? Perhaps not."

There are several phrases or descriptive words being used above. A *definite event* in the Church, an *event* in the Church, a *great event* in the Church, *preceded by a special happening, something like a schism, a particular, specific, or definite event* have all been addressed over the last sixty years. Logic would say it is imprecise on the **exact event**, but one thing is certain. There is some significant event that will impact the Church. Based upon the young visionaries speaking about dire circumstances coming to the Church, the event appears to be very negative. The most probable is a **schism**, as that exact word was used by Conchita. However, this is before the Warning. Another tier of a major event seems to be at the time of the Miracle. It was said there would be "the reunification of Christians." The conclusion may be there are two major events at different times, and one is negative, and the other is positive.

The Issue of the Number of Popes

After Pope John XXIII died, Conchita said that Our Lady told her, *"After this pope there will be only three left, but there would be a fourth pope who would govern the Church for a short time, then it would be the end of times" (el fin de los tiempos).* At one point, Conchita said there would be three popes, and then, "el fin de los tiempos." This comment needs to be broken down into two separate components. The first is the issue of three or four popes? The second is, "then it would be the end of times." A significant issue is what does an "end times pope" really mean? It is a new phrase in the Church, in private revelation, and is certainly not mentioned in the Catechism or magisterial doctrine of the Church. Both versions of whether there would be three or four popes can be correct.

The bigger issue is, who is the end times pope? Did it start with Benedict XVI, or begin with Pope Francis? If it started with Benedict XVI, it would logically follow that Pope Francis is also an end times pope. So what is the start date of an "end times pope?" Over what span of time does this consist? What constitutes an "end times pope? If one considers there may be the issue of a pope who reigns just a short time, that would mean Pope John Paul I was in that chain of popes. If three, it would make Pope Benedict XVI an "end times pope." If four, that would make Pope Francis the continuation of an "end times pope." Nowhere was it ever said the papacy would end.

On one occasion, Conchita mentioned four popes and then, *"el fin de los tiempos."* This was said in an interview with Bishop Garmendia of New York in 1981 (see below). However, both of these statements on the number of popes could be true when one factors in the statement, *"And one would govern the Church for a short time."* If one were to look at this from a macro view, we have presently arrived at *"el fin de los tiempos,"* no matter who is pope now. Looking critically at the language of both versions, three or four popes could simultaneously be correct.

In October of 1966, Conchita became a boarder in the college that the teaching sisters of the Immaculate Conception have in Burgos, Spain. On November 1st, the Feast of All Saints, she talked confidentially with the director of the center, Mother Nieves Garcia. Among other things, she said this, which the religious sister wrote down very carefully, "One day I said to the Virgin, will the end of the world be during the time of these events? And she told me, No, the end of times. After Paul VI, there will be **only two more popes**; and then the end of the times will come."[91]

"One time she told this to the eminent professor, Father Lucio Rodrigo at the Pontifical University in Comillas. For some time, Aniceta and Conchita traveled regularly to the seminary in Comillas—taking advantage of the cars of friends and acquaintances—to have their confessions heard by this priest."[92]

Because the meaning of these words "the end times" is not yet fully understood, it would be well to point out that when the visionaries speak of the end of times, they are **not** referring to the end of the world, but rather to **the end of an era or epoch of time.** Prophecy often has a veil over it until the actual event(s) occur. Have we entered the New Times? For example, in the Old Testament, God the Father spoke to us through the prophets, sometimes referred to as the era or times of the Jews. In the New Testament, God the Son spoke to us directly during His public life on earth, known as the time of the gentiles or the era of time that Saint Paul preached. Today, God is speaking to us through Mary, the Mother of God. Pope John Paul II called the 20th century "Marian Times." The reason it may not make a difference on whether it is three popes or four popes could be in the interpretation of what constitutes the *end times pope,* and our lack of the mystical understanding of what Heaven intends, or means by the exact expression, because with either pope, whether it be three or four, we are in the *end times.* That phrase seems to be the more profound meaning of the issue Heaven is conveying. If the prophecy is true, we are in the *end times.*

Conchita said: "After Pope John XXIII died, Our Lady told me, 'after Pope John, there will be three more Popes, one will reign only a short time, and then it will be the end of times.' When Pope Paul VI became Pope, Our Lady mentioned this to me again. She said, 'Now there will be two more Popes, and then it will be the end of times, but not the end of the world." With the election of Pope Benedict XVI, this has caused confusion. One plausible explanation is "three more popes and then the end of times" refers to Pope Benedict XVI as the Vicar of Christ in place as the end times Pope.

Since John XXIII, we have had Paul VI, John Paul I, John Paul II, Benedict XVI, and now Francis. We do know that John Paul I governed only thirty-three days, which is an amazingly accurate prophecy in light of that fact it did happen. If the above is true, then that would mean the conclave electing

Pope Benedict XVI ushered in the "end times." With the death of Benedict XVI on December 31, 2022, more confusion was experienced. What is the start date for an *end times* pope is the unanswered issue. It is a plausible scenario where everything Conchita said is accurate. It was never said that the papacy would end, but that it would be at some point, "el fin de los tiempos." The fact is, right now the Church is in a place it has never been before.

Listed below is the chronology of recent popes for more clarity:

1. Pope John XXIII. Opened up the Second Vatican Council. Died June 3, 1963. The prophecy was given when Pope John XXIII was pope.
2. Pope Paul VI. Closed the Second Vatican Council. Died August 6, 1978.
3. Pope John Paul I. Died September 28, 1978. His pontificate lasted only 33 days.
4. Pope John Paul II. Died April 2, 2005.
5. Pope Benedict XVI. Elected pope April 19, 2005. Abdicated his papacy February 28, 2013. Died December 31, 2022. If the prophecy is true under the three popes, this means that Pope Benedict began an era of "end times" popes.
6. Pope Francis — Elected March 13, 2013.

On August 27, 1981, Conchita sat for an interview with Bishop Garmendia of New York. Conchita was asked by the Bishop, "are there any other relationships between Rome, the Holy Father and the Miracle that you would like to talk about?" Conchita said, "Yes." The Virgin told us something related to the Holy Father, and it was that before the Miracle, there would be only three more popes. The Virgin said, three more popes are left: there will be only three more popes."

Was one omitted because he would only live for a short time (Pope John Paul 1)? This issue of three popes mentioned and other times four popes has caused concern for many who are critical of Garabandal, but it must be asked, do people have all the information to make an informed decision?

Interview with Conchita Gonzalez and Bishop Garmendia, New York, August 27, 1981[93]

See the interview below which addresses the issue about the number of popes, among other things.

Bishop: Does the general public have doubts about the apparition?

Conchita: The Virgin told us that before the Miracle, many people will stop believing.

Bishop: So you believe in the Virgin blindly and you always refer us to what she told you. There's another subject I'd like to bring up, Conchita, and that is Holy Communion. I understand that the Virgin told you girls that if there are priests present, the Angel would not give you Communion; that the Angel would only give Communion when there were no priests present. However, I understand that on the day of the Miracle of the (Visible) Communion there were some thirty priests in Garabandal. Can you clarify this?

Conchita: The Virgin never told us that the Angel would not come if there were priests in the village. It is the Angel who did not come when there were priests in the village. Only that day, the Angel came, even though there were priests in the village. I can't explain why.

Bishop: So, the Virgin did not categorically tell you the Angel will give you Communion only when there are no priests in the village, did she?

Conchita: No. Because whatever the Virgin says, happens just as she says it…

Bishop: As for the present Bishop of Santander, is he going to have a special sign before the Miracle? Will it be something that happens in nature or something in general?

Conchita: The Virgin said that she was going to send proof to the Bishop of Santander so that he will allow priests to go to Garabandal.

Bishop: What kind of proof?

Conchita: She didn't say. This sign of the truth of the apparitions will be something private for whomever is the Bishop of Santander at the time of the Miracle.

Bishop: So, it will be for the one who is Bishop at the time of the Miracle?

Conchita: Yes, he will receive a sign.

Bishop: So the Bishop will receive a sign and he will know that Garabandal is true. This is clear now. You know, Conchita, that we are attracted to Garabandal because we love the Virgin. We know she utilizes humble people and means like at Lourdes and Fatima and other apparitions. It has been said that the Virgin told you the Miracle will be on a Thursday. Is this true?

Conchita: Yes. The Virgin said it will be on a Thursday, and she also gave the day, month and year.

Bishop: I am so glad to hear this. I had been told that you knew it was to be a Thursday, and began to guess at the dates. But the Virgin told you the exact date, the exact month, and the exact year. No one need have any doubts now. If everything in life were so perfectly clear there would be no problems. I heard you were in Rome.

Conchita: Cardinal Ottaviani sent me a letter through Princess Cecilia de Bourbon-Parma and I went to Rome with my mother.

Bishop: I don't want to press you, but what happened?

Conchita: They interviewed me for two hours and told me that it would be better to keep secret all that was said. I don't remember now all the questions they asked me, but I remember it was for two hours.

Bishop: Can you tell us your impressions of Rome? I imagine a girl from Garabandal, a remote mountain village, would have a lot to say about Rome, right?

Conchita: No, not really. I went there because they called me. They asked me questions and I answered them; that was all. After seeing the Virgin, I find it difficult to be impressed by Rome.

Bishop: … Are there any other relationships between Rome, the Holy Father and the Miracle that you would like to talk about?

Conchita: Yes. The Virgin told us something related to the Holy Father, and it was that before the Miracle **there would be only three more Popes.**

Bishop: I want this to be very clear to all who hear this tape. Conchita was very precise. The Virgin told you that before the Miracle…?

Conchita: At the time, Pope John XXIII was living. **The Virgin said, "Three more Popes are left; there will be only three more Popes." She was then speaking about the end of the times.**

Bishop: So after John XXIII came Paul VI, and then John Paul II. So look out, the noose is tightening! It's the Virgin who is speaking.

Conchita: The Virgin was talking about the end of times. She also spoke to us about France. I don't know if you remember but it was being said that a world war would break in 1962. At the time, everyone was afraid, including me. Then the Virgin appeared and addressing our concern said: **"Don't be afraid, there will not be another world war."**

Bishop: So she said there would not be another world war. There have been local conflagrations, and much has been said about a coming world war. The situation is very tense, but a world war would be the end of nations.

Conchita: I don't remember anymore. I would like to add, however, with reference to Rome, that some priests or people are putting too much pressure on the Church to approve Garabandal. I believe it would be better that this be left in the hands of God. Let them speak about and spread the Message of the Virgin, but leave the rest in the hands of God.

Bishop: You caution against rushing things and speculating. You prefer that all be left in the hands of God. You have complete confidence in Him.

Conchita: Yes. Before, when I was so concerned about whether Rome would believe me or not, the Lord Himself told me: "Don't worry about being believed, especially Rome. I will do everything." I would like to tell this to all those who want the Bishop and Rome to hurry ahead in this matter.

Bishop: People are always looking for new things. I agree with you; let God and the Blessed Virgin handle it in their own way. You aren't searching for great things, you are simply living a Christian life just as the Blessed Virgin said to.

Conchita: Yes, every day, and waiting for the Miracle.

Bishiop: Each day you live it.

Conchita: Yes.

Bishop: That is what the Gospels and Our Lady say; to live the Christian life every day. This is what you mean right?

Conchita: Yes. Live every moment of the day with true faith and devotion.[94]

CHAPTER 14

The Sentiments and Actions
of the Bishops to the Present Day

Shortly after the apparitions began in 1961, Bishop Doroteo Fernandez, Apostolic Administrator of the diocese of Santander, set up a fact-finding board of inquiry consisting of three priests and two doctors to study the apparitions. Psychiatrist Luis Morales Noriega and Father Francisco Odriozola led the study. This study was not considered a Canonical Commission. Included in the group was Father Juan del Val Gallo, who was later to become the bishop of Santander. During the four plus years of apparitions, the members of this group went to the village on only three occasions. They never met as a body nor did they ever issue a definitive report. Dr. Luis Morales, the leading expert on mental health in Santander, declared that the events had a natural explanation based on *"psychological theory,"* which created negative impressions of the apparitions.

In 1961, Our Lady told the visionaries, "A time will come when all four of you will contradict yourselves one with the other, when your families will also contradict themselves about the apparitions; you will even deny that you have seen me or Saint Michael." On this occasion, witnesses heard the four visionaries while in ecstasy say, "How is it that one day we will say that we did not see you, since we are seeing you now?" Our Lady told them, "Because you are going to pass through the same confusion as the Church." The children later did deny receiving apparitions as Our Lady had warned them in 1961. Thus, the Bishop and his successors had cause for serious reservations about their authenticity. Bishop Fernandez and his immediate successor, Bishop Eugenio Beitia, issued "Notas." These "Notas" advised caution and restricted priests from visiting the village without permission. They stated further that there was no evidence that any supernatural events had taken place. The young children's denial would naturally come from ridicule of people who put pressure on them. This brief denial reminds one of Peter denying Jesus three times in His hour of trial.

A list of the Bishops of Santander, Spain, since 1961 to the present day is as follows:

1. Jose' Maria Equino Trecu, October 2, 1928–May 7, 1961 (the apparitions had not begun when he was Bishop.
2. Eugenio Beitia Aldazabal, January 27, 1962–January 23, 1965
3. Vincent Puchol Montis, 1965–1967
4. Jose Maria Cirada Lachiondo, 1968–71
5. Juan Antonio del Val Gallo, 1971–91
6. Jose Vilaplana Blasco, 1991–2006
7. Vicente Jimenez Zamora, 2007–14
8. Manuel Sanchez Monge, 2015–present

However, it is significant to note that Bishop Beitia, in his notes on July 8, 1965, stated, "…We would like to say, however, that we have found no grounds for an ecclesiastical condemnation either in the doctrine or in the spiritual recommendations that have been divulged in the events and addressed to the Christian faithful. Furthermore, these recommendations contain exhortations to prayer, sacrifice, devotion to the Holy Eucharist, and devotion to the Blessed Virgin under traditional, praiseworthy forms; there are also exhortations to a holy fear of the Lord, offended by our sins."

Bishop Puchol Montis, who succeeded Bishop Beitia, was not as favorable. He denounced the events throughout the province with a media campaign. Due to Bishop Puchol's untimely death in an automobile accident on May 8, 1967, Enrique Cabo, the Vicar Capitular, headed the diocese until a new Bishop could be appointed. The new successor, Bishop Cirarda, similarly discredited the apparitions by sending a letter to all the bishops of Spain, through the Church's Secretary of State, yet never condemned them.

Bishop Val Gallo was a pivotal figure in the Garabandal investigations from the beginning. As a young priest in 1961, he was selected to be a member of the original commission to investigate the apparitions. However, he resigned in protest on the way the investigation were conducted. Now Bishop, he felt a new investigation was needed, and in 1986, he appointed a new commission that was never made public. He announced to the Vatican during his visit to Rome that he was quietly reopening the investigation on the events of Garabandal. He was always clear that he was supportive, until his death in 2002. Over time, he treated the visionaries with warmth and sincerity, and was sympathetic to what happened there.

The next was Bishop Vilaplana Blasco, who maintained Bishop del Val Gallo's position of not condemning them. Archbishop of Oviedo, Carlos Osoro Sierra was made Apostolic Administrator of Santander, and gave priests the ability to say Mass and hear confessions in Garabandal.

One of the prophecies of Garabandal stated that a future Bishop of Santander would at first not believe in the apparitions. However, after receiving a sign, he would lift all restrictions that forbade priests to visit Garabandal. In January of 1987, Father Gomez, the pastor of the church in San Sebastian in Garabandal, was instructed by the Bishop to allow visiting priests to celebrate Mass in the village church. This change in policy lifted the restrictions of 1962. The Bishop, in a statement carried by the Catholic News Service, explained that his decision had no connection with his belief in the apparitions, but was merely out of respect for the priests who arrive with pilgrims. After this imposition was lifted, Conchita said, "that the time of The Miracle is very close." "The rest," she said "will not be long in coming." In 1991, all studies were completed and submitted to Rome by the new Bishop. This statement is confusing to many that she would say as far back as then the events were very close. However, in spite of that, Garabandal has had the support of many prominent people in the Church, and may have been a factor in protecting them.

Dr. Luis Morales Recants His Early Testimony

A dramatic turning point in the events of Garabandal occurred on May 30, 1983, the eve of the Feast of the Visitation. Dr. Morales, the leading psychiatrist in Santander, delivered an historic address in which he retracted his original negative judgment and defended the reality of the apparitions. This startling reversal of judgment ended the twenty-two years of silence imposed by the Church authorities of Santander. In his opening remarks, Dr. Morales said: "I am here today to speak to you on the apparitions of Our Lady at Garabandal. It is because she herself has worked this change of attitude in me. Moreover, I am speaking with full permission of the ecclesiastical hierarchy." He concluded by saying, "I will end my conference pleading with the Virgin of Garabandal, that for the rest of my days, she may keep me under her mantle and have mercy on me."

Criteria for Decisions by the Bishops

"How wonderful is the power of prayer! It is like unto a queen, who, having free access to the king, obtains whatsoever she asks."

ST. THERESE OF LISIEUX

Bishops by their nature are cautious when it comes to private revelation. This is usually a healthy position for the Church, yet often frustrating, as many feel the Church moves too slow to set up commissions to study the messages. If the Church rules incorrectly, it can do harm if it rushes findings. The faithful could lose trust based upon potentially poor decisions by investigating commissions. If a Bishop were to formally commission a study on the apparitions and make a public declaration, there are three possible outcomes:

1. **Constat de Supernaturalitate,** affirms the supernatural origin of the events;
2. **Non Constat de Supernaturalitate,** expresses a decision based on the insufficiency of facts and elements of proof to either affirm or negate the supernatural character of a presumed private revelation;
3. **Constat de non Supernaturalitate,** negates the supernatural character of the facts/events which were examined.

Since 1961, no Bishop has ever condemned the apparitions. Bishops have taken different positions of sentiment and affection for what happened at Garabandal. In the early years, priests were precluded from visiting the village, then Bishops opened it up for their priests, eventually to Bishops celebrating Mass there, appointing commissions to study it further, and so on. To date, with three of the four visionaries still alive, and events prophesied to happen, there has never been an outright condemnation or approval, hence categorizing Garabandal is number two above: **Non Constat de Supernaturalitate**. This is the wisest and best position to take under the circumstances. As far as the Church is concerned, there is not enough evidence at this time to rule definitively for or against supernaturality.

While we await the final judgment of the Catholic Church, we should be guided by what Conchita wrote. On September 14, 1965, she said, "The Virgin Mary likes it very much that we spread the message, and she promised to reward everyone, but obedience to the Church must always come first, because this will give more honor and glory to God."

In a letter dated May 7, 2007, the Archbishop of Oviedo, Spain Carlos Osoro Sierra, the Apostolic Administrator of the Diocese of Santander, wrote to an American named Edward Kelly. Mr Kelly had sent a book he had written on Garabandal, and he received a letter in response. Kelly was an American who married a woman from Garabandal, and then lived in California.[95] Bishop Sierra wrote, *"I encourage you to continue maintaining this devotion to Our Mother.... I am open to all information and to every consideration about Garabandal."*[96]

On the 50th anniversary of Garabandal in 2011, the Diocese gave its blessing for celebrations of the events.

In 2012, Bishop Vicente Jimenez Zamora of Santander personally celebrated Mass in the village. Again, he did the same on May 12, 2013, and kissed the crucifix belonging to a man in the village that had been allegedly kissed by the Blessed Mother. He was the first Bishop to ever say Mass in the village since the events began in 1961. In 2014, Bishop Manuel Sanchez Monge was appointed as the new Bishop of Santander and left everything as it had been in previous years concerning the position of the Church. On October 20, 2022, he stated, *"My position, like that of my predecessors, is that Rome's assessment remain valid: there are no signs of supernaturality."*[97]

There is a pattern that is obvious. Over time, clergy in general, and some Bishops have softened their position on Garabandal. There may be several reasons for this. First is seeing the prophecies undeniably coming true concerning the state of the Church and the world. Second, is observing the fruit from what was said with people in fidelity to the faith, nothing was said that was doctrinally wrong. Third, many notable people in the Church have supported what happened there and have been open in their defense of it.

Has Garabandal Been Protected from a Negative Declaration by the Church?

Has Garabandal been protected from being condemned because it had such support from many well-known clergy and saints? Did this support prevent the hierarchy in Spain from moving imprudently like some others in history where they gave an early critical judgment? Benedict XVI was aware of Garabandal, but never made an announcement that I have ever seen. Josemaria Escriva, the founder of Opus Dei, made three trips there as a priest, as he was often in nearby Navarre, Spain. He also never made a declaration one way or the other from what I have read.

The commissions to investigate the apparitions would often come from Madrid and other large cities in Spain, and those appointed would often never investigate or even go to Garabandal to get first-hand accounts of what happened. Instead, they mingled in the cafés and restaurants in beautiful downtown Santander, overlooking the Bay of Biscay. Over the years, investigations of alleged apparitions by the Church have generally been lackluster and inadequate. However, the Church, showing prudence has waited to see if the prophesied events happen before a judgment is rendered.

Interview With Conchita, 1973

Conchita Gonzalez Keena does not grant interviews today and this is understandable. What could she add, at this late date, to what she has already said or already been written? What Conchita has said on previous occasions is still of interest. The following is an interview with Dr. Jeromino Dominquez (1936-2008) in May 1973, as provided in the *Garabandal Journal*. No attempt was made by the author to change any language used during the interview.

Doctor Dominquez: What did you feel when you saw the Virgin? Were you afraid or was she like a friend?

Conchita: Whenever she came we felt a great joy. It was as though she had been away on a trip and had just come back.

Doctor: So how did you feel toward her as to a friend?

Conchita: I felt toward her as to a friend, or just as if she were my mother.

Doctor: Did she always appear with a white dress and blue mantle or did she sometimes appear dressed another way?

Conchita: She always wore a white dress and blue mantle. I remember once we asked her why she dressed this way since the statues we were used to seeing of Our Lady of Mount Carmel showed her dressed in brown. On the next day, or perhaps it was several days later, I don't remember exactly, she came dressed in brown. After that she always appeared with a white dress and blue mantle.

Doctor: Did the Virgin wear the scapular on her wrist all the time or just sometimes?

Conchita: Always! She always wore it.

Doctor: Do you remember if the Virgin asked you to bring religious objects for her to kiss?

Conchita: Yes, she used to ask us to kiss them. She said that those who wore these articles would do their purgatory here on earth. She also said that through these objects miracles or prodigies would be performed. I think she said prodigies not miracles.

Doctor: Do you recall any miracle or prodigy that resulted from a rosary that the Virgin kissed?

Conchita: I remember one regarding a medal. A little girl was in a coma and everyone was just waiting for her to die. A lady brought the girl a piece of pine from the tree where the Virgin appeared, and the medal. The girl was completely cured between that night and the following morning. She is now married, has children of her own, and is completely normal.

Doctor: Did the Virgin ever talk about the rosary?

Conchita: Every time we saw the Virgin we would say the rosary with her. She taught us how to say it.

Doctor: How did she teach you? Did she take the lead in praying it?

Conchita: Yes, she would lead us in praying it and we would repeat her words.

Doctor: Did she pray it slowly or quickly?

Conchita: Slowly, very slowly.

Doctor: Is that the right way to say it?

Conchita: We thought it was the right way at the time.

Doctor: Do you remember the rings? Did the Virgin ask for wedding rings to kiss?

Conchita: Yes. People would give us wedding rings for the Virgin to kiss. Sometimes we would have rings on every finger, then when we saw the Virgin, we would give them to her to kiss. She would tell us to put each ring on each owner's finger. She would say: "This ring is for this person." We wouldn't see the rings or the persons, but we followed her directions.

Doctor: That's unusual because you are in ecstasy looking up. How could you tell if you had the ring since your hands were full of them?

Conchita: She would say to us, "not this ring but the one on your little finger" and so on. Let me tell you of a case involving the rings. A couple gave me two rings for the Virgin to kiss. I presented them to the Virgin, but she didn't kiss them. Instead, she gave me a message to be delivered privately to the couple.

Doctor: What was the message?

Conchita: The message was that they were not married, but just living together. When I told them they cried. Later they got married.

Doctor: (Showing Conchita a picture of herself in ecstasy giving the crucifix to a man). Do you remember these events such as this one with you holding out the crucifix?

Conchita: I do remember very well that we held out the crucifix for the people to kiss. I never knew the people who kissed it. The Virgin would say, "Extend your arm" and the crucifix would be kissed by whomever the Virgin wanted.

Doctor: Wasn't there something that once happened with a small crucifix?

Conchita: Yes. One day a man gave me a very small crucifix about the size of a fingernail. When I went to give it to the Virgin to kiss, it fell to the ground and I lost it. When the man came to ask me for the crucifix, I told him that I'd lost it, but not to worry because I would ask the Virgin to help me find it again. Several nights later I found it. (During an ecstasy) the Virgin said to me: "Bend down and pick up that object." So I bent down and picked up something that was covered with mud, and it was the crucifix that I had lost.

Doctor: What did you do with it?

Conchita: I gave it back to the man.

Doctor: What do you remember about priests during the time of the apparitions?

Conchita: I remember that many priests came to the village (to see the events) and many were dressed in civilian clothes. I don't know how, but we always knew who the priests were even if there were a lot of people. One night in particular when we were seeing the Virgin, there were a lot of people present. The Virgin told us to hold out our arms (with the crucifix), which we did. When it was over, we learned that all those to whom we had given the crucifix to kiss were priests dressed in civilian clothes.

Doctor: (Showing Conchita a picture of the girls in ecstasy at the village church door) How come you were at the church door?

Conchita: In the beginning (of the apparitions) we used to enter the church. But then because of the disturbance made by people who wanted to be first when we held out the crucifix for veneration, the Bishop said we could no longer go inside while in ecstasy. From then on, the Virgin never led us inside.

Doctor: You mean from then on the Virgin only led you up to the door?

Conchita: Yes.

Doctor: Was this her way of saying the Bishop had to be obeyed?

Conchita: Yes, I think it was an example of obedience we owe to the bishop and also to each person to whom we owe obedience.

Doctor: At what time of the day did the Virgin appear, when there were people present?

Conchita: She appeared at all hours of the day or night: eleven or twelve at night, or one or five in the morning. There was no definite time. Sometimes there were many people, even at five in the morning. Sometimes she appeared to us when we were alone.

Doctor: How did you know when she was going to appear at night?

Conchita: She would alert us by three calls, but please don't ask me about them. It's something I have never been able to understand; that's all I can say.

Doctor: Was it something you felt inside?

Conchita: I have never been able to explain it. It was like an immense joy that brings you to a place without your knowing where you are going, only that you have to go there.

Doctor: During all these spectacular events there were messages. There was one in 1961. Can you repeat what the Virgin said in that first message?

Conchita: Yes. The words of the Virgin were: "We have to do much penance and make many sacrifices. We have to visit the Blessed Sacrament often. Above all, we must be very good. **The cup is already filling up. If we don't change a great punishment will come upon us.**" This is the way I understand it, although the Virgin didn't say it this way. With respect to penance and sacrifice, penance is what we impose on ourselves; sacrifice is giving up things as a situation suggests. For example, when a person scolds us, not to answer them back. Or if we receive a blow, to offer it to God. For me this is self-imposed penance and sacrifice.

Doctor: On the subject of penance and sacrifice, wasn't there an incident regarding a piece of gum?

Conchita: Yes. The day of the last apparition, on November 15, 1965, I had a piece of gum in my mouth. The moment I saw the Virgin, I stopped chewing it and lodged it against the inside of my cheek. But she said: "Why don't you get rid of that gum and offer it as a sacrifice for me?" (Note: In an account of this apparition that Conchita wrote for Father Jose Maria Alba, S.J., on December 10, 1965, the words of Our Lady are more accurately recorded: "Why don't you get rid of your chewing gum and offer it up as a sacrifice for the glory of my Son.")

So I took the gum out of my mouth. I understood from this that the Virgin was not asking for big sacrifices, but small ones that we can continually offer them out of love for her.

Doctor: So little sacrifices are good when made in the presence of God. After all, gum is not bad, right?

Conchita: Not at all, but giving it up is an act of love for God.

Doctor: The Virgin also said in the message that, above all, we have to be good. What do you think she meant by that?

Conchita: I don't know what the Virgin meant. I understood it to live moment by moment offering everything to God. Living like a Christian the way our conscience tells us is what I think she meant.

Doctor: So everyone can be good.

Conchita: Sure. Everyone in the practice of religion, in their environment, in their family, their job, knows how to be good because each person has his own conscience and God speaks to each one through their conscience.

Doctor: Each man and woman knows what is right or wrong whether it's here (in New York) or a little village like Garabandal.

Conchita: I am sure that each person knows when they do something good or bad.

Doctor: The message then was the important thing in all these apparitions. What have you done or what have you tried to do to live the message?

Conchita: What would give the Virgin great happiness is a very difficult thing for me. That is to live each moment of the day doing everything for God.

Doctor: Do you think you and I are living the message?

Conchita: I think I am, but you have to answer for yourself.

Doctor: You work as a nurse. (Note: At the time of this interview, Conchita was a nurse in a clinic run by Dr. Dominquez in New York.) Do you fulfill the message in that capacity and if so how?

Conchita: I try doing my work to the best of my abilities and by treating the patients the way I should.

Doctor: How about a housewife with three or four children who is busy all day? Can she fulfill the message?

Conchita: Surely, according to the perfection in which she accomplishes her duties, offering all her actions to God.

Doctor: Offering to God all the little things she does during the day. So it's not what you do but how you do it.

Conchita: How you do it, that is true.

Doctor: How about a person working in an office?

Conchita: You can fulfill the message anywhere. You can always be good and offer praise to God.

Doctor: One of the things you have done in New York is give out scapulars. Why do you do that? Do you like giving out scapulars in the office and on the streets?

Conchita: Ever since I was a little girl, I've worn the scapular. It's a devotion my mother taught me. But more than that, I wear it because whenever the Virgin appeared, she had the scapular on her wrist.

Doctor: All that you have said so far deals with the first message. Wasn't there another message on **June 18,** 1965? Can you tell us about that one?

Conchita: Certainly. The Virgin's Message delivered by Saint Michael said: "Because my message of October 16, 1961, had not been fulfilled and that the world didn't know about it, I'm telling you that this is the last one. Before the cup was filling up. Now it is flowing over. Many priests, Bishops and Cardinals are on the road to perdition and are talking many souls with them. Each day less and less importance is being given to the Eucharist. You should use all your efforts to avoid God's wrath. If you sincerely ask for pardon, He will forgive you. I your mother, through Saint Michael the Archangel, ask you to correct your ways. You should sacrifice more. Think of the passion of Jesus.

Doctor: What do you think about the statement that Cardinals, Bishops and priests are on the road to perdition?

Conchita: I think every day the Virgin appeared, she mentioned priests and that we should pray for them. We never understood why. For us, priests were like saints because we never had many come to our village.

It was considered a privilege whenever one came. Regarding Bishops and Cardinals, we thought it strange, but we would repeat it the way she said it.

Doctor: (Showing Conchita a picture of her receiving Communion from Saint Michael) Here you are, but we are not able to see the Host. The angel brought you Communion many times, isn't that right? Do you remember how many times?

Conchita: Not that many, maybe forty times. Usually there was a priest in the village and the angel only gave us Communion when there was no priest. Regarding Communion, the Virgin taught us the value and the importance of the Eucharist. After the apparitions started, we never missed a day without receiving.

Doctor: Since only priests can consecrate, did you ever ask the Virgin where the angel got the Hosts?

Conchita: Yes, we did ask because a priest told us to. The Virgin said that the angel took the already-consecrated Hosts from the tabernacles of the earth.[98]

CHAPTER 15

The United Nations Attack on the Church and the Culture — The Daily Incremental and Relentless Assault of Communism

And this is the judgment, that the light has come into the world, and men loved darkness rather than light, because their deeds were evil. For everyone who does evil hates the light, and does not come to the light, lest his deeds should be exposed.

JOHN 3:19-20

The encroachment year after year, of well-placed globalists advocating socialism and Communism, with world bodies attempting to eradicate Christianity is well organized. It is relentless, intrusive, insidious, and Luciferian, catapulting civilization to a place it has never aspired to, nor worked towards. The goal of the self-appointed global elite is total replacement of biblical values in Western Civilization. The United Nations is now going full throttle in its attack on the Catholic Church. The Roman Catholic Church is the last remaining obstacle to achieving world government. Their goal is very simple: eliminate the Christian concept of living a moral and faith-filled life for a new model of total atheist state control, especially where the family is concerned — from cradle to grave. All of their efforts are escalating in a profound way. This aggressive global agenda against the Church started primarily with The International Conference on Population and Development in Cairo, Egypt, in 1994 (Commonly referred to as the Abortion Rights Conference), in conjunction with the United Nations steadily seeking to discredit Roman Catholic Dogma and Canon on homosexuality, abortion, pedophilia, and contraception. On March 8, 2023, the United Nations released a report that says, *"With respect to the enforcement of criminal law, a prescribed minimum age of consent to sex must be applied in a non-discriminatory manner. Enforcement may not be linked to the sex/gender of participants or age of consent to marriage.*[99]

This is an open door to legally normalize sexual relations with minors, supported by government. If anyone thinks this may be to extreme an interpretation, look at the gradual drift over just the last twenty years, where now a segment of the population is tolerant of this agenda, if not openly promoting it. As the years go by, the United Nations is more open to the public about what it is promoting to normalize LGBTQ+ activity in schools. Generally, the younger the age group, the more they have been supportive of this pagan agenda.

It's quite a simple approach when one thinks about it. Infiltrate and make the Church irrelevant, and marriage and family will corrode, and vice versa. Since marriage and family are the foundational structure for a civilized society, when that is removed, all that will be left is rubble. The agendas that are being promoted today are pagan acts reminiscent of Moloch on ancient altars. Institutions, large and small throughout the world, are codifying pagan behavior into law, and more people are accepting these practices as normal.

The Roman Catholic Church remains the final thorn in the side of the godless globalists, preventing them from fully implementing their goals. The globalists must tear down the authority of the hierarchy and the role of the papacy itself, rendering it powerless, before they can rule the world on their terms. It has long been a goal of secret societies of all kinds to denigrate established Church doctrine and replace it with *"radical inclusiveness,"* free of any moral boundaries.

Animosity and public hostility towards the Church over the last twenty years has increased over the issue of pedophilia in the priesthood, and the perception of Church doctrine in general. Government, non-governmental organizations (NGO's), wealthy foundations, radical leftist philanthropy, think tanks, corporations, and other institutions are building anti-sentiment on Church dogma — and it is organized. This is the agenda global policy makers are pushing to enact laws to end the supremacy of any moral authority. In no way is this an apology for the issue of pedophilia in the Catholic Church, but other faiths are infiltrated with this evil as well. Yet, they are rarely, if ever mentioned alongside the Roman Catholic Church abuses. No one group, or denomination, has a monopoly on this sin.

The UN has a goal of preventing the Church from having a seat at the table as an authority figure defending parental control of one's own children. The goal of the United Nations is universal access to abortion, gender neutrality, homosexuality, parents losing rights to their own children, control of curricula in the classroom, and removing Catholicism from any influence or position as a voice in the community of nations.

In February, 2014, the United Nations Committee on the Rights of the Child Report went into direct assault on the Church and families. The committee chair on Children's Rights, Kirsten Sandberg from Norway, said the following: "We urge that the Holy See review its position on abortion which places an obvious risk on the life and health of pregnant girls, and to amend Canon 1398 relating to abortion with a view to identifying circumstances under which access to abortion services can be permitted. The Church needs to assess the serious implications of its position of adolescent enjoyment of the highest health standard and overcome all the barriers and taboos surrounding adolescent sexuality that hinder their access to sexual and reproduction information." This demonically inspired statement is open warfare against the Church and family, and its positions on the sacredness of life and marriage. The existing structure of the Church has to be torn down to install their radical globalist agenda with new structures and monuments of immorality and doctrine.

Sandberg went on speaking about the fact the Church must change its views on homosexuality and other doctrines held sacred by the Magisterium. Over the last generation, their pursuit of this agenda has been relentless. With the moral climate deteriorating much more rapidly, it is easier to foresee this agenda being realized, as some clergy and laity in the Church capitulate to the State and the requirements of global elite corporate interests. The goal of the United Nations is to indoctrinate young children about sexual matters and make the killing of the innocent readily accessible in every country of the world.

At this point, no one knows how many abortions have taken place in the world over the last forty years, yet it is estimated to be well over two billion. The number is growing exponentially, due to governments worldwide promoting abortion through state sponsorship and funding. When we factor in sterilization, Plan B (morning after pill), and other methods of chemical abortion, the numbers just keep growing. A person can now go to a pharmacy and just get Plan B and walk out the door. It is now as easy as buying a bottle of baby aspirin or a bottle of shampoo in an American drug store.

The Food and Drug Administration is proposing that the birth control pill no longer need a prescription from a doctor, but should be available over the counter. This corresponds to **"the cup is filling up,"** and the message of **"the cup is flowing over."** Abortion is an integral part of the message of Garabandal, bringing chastisement to the world. This brings up the question of whether we are bringing judgment upon ourselves through our sins, or is it God's wrath punishing people. Isaiah writes, *"It has been your sin that separates you from God"* (Isaiah 59:2). We can see now **"why"** The Warning and The Miracle will be worldwide events for a correction of the conscience of the world.

The confluence of evil globally is making this scenario of irreparable harm to children more plausible. It reminds one of what Jesus said, *"Whoever causes one of these little ones who believe in Me to sin, it would be better for him if a great millstone were hung round his neck and he be thrown into the sea"* (Mark 9:42).

This heinous plan is the epitome of Satan's agenda to destroy civilization and corrupt the very youngest through indoctrination and brainwashing at the hands of the state, creating a moral breakdown of the child. This is being imposed by unelected officials with a diabolical agenda to dismantle any resemblance to virtue in culture. Billions of dollars are behind the U.N., through member state contributions and organizations such as the Bill and Melinda Gates Foundation, The Rockefeller Foundation, The United Nations Population Fund, International Planned Parenthood Foundation, CARE International, Save the Children, the World Health Organization, Soros funded entities, and dozens of other groups promoting an agenda attacking long standing Christian doctrine. A world without God is their policy program and unstated goal. The seers of Garabandal spoke of the world being **Communist** at the time of the Warning. It has, in essence, already happened through existing globalist deep state government policies, a secular practical atheism.

Conchita asked **why** the Miracle was coming. Jesus told her, *"To convert the whole world."* Conchita also asked, *"Will Russia be converted?"* Jesus told her, *"It will also be converted, and so everyone will love Our Hearts."*

To avert these disasters coming to the world, the Blessed Mother at Garabandal asked for Mass, penance, fasting, confession, conversion, amendment of life, sacrifice, visits to the Blessed Sacrament, and praying the Rosary every day.

Central Bank Digital Currency (CBDC), the Vaccine Passport, the Globalist Goal to Control Mankind — The Ultimate Clash of God vs. Satan

"My Kingdom is not of this world."

JOHN 18:36

It is much easier to manipulate and control an individual who does not acknowledge the truth of Christianity, which is precisely why Christ must first be removed by tyrants. We have seen the brutality of Communist regimes in the recent past, from the USSR and China and other brute dictators, but Communism is a government where God cannot be publicly displayed. Through sophisticated social engineering, much of the West, and the world at large, exhibits a form of theoretical and practical atheism — or Communism as it comes to everyday living. This diabolical genius of social engineering has so thoroughly indoctrinated the last several generations of people, they are now easily manipulated. A world without God is the Communist (the National Security State) goal. Social engineering, or manipulation of the masses is no longer a theory or practice, it is a predictable science. With the increasingly further sophisticated developments in Artificial Intelligence (AI), the world is increasingly becoming more dangerous for believers unwilling to comply with state tyranny.

One impending initiative that will have global implications is **Central Bank Digital Currency** (CBDC), wherein buying and selling by all citizens will be impossible unless done digitally under Central Bank (government) control. The United States, the West and China are far down this road already. In many circles, the term used is **FinTech** which means Financial Technologies. Fintech is the large spectrum of financial instruments, software and hardware, to automate and deliver the systems the government wishes to implement more efficiently. No country is further along than China where this type of control of banking and financial transactions is already in operation, tying the right to conduct transaction to an individual's social credit score. Many years ago, Google helped China reach its technology goals to implement it. Australia and England are well down this road to being the first non-Communist countries to implement the first stages of such a system for their citizens. CBDC will be ushered in by an unholy alliance of Big Finance, Big Pharma, Big Government, Big Tech, Big Social-Media, and Big Climate all working as one.

Even before the introduction of the CBDC in the U.K, in June of 2023, banks in England de-platformed (some are now calling it de-banked) well known British conservative firebrand Nigel Farage, and several other outspoken critics of woke and New World Order political policies, barring them from banking institutions throughout England. Farage said, "after banking for several decades in certain banks, I was rejected at seven different banks in the trend of de-banking, as this practice is more common..The letter came through and simply said, We are closing your accouns." After serving as a former British member of the European Parliament, Farage is the highest profile figure to be refused banking services. He says, "If this can happen to me, it can happen to anyone," and claims the UK is trying to force him to leave the country by closing his accounts. In the month after this incident became public, the banks did not debank him due to public outcry. However, Farage sees this as a growing trend, that in time will impact more people.[100]

On November 9, 2023, the European Parliament and the majority of the member nations reached a provisional agreement on the establishment of the European digital ID or "eID"—the first central and fully digital identification systems for all Europeans. The vocal are in the forefront against tyranny, thus they will be the first people the state will pursue. Fear of being a target is the primary reason most people stay in the background and not out front in the fight. The fear of not speaking up when tyranny is at your door step, is what will ultimately bring our destruction. Had more people spoken up about what Hitler was doing in the 1930's, it would have never gone as far as it did. However, the vast majority of the nation's citizenry watched in silence, and said nothing until death was in their own home.

The Garabandal prophecies on Communism are being fulfilled with state control of social structures on a global basis. **Central Bank Digital Currency** with associated enforced Social Management technocracy and Digital ID's would constitute Communism. Artificial Intelligence (AI) which is very advanced, using blockchain technology that is interoperable among member institutions and nations, will enable CBDC tyranny. Combine this with the vast amount of biometric schemes currently planned and implemented, and digital currency will end freedom and liberty in ways that nothing else could ever accomplish, because non-elected bureaucrats will determine what type of behavior is acceptable for a financial transaction to be allowed. For Americans, this will be the end of America as a Constitutional Republic, imposing ultimate government control of an individual's daily actions.

CBDC is where people cannot buy or sell without the knowledge of government bureaucracies using technology that is easily monitored and controlled. It is the ultimate goal of the globalists to seek control of their citizens. Programs are firmly in place administratively to allow this to happen. Digital currency and Digital IDs are supported by central banks and the'U.S. Federal Reserve. It will not be a *mandate* as it was for the Covid vaccine, but enforced through socially coercive means if there is non-compliance. Everyday transactions will be impossible unless there is compliance, thus making it hard to live. CBDC is the vaccine issue on steroids and has biblical significance. Heaven sees this in advance and has a great plan where people must trust. It will appear all is lost as we move closer and closer towards this state control.

In April, 2023, President Joseph Biden signed an Executive Order to implement a social justice credit score in the name of environmental justice for US. Citizens. This builds on previous Executive Order Number 14008, called *Tackling the Climate Crisis at Home and Abroad,* which is the U.S commitment to deal with environmental injustice. Western Governments are calling the climate crisis a matter of National Security. Tie this to the *Digital Currency Monetary Authority* (DCMA), which is the new CBDC called the *Universal Monetary Unit* (UMU), also now known as *Unicoin,* and the system is in place for tyranny like the world has never seen with a cashless digital currency.

The International Monetary Fund (IMF) say they are supporting CBDC to protect the financial integrity of the international banking system. Merchants and trading partners will be able to accept UMU as a form of payment for goods and services priced in any national legal tender.

Although the UMU was announced at the IMF Spring, 2023, meetings, it was not launched by the IMF. The currency exchange will be fully interoperable using U.S. SWIFT codes for transactions. The planning is no longer in the early stages, but the execution is. I would expect Unicoin to have several more name iterations or changes before it becomes fully operational in the coming years under the auspices of global banking. Other related words presently being used are *World Coin* and *World ID.* Whatever the system finally will be called is irrelevant. This is the tyranny Heaven is fighting as we near the end game for the battle of all battles in the Heavens.

Speaking at the G20 *One Future Forum* in India in 2023, European Commission President Ursula von der Leyen said, "The world needs international digital ID systems like coronavirus passports and Artificial Intelligence should be regulated by a global body similar to the United Nations Intergovernmental Panel on Climate Change. More globalist institutions will be needed to set boundaries and regulations.

The future is digital. I passed two messages to the G20. 1. We should establish a framework for safe, responsible AI, with a similar body as the IPCC for climate. 2. Digital public infrastructure are an accelerator of growth. They must be trusted, interoperable and open to all."[101] This is just another relentless push to ram through an agenda by unelected bureaucrats to establish world government, and using digital technology and climate change as a driver.

In the $1.7 trillion Omnibus Bill signed by President Joseph Biden on December 29, 2022, there was $772.5 billion for non-defense discretionary programs. This is on top of several trillion previously set aside under Covid relief and other programs where the U.S government and the Office of Management and Budget (OMB) have the ability to funnel cash to pet ear-marked projects. Included in the Omnibus Bill is money allocated for automobile companies to automatically shut a car off for a late payment, or other nefarious agendas that will creep in when people in the near future are declared enemies of the state. A more encompassing and accurate term than the Deep State is the *National Security State,* which encompasses all aspects of technology, government mandates, citizen compliance, a social credit score for all tax payers, and knowledge of all activities on buying. spending, or selling — in other words *all* financial transactions. The infrastructure laws and programs are in place for a final coup d'etat against humanity, so as to implement a more godless agenda. It is Satan's crowning achievement to enslave mankind.

We saw this in Canada in the early winter of 2022, when hundreds of ordinary citizens supported the truck convoy driving across Canada met in Ottawa to protest vaccine mandates by the Trudeau government. Trudeau implemented the Emergency Powers Act to crush any dissent against his policies during Covid. If someone helped a protestor, either by giving them cash for gas or food along the route, they had their funds frozen and were electronically fined directly through their bank accounts. Others lost their employment. This is a harsh sentence for a basic civil right of free speech. The plan is clear now: cross the government and you are going to pay financially in some form.

"The really efficient totalitarian state would be one in which the all-powerful executive of political bosses and their army of managers control a population of slaves who do not have to be coerced, but because they love their servitude."[102] It is precisely for this reason CBDC will be rolled out under the premise that it will protect us from fraud, and will be good for us, while giving us another level of privacy and personal security. This is precisely how the globalists primed the pump for widespread public acceptance by a generally unsuspecting population for the Covid vaccine, before efficacy and safety were established. As Benjamin Franklin famously said, "Those who would give up essential liberty to purchase a little temporary safety, deserve neither liberty nor safety."[103]

Former Secretary of State and long-time presidential advisor Henry Kissinger at one point said, "If you give Americans the choice between security and freedom, they'll take security." Kissinger has been a perennial architect of strategy and policy formulation for a New World Order — largely run by unelected leaders — for nearly seventy years. He has been working for the utopian dream of global government for a lifetime. Turning 100 in 2023, he is still going to annual meetings of the Council on Foreign Relations, the Trilateral Commission, and the World Economic Forum. Kissinger states the agenda as clearly as anyone could that the goal is *a "community of nations"* under an umbrella of godless policy wonks and billionaires looking to shape the world in their image. He writes, "In 1961, as a young academic, I called on President Harry S Truman when I found myself delivering a speech. To the question of what in his presidency had made him the most-proud, Truman replied, 'That we totally defeated our enemies and then brought them back to the community of nations. I would like to think that only America would have done this.' All of Truman's successors have followed some version of this narrative and taken pride in similar attributes. American presidents of both parties have continued to urge other governments, often with great vehemence and eloquence, to embrace the preservation and enhancement of human rights."[104]

Here is the conundrum and paradox in a world where intentions are manipulated to control the masses. It is a lofty and sublime goal for any individual to want peace and harmony of all peoples and nations, and even reminds one of the words of Jesus, "blessed are the peacemakers." However, under the tent of this stated goal is a nefarious and hidden agenda to control and implement policies detrimental to those with faith in God. The result of this agenda is the tyranny we see today exercised by sovereign governments globally. The Trojan Horse is the ideal of peace and basic human rights, but with an alternative agenda to use this against nations once their preselected people are in power. President Harry Truman had an illustrious career in politics as a United States Senator and Vice President under President Franklin Roosevelt, before he became president upon the death of Roosevelt. At the very end of his career, he became Grand Master of the Lodge of all Freemasons in the United States, and he said that this was the greatest honor in his entire life.[105] In 1945, Truman endorsed world government in a speech saying, "It will be just as easy for nations to get along in a republic of the world as it is for us to get along in a republic of the United States."[106]

This is similar to a college freshman coming home from his or her first semester after an introductory course on Marxist Theory, after reading *Das Capital* or the *Communist Manifesto* by Karl Marx. It works like a charm on paper in the classroom but not in the streets. Striving for peace and being a peacemaker is very different than thinking godless unelected bureaucrats placed in power by elites should rule a nation. The fall of man and original sin will never allow the community of nations to become an admirable goal, because as soon as someone gets power and authority, it is almost universally abused. Thus, the utopian dream since the time of Plato, has always failed miserably, and brought nothing but chaos and bloodshed to those trying to implement it.

The next stage of government is to not just marginalize individuals for dissenting from progressive government policies, but designed to have complete control over all their banking transactions. How an individual thinks is how they act, and the government wants to control both. Church Fathers spoke of this connection of how a person believes. Train a person to think collectively, and they will act as they are told, because they believe as they think. The World Economic Forum (WEF) is known for the famous statement of Klaus Schwab, *"In the future you will own nothing, and be happy about it."* Schwab was the founder of WEF in 1971, with mission to set the agenda of the elites *to improve the state of the world,* grooming young leaders with his ideology.

The WEF's annual meeting each year is in Davos, Switzerland, where the rich and powerful network and exchange ideas. A favorite in the inner circle of Schwab is Yuval Noah Harari. Listening to him speak and reading his literature is like taking a swim in a cesspool, where the synapse of his brain misfires with his every godless thought. Harari goes about the day making up new language, and his ideas are so far out in left field, you are left scratching your head to find any logic at all in his thinking. Speaking at the World Economic Forum 2018 meeting, a quote of Harari's dystopian Darwinist view is, *"History began when humans invented gods, and will end up when humans become gods. We are probably the last generations of homo sapiens within a century or two, earth will be dominated by entities that are more different from us, than we are from Neanderthals or from chimpanzees. Because in the coming generations, we will learn how to engineer bodies, brains, and minds. That will be the main products of the 21st century economy.* Harari and Schwab are the types of people Heaven is battling with their atheistic humanist agenda permeating society.

The World Economic Forum is openly advocating for a chip being implanted under your skin if a person wishes to participate in society. They now promote a microchip to do the most basic things as purchase food or water which in turn will be joined to a digital CBDC technology, that is directly connected to a person's social credit score. Professor Richard A. Werner, an economist who has worked at Oxford University, the Bank of Japan, the Development Bank of Japan, the Asian Development Bank, and he is considered a leader in the implementation of digital currencies. He said, **"You have to think of CBDC as a control system, or a permit system, not a currency. It's a conditional currency based on you actually getting that permit.** If you happen to be a critic of government policy or a critical of central banks this could be difficult for the individual. Of course, these are things we have already seen in China. There are plenty of videos where somebody tries to use it to buy a ticket and it doesn't work because his social credit scores are low."[107]

The concept of a chip under the skin to track people is not new. The technology is already developed to implement it as a policy if the government mandates or makes it law. It is no longer science fiction as a concept. The North American Masonic Lodges have an initiative called the Masonic Child Identification Program (MYCHIP), staffed by law enforcement, volunteers, and dental professionals which take digital fingerprints, digital video, and mouth swabs in case a child is abducted. The Program is administered by Freemason proprietary software. Since its inception in 1988, they allege the Masonic Youth Child Identification (MYCHIP) has helped to identify 300,000 children since its inception in 1988. The Masons of Massachusetts partnering with the Massachusetts Crime Prevention Association donate MYCHIP resources to make the service available to the public. MYCHIP is working in conjunction with the Most Worshipful Grand Lodge of Ancient Free and Accepted Masons in the Commonwealth of Massachusetts.

The World Economic Forum held its annual summer meeting in Tianjin, China in June 27-29, 2023, where there were approximately 1,500 participants. It is routinely called *The Annual Meeting of New Champions* or *Summer Davos*. The outcome of the meeting is that the world body of leaders are going to be asked to more heavily "promote multilateralism and collaboration in a fragmented world with a global transition to a green and renewable economy, and more heavily use surveillance." Schwab's excitement could not be contained as he lauded the Chinese leaders for their tough Covid policies with lockdowns, as a role model for other nations.[108]

CBDC is controlled by the Federal government, which controls the banks, which could easily affect employment, and freezing inbound and outbound flow of funds from any financial institution. Every bank, credit union, and financial institution in the entire country must comply with Federal policy or they will be outside the law and will need to close their business, because the source of their funds is directly from the United States Federal Reserve and the U.S. Treasury. Think of not being able to receive Social Security, Medicare or Medicaid, or to cash a state or Federal check, visit a dentist, a doctor, enter a hospital, register your car, or renew a driver's license. All government contractors and businesses will not be able to conduct business, not be able to pay an electric or water bill, buy or sell a car, enter into any government building, or enter a military base. Think for a moment how draconian it would become if the health care and medical profession could deny filling a medical prescription, no matter how small or significant that may be, based upon an ESG (environmental, social, governance) credit or reporting score. With the hundreds of billions of dollars in revenue streaming into the purchase of drugs, the health profession has extremely organized data bases on U.S. citizens, their buying habits, and prescriptions. If you think people got weak in the knees regarding Covid policies and had difficulty making decisions in the face of the demands of the state over an experimental drug serum, what do you think will happen if government wishes to implement CBDC? The banking establishment in Australia has publicly announced that they will be eliminating cash and checks by 2030. What does this have to do with Garabandal? Garabandal spoke of Communism and radical changes coming to the Church and the world, and these are principal elements of those changes.

The Federal Government has been deeply embedded in telecommunication companies since World War II. There was heavy cooperation in wartime conditions to get as much information as possible on the plans of America's enemies and tactics— in other words, spying. This has not only continued, but flourished in the commercial sector for widespread information gathering on citizens with intel agencies having representatives from telecom communications dedicated to government agencies. If the government mandates people to have cell phone service terminated, it can happen — instantly. The same for obtaining a new passport or using one still valid. With the stroke on a keyboard you can be placed on a no-fly list where airlines and customs no longer recognize your passport.

With the implementation of CBDC, a world government agenda, and groups like the World Health Organization (WHO) putting pressure on governments to implement a vaccine passport, or Digital ID of some kind; this will be the ultimate tyranny. Presently, these health passports are being released in Europe with cooperating nations. The Global Digital Health Certificate has an elaborate network to protect citizens across the globe from all future health threats. Citizens of the world will be in the WHO health database to determine who has not received all the necessary vaccinations they demand, or they will be blocked from commerce and travel. Vaccine passports are the ultimate tracking device designed to control an individual's behavior. Covid 19 was the dress rehearsal to see who would succumb to state mandates. Every major branch of the U.S. Government has a database of who refused the Covid vaccine, and it is now centralized.

The U.S has signed onto the UN World Health Organization's Pandemic Treaty vaccine passport agenda, with instructions to implement the Vaccine Passport at borders, closures, and quarantine measures. **It is designed for future pandemics**. The Treaty is in the draft phase and won't be under consideration until May, 2024. Now add on Artificial Intelligence (AI) capabilities and no stone is left unturned for tracking and government reconnaissance of every individual. Article 19 of the WHO Constitution allows the WHO General Assembly to adopt binding agreements for all member states by a two-thirds majority. Behind the agreement is the Bill and Melinda Gates Foundation and U.S. billionaire Marcel Arsenault.

The agenda for government control never ceases, and the assault is on many fronts. The relentless push of technology and ideology continues to encroach on privacy and rights. Former President Barack Obama said, "And the need for us, the general public, I think to be more discriminating consumers of news and information, the need for us over time to develop technologies to create watermarks or **digital fingerprints so we know what is true and what is not true.**"[109] The public will be told this is for their financial safety and security. This is now at this point getting into biblical concepts of what has been warned about in Scripture, where people will not be able *"to buy or sell without the Mark of the Beast"* (Revelation: 13:17).

Your cell phone and computer are your tracker. You can be placed in any location if you have your cell phone on you (even if it is turned off), your location can be detected through surveillance methods, GPS, or satellites. Every click on your computer, every text, every web site you have visited can be tracked, and cell calls you have made have been logged into a database, using algorithms that are so precise a profile of all your interests and habits has been assembled. Eric Schmidt, the former president of Google, once said, *"We know more about you than you do."* The technocratic state will increasingly become the enemy of the righteous who will be outside the system of what is acceptable by godless government bureaucrats. Every spending habit will be in your profile, and it will be so exact, it can tell your discretionary spending with 99% percent accuracy, and 99% of your intellectual interests, all the way down to health data and what ails you.

Black-market transactions will gain popularity in a CBDC economy, but they will only take you so far. Operating under the radar will be nearly impossible because a person's needs will be so great. Escaping to a refuge is not a long-term option. Over the last thirty years technology advances are now much more coordinated with government funding for public private partnerships. They are light years beyond what they were when they found Unabomber Ted Kaczynski hiding out in the Montana woods in a cabin with no water or electricity. The line today between what is government and what is corporate has increasingly disappeared, primarily because of mutual goals.

Those who think these assertions may not be factual may want to do some research into the **Fed Now** Program that started beta testing in July 2023. The financial monitoring system has been under development for years in joint cooperation with the United States Federal Reserve, the New York Federal Reserve, The Massachusetts Institute of Technology (MIT), MITRE Corporation, along with dozens of U.S. multi-national and transnational corporations. In addition, the surveillance state is well under way electronically. The globalists will attempt to usher in the digital currency with some sort of a cataclysmic event in the world. It could be a nuclear exchange, a world-wide sovereign debt crisis, or a new killer virus. It will most likely involve a major portion of the world. Russia, China, Ukraine, the United States, and NATO will probably be involved to some degree. Due to the interconnectivity of the world economy, it will have a profound impact on everyone overnight. As a result, the crisis will activate governments through the fiscal policies over bankers they now control, demanding them to implement their plans. As the age-old Masonic saying goes, *"out of chaos, comes order."* This plan was used to perfection in the French and Bolshevik Revolution to bring change. CBDC is just another plan to create chaos to bring a new order on terms would-be masters dictate to control the masses.

In 2022, it was discovered the Federal Bureau of Investigation (FBI) was planting operatives in Catholic Churches in the Diocese of Richmond, Virginia. Their goal was to gather information to determine if conservative Catholics were potentially enemies of the state. It was later discovered the same thing was taking place in Los Angeles, California, and Portland,

Oregon in a coordinated effort, not just one rogue agent as they had indicated earlier. As far as the FBI was concerned, these people were considered either white supremacists or future terrorists. It was a monitoring operation that went all the way to the top of the FBI. It was well established through leaked documents this was true, and Rep. Jim Jordan (R-OH) conducted a hearing in the House of Representatives on the seriousness of the issue. The Federal government were surveilling conservatives for information gathering. These are Stalinist and Nazi strategies that progressed to draconian practices as time went on with state abuse of power. This is now what the Federal law enforcement agencies are engaging in, and will be a part of the social credit score under a CBDC system of governance. Anyone who thinks this is not possible in the U.S. may want to look at the incremental eradication of religious and civil rights over the last generation at the local and federal level that has penetrated to nearly every agency and school board in the United States. If it is a blue state, it has been for the most part captured by socialists/ Communists.

CBDC is an interoperable empire because it is a form of digital control. It is transnational in every aspect, independent of borders. Buying and selling will be determined by someone you have never met. Governments and business will fall in line with one another because the system is so far advanced by airlines, major corporations, central bank clearing houses, and world lending institutions. A country is at the mercy of the global elite if in need of financing for infrastructure projects, or just everyday lending, and if a business does not comply, it will cease to exist. Conformity to a world body of regulatory requirements will drive compliance. Groups like the Bank of International Settlements (BIS) in Basel, Switzerland, the central banker's bank, have had this agenda for a long time. Transaction clearance will be under their control through member banks.

For those thinking ESG enforcement may be impossible or even imaginable, Larry Fink, CEO of BlackRock, the largest company in the history of the world with $10 trillion under management, operating in 30 countries, and with clients in over 100, said the following: "**ESGs are about Forcing Behavior and bending the knee to Diversity Equity and Inclusive (DEI) policies. The attacks are now personal for the first time in my career. They are trying to demonize issues.**"[110] Fink also sits on the board of the Council on Foreign Relations (CFR), and the World Economic

Forum (WEF), and has a net worth over $1billion. If a person has a low Environmental, Social, and Governance (ESG) score, they will be a target for marginalization and become future targets by government.

G. K. Chesterton once said, "Unless a man becomes the enemy of evil, he will not even become its slave, but rather its champion." C.S. Lewis said, "One of the most cowardly things ordinary people do is to shut their eyes to the facts."

A goal of the global elites for several generations has been to destroy the United States. The reason is quite simple to understand if you can grasp their ideology. The U.S. superiority for several generations was unmatched in nearly every sphere of power and dominance — militarily, technologically, academically, and other areas in standards of living. The United States has been the equivalent of a 900-pound gorilla on the world stage, and for global government by a council of rulers looking for equality, this had to be eliminated. This gradually began to happen when countries like Cuba, Malta, Albania, Gabon, and Ghana were placed on the United Nations Security Council and given a vote equal to the United States, determining policies going forward. This was all designed to take away U.S. hegemony from having the clout of previous decades. Gradually, the world body chipped away at U.S dominance to reduce it to the level of less influential nations. A major part of that plan was to destroy the dollar as the reserve currency of the world so America could no longer exert its authority anywhere. Having a global digital currency is another element of leveling the playing field, ending U.S. influence globally. At this moment in time, the U.S. is in a moral, economic, and structural death spiral and doesn't display command in nearly any area. Unless something happens suddenly, the U.S. is riding into the sunset as a superpower. This has been the plan of the globalists and it is succeeding.

The Divine Reset of Garabandal is Heaven stepping in to prevent the enslavement of people. The young visionaries described the times of tribulation as *"the return of Communism."* A digitally controlled transaction system of government is the fullest expression of Communism. Trotsky, Lenin, Stalin, Marx or Engels never could have envisioned such a mastery of thought when they published their Communist Manifesto in 1848. The above system of digital mastery of humanity is the final leg of a long sociological, evolutionary, Orwellian journey that Heaven will prevent from happening.

Heaven has a plan, and that will begin with the Warning and the Great Miracle to give desperately needed hope, to reverse this cycle of dystopian Luciferian evil. This is the battle of all battles and the "time of times." This is why the world waits for the Mercy of the promises of Garabandal to turn this tide of evil through repentance of people to see the wrong they have done. This exposure of evil in society is a necessary but painful step towards people coming to the realization that evil does exist in human form on a widespread basis through corrupt organizations.

All of these developments over the last several generations reminds one of the documentary *The Last Days,* with the quote from a Hungarian Jew. It said, "People wonder how it is we didn't do something. We didn't run away, we didn't hide. Well, things didn't happen at once. Things happened very slowly. So each time a new law came out, or a new restriction, we said, well just another thing. It will blow over. When we had to wear the yellow star to be outside, we started to worry." The ultimate goal of the people behind this agenda is to totally remove God from all institutions on earth, and control every aspect of our lives by putting us in a digital cage. This is not the work of man, but of Lucifer himself. Even secular pundits seeing the escalation of chaos at an accelerated pace, who have never professed having a spiritual outlook on the news, are speaking in religious terms now saying that what is now happening is evil.

Evil operates in incremental stages working inside the administrative system of government. Lenin understood how to gradually take over from within when he said, "The way to crush the bourgeoisie is to grind them between the millstone of taxation and inflation." Once those means are exhausted, and they feel a path is blocked, Marxist Communism will then burn down or blow up existing structures to achieve its goals.

CHAPTER 16

Stalin and The Communist Goal to Control Spain, The Spanish Civil War: Prior to Garabandal

"There is no fear in love, but perfect love casts out fear. For fear has to do with punishment, and he who fears is not perfected in love."

I JOHN 4:18

If it had not been for the famous book by Ernest Hemingway *For Whom the Bell Tolls* (1940), which was then made into a film starring Gary Cooper and Ingrid Bergman by the same name (1943), many Americans may not have known about the Spanish Civil War. Hemingway, Cooper and Bergman were established names in America to literary and film audiences at the time, and the book and the film made the war more recognized in the United States. The movie is about a small incident during the Spanish Civil War with a group of misfits fighting against Franco. In 1937, Ernest Hemingway went to Madrid to report as a war correspondent in sympathy with the Republicans. In total, he sent a total of 31 dispatches to foreign outlets on the war. Hemingway was not new to wartime conditions. He had volunteered to drive an ambulance for the American Red Cross in Italy in World War I, and was on the side of the Spanish Republicans backed by the Communist party throughout the world. In June of 1918, Hemingway was wounded by Austrian mortar fire when the war was months away from ending. His musings about his wartime medals and experiences were suspicious to people knowledgeable about his exploits. Whether it was an intellectual pursuit, a desire to see combat to write about emotions, a true ideology of the Communist cause, being a mercenary, the adventures of war, or other complicated reasons, one may never know. One thing is certain: Hemingway was an adrenaline junkie.

For decades, the Hemingway family has been plagued with addictions such as alcoholism, drugs, eating disorders, and mental illness. A total of seven family members over four generations have taken their own lives, including his famous supermodel granddaughter Margaux Hemingway, who died at the age of 42 in 1996 by suicide from a drug overdose, after suffering from depression. Hemingway is spoken of at some length because he is emblematic of a rudderless lost soul looking for answers in all the wrong places, which is exactly what a fervent Communist does.

The Spanish Civil War started in July of 1936 and ended in April of 1939. It was the largest atrocity in Europe post-World War I. In total, an estimated 200,000 people died (this number varies by historians, as some say much larger) from the war that tore Spain apart. As with all wars, the scars have generational consequences, both prior to war and in the aftermath. Millions of Spaniards were displaced and had their lives severely disrupted. Nearly 500,000 fled to France for refuge while an estimated 15,000 Republicans ended up in German concentration camps after 1940, as Hitler was anti-Communist, and anti-Russia. The Republicans murdered 4,200 priests and seminarians, 2,400 monks, nearly 300 nuns, and 13 bishops for a total just shy of 7,000 religious. Some historians put that number closer to 8,000. Communism seeks to wipe out at the outset of a conflict all Christian views it perceives as anathema to their goals. Franco had seen the national elections were corrupt and were rigged by the Communists, and he felt this had to be corrected to save Spain. However, with all wars, corruption is rampant, with both sides having legitimate grievances on the origins of the conflict, thus the battle goes to the streets. No regime in power is ever exempt from corruption, and the longer a party is in power, the corruption increases.

The war was a classic example of aggressive and powerful governments looking to carve up a nation and expand territories for their own political gain during a time of internal division. With Nazi Germany and Russia seeking control on opposing sides, the choices were not ideal to fight for one side or the other for an American audience. The Republicans backed by Communists (Russia) were killing clergy, seeking to wipe out the Church. The Communist Party of the Soviet Union was now firmly established as a formidable power since the Bolshevik Revolution of October, 1917. Nazi Germany and Mussolini of Italy backed the Nationalists. The irony of war was obvious.

Communists all over Europe and around the world were interested in Spain, as they could feel the apple was ripe to drop in their lap, and fully implement their system of government on a broader scale in a western country. Stalin gave the Republicans their needed support. A leader in the British Communist Party spoke of their practices to defeat capitalism, Franco, and the Church with a highly organized campaign. Douglas Hyde, wrote in his book how the Communists organized to take over Spain, explaining how they employed revolutionary tactics and raised money for Spain. His conversion story is one of the most moving and articulate conversion stories ever told. In his book *I Believed — the Autobiography of a Former British Communist,* he writes, "Communism had become our aim and we said so. It could only be achieved by bloody revolution, civil war and Red Terror — and we made no bones about it. The capitalist world was rotten, we hated its traditions, we rejected its conventions, its morality, and we did not hesitate to proclaim and to practice these things. As Communists we publicly defied all 'bourgeois'" conventions and glorified in being "outrageous."[111]

Hyde continues, "By the time the Spanish Civil War began in July of that year, I had the movement already established, organizing a wide variety of well-intentioned people. The events in Spain were a challenge and a showdown. Here was the war and fascism against which we had warned, already beginning in one corner of Europe. Who knew where it might end if all those who stood for peace and democracy failed to unite? All over Britain and right across Europe, recruits to the party came thick and fast — the sensitive intellectuals, the troubled and disillusioned pacifists, and solid working class, trade union types who distrusted us in the past, but now believed that, if what they stood was for one day to be defended, arms in hand, it would be the Communists who lead and fight as no one else."[112]

Hyde states how they operated and how lost souls following Communism expressed their passion: "the Communists went to Spain for quite different reasons from those of the non-Communists. **We saw it as a chance of learning the art of insurrection in practice so that it might one day be applied at home; to get experience of the barricades, to learn to use the modern weapons of death and destruction for the cause of Communism.** Every Communist Party in the world sent numbers of its members there to gain such experience. The leaders went out one after another for a few months experience. Very few lost their lives or received serious wounds.

The types of jobs they took were calculated to make this not likely, and every party member felt that the leaders should not light heartedly be thrown away.

"The rank and file died in great numbers in the early days and set an example of heroism. Too many died for the Party's liking. It was not intended that party members should be slaughtered wholesale. Dead men could make no contribution to the fight for Soviet Britain."[113] Hyde goes on to explain how the British Communists raised money for the Communist cause in Spain by supplying logistical support for ambulances and things needed in wartime conditions.

Hyde writes as an insider who orchestrated plans at a senior level for over twenty years before he had a Damascus-road incident. As the editor of the Daily Worker in England, he understood the intellectual side of the arguments of what Communist goals were and how to achieve them. Hyde writes about the mentality of a Communist: "As a Communist I had a vested interest in disorder, in economic crisis, social injustice and chaos, military defeat, my hopes had been pinned on world unrest and national instability. The aggressiveness of the leaders in the East, the growing problems of the West would have raised hope of an early victory for Communism. Marxism had always provided easy answers for difficult situations.

"The world had not consisted of millions of imperfect men striving for something better, but of two warring classes out of whose conflict would come our new order. The problems and solutions had been simpler, more clear-cut and utterly phony."[114]

"The Communist may be able to put his finger on what is bad in our society, but only the Christian is fitted to expound the good. One of the great errors of our time was to put into words by those who grandly disposed of the Soviet rejection of religion with the statement **that there the worship of God has been replaced by the service of man. It has been that sort of facile thinking which has opened the way to the destruction of the culture of the West.**

Marx, in his famous Eleventh Thesis, declared: The philosophers have only *interpreted* the world in various ways; however, it is their goal to change it. With its combination of intellectual arrogance and emotional appeal it was calculated to attract both the new, pagan intelligentsia and proletarians looking for an ideal."[115]

At Garabandal, as heralded at Fatima in 1917, the Blessed Mother saw the immediate threat and intervened to alert people about the scourge of Communism, and the physical and spiritual death and destruction it brings to humanity. The essence of her interventions in the world is a supreme act of love and mercy to give **solutions** for an alternative way to live a more abundant life. This is what Heaven is fighting. Communism is raising its ugly head again, albeit in a more calculated and sophisticated way through the legislature, and thus administration of unjust laws.

Hyde highlights this point after his conversion when he writes, "It would be tragic enough if there were increasing thousands of already bad men going year by year through this process. In a way it becomes even worse when it is realized that the majority are essentially good and come with good intentions."

"When I look back on the people who were for so many years my comrades and friends, I know that among them were some who were super-careerists, some who were bad who came to Communism because they were bad, and were attracted by the bad that was in it. I know too, that the majority would make magnificent Christians **if once they were given a better cause in which to believe. And I am certain that millions more could be prevented from ever joining the Communists ranks if they were made more aware, of something superior, something even to make greater demands upon them, claiming the whole man and using him for a noble instead of ignoble ends.**"[116]

"As a Christian I now believed that our current problems were the outcome of the failure or inability of nations to live up to the ideals they once had held, and of men to live up to the faith which some still retained and others had scornfully rejected."[117]

The war engulfed the prevailing powers in Europe at the time as the politics of previous decades erupted into a ferocious civil war. Wars take generations to germinate, and then suddenly explodes like a volcano, as was the case with Spain. The Nationalists were mostly comprised of Roman Catholics, landowners, business owners, military leaders, and people devoted to the Church. As with all wars, there are legitimate reasons for conflict coming from both sides. Had there been generational abuse and corruption with these groups that warranted a war? To the Republicans the answer was yes. Wars are generally fought over someone wanting what the other has, gained illegally or legally, continued legislative abuses, patronage and nepotism, or unjust laws favoring the power that is in place.

The Republicans attracted conscripts like Hemingway and Douglas Hyde, men who had a romantic and a utopian idea of life, often void of any religious convictions. Hemingway lived a life of narcissistic hedonism with few boundaries and no affiliation of any public declaration of faith. He had enjoyed the fruits of all the world had to offer in later years with world-wide fame. In the vernacular of the lore of centuries ago, he was a *"worldling."* From the bulls of Pamplona, the conviviality of the night life of the Café Vendome on the left bank in Paris, the blue marlins of Cuba, the boat culture, the alcohol consumption, the trout streams in Ketchum, Idaho, the hunts and safaris in Africa, infidelities, four marriages... he licked the earth for all it had to offer. In the end, he went into his bathroom, loaded his double-barrelled shotgun and blew his head off, leaving his wife to clean it up. The utopian dream of solving conflict through war had eluded his soul and only satisfied his flesh, as this is exactly what Communist ideology does. He, as others, looked for justice through imperfect models outside of faith, love, humility, and the truth that only the gospel can bring. In the end, the Communist way only brings personal desolation, loneliness, and destruction.

There could be a lot more said here about the war and to explain why the apparitions of Garabandal happened, in of all places, a tiny mountain village about an hour's drive from Santander on the Bay of Biscay. The question must be asked, **Why There? Why Then?** At the time of the apparitions in 1961, it was just twenty-two years after the Spanish Civil War, and just sixteen years after World War II, and the country was still healing. Inhabitants in the village of Garabandal all had been involved emotionally and spiritually, if not some on active duty.

Another story of note, like Douglas Hyde's, and one closer to home in the United States, is that of Whitaker Chambers (1901-1961), the American spy and Communist, who had a falling out with his idealistic views of Communism. Growing up in a dysfunctional home and being heavily engaged in the Communist ideology as a young man, Whitaker Chambers was another, who like Hyde, began to see the lies of Communism after observing Stalin's Purges in the late 1930's. He eventually left the party and told his story.

In Chambers' memoir titled, *Witness,* he provides his heartfelt emotions of his growing disillusionment with his previous activities. After an emotionally troubled childhood, Chambers poured his energy into the black hole of nihilistic Communism. Through moral and intellectual reasoning, his heart began to change and he wrote: "One thing I knew: I was no longer a Communist. I had broken involuntarily with Communism at the moment when I first said to myself: it is just as evil to kill the Tsar and his family and throw their bodies down a mine shaft as it is to starve two million peasants or slave laborers to death. More bodies are involved in one case than the other. But one is just as evil as the other, not more evil, not less evil. I did not know at what point I said this. I did not even know that with that thought I had rejected the right of the mind to justify evil in the name of history, reason or progress, because I had asserted that there is something greater than the mind, history or progress. **I did not know that this Something is God.**"[118]

No one can begin to understand WHY Communists hate the Catholic Church until they understand how detached it is from a moral philosophy that comes so naturally to so many other people. Communism is the enemy of the Church because it is an alternative religion, seeking to rule without God, and it is a principal reason for their passion. Energy for a Communist needs an outlet. It is an empty soul seeking their own ideal of an earthly utopia void of a willingness to submit to a Supreme Authority. It is the supreme element of a humanistic manifesto. It is a mistake to think it is merely a *form of government.* If that were the case, the Blessed Mother would not mention it so consistently as an enemy of Christendom. Author Frank Myer explains the Communist goal: *"Right is might* must be integrally conceived with *Might is right."* The individual Communist believes that what he does for the proletarian revolution is fated to be victorious; and that it will be victorious because what is done to bring it about is right. There is no dilemma, therefore, between the *Inevitability of socialism* and the duty to act to bring it about."[119]

Awareness of the history of Communism is essential to understand the prophecy of Garabandal: namely, the world has experienced, and is heading toward, another virulent strain of Communism, with its brutal enforcement methods and hatred of God and religion. Russia was central to the Fatima message with its prophecy that Communism would be the scourge of the earth. This was also said at Garabandal over forty years later. Understanding the Communist mentality is crucial to recognizing and combating its insidious methods. Communists have taken control by never using the word Communist, but employing its methods.

Soviet Expansion Under Stalin's Communism

At the time of the Spanish Civil War, Stalin was hell-bent on expanding Soviet ideology and territory with an atheistic Marxist state agenda. Few in history would rival his brutality. Lenin died in 1924, and by 1936 Stalin was flexing his powerful muscles with new lands to conquer. The USSR spanned eleven time zones, from Vladivostok in the east to St. Petersburg in the west. For Stalin to assume more power, he had to subjugate and crush all Catholic countries within reach and undermine Vatican authority. He set his sights first on the Church. To become the only Soviet god, he arrested 168,300 Russian Orthodox clergy during the purges of 1936-1938 alone, with 100,000 being shot. The Russian Orthodox Church had approximately 55,000 parishes in 1914. These were reduced to 500 by the late 1930's.[120]

This had been precisely what the Blessed Mother warned about at Fatima to the three young children. *"Russia would spread her errors..."* Analogously, she warned at Fatima about the future direction of the Church if there was not obedience to Her Son.

Stalin's purges in the Baltic States were at the exact time when Spain officially went to war with overwhelming Soviet support for Republican Spain. Stalin had starved Ukraine through a man-made famine in 1932-33 to implement Soviet collectivism. Approximately 3.9 million people died in Ukraine alone. Having furthered Soviet dominance to his south, Stalin then set his sights on the Baltic States. They were the furthest west, bordering Poland, and heavily per capita Catholic. Stalin was clear there was no room for the God of Pope Pius XII or the Vatican during his reign. Stalin could not dethrone the pope for obvious reasons, but that did not deter him from trying to conquer land further west, so he decided to wipe out the Catholic churches — for the churches posed a threat he could not tolerate. And as he had done in Russia and Ukraine, he now wanted to expand his empire.[121]

Stalin's strategy was to dispatch his favorite hangman, Andrey Vyshinsky, to Sovietize the Baltic States, and, in the process, destroy the national Catholic churches. Vyshinsky was old political police (NKVD) who had worked wonders in purges of the Russian Orthodox Church from 1936-38. Vyshinski knew what he had to do. More than seven million people had been sentenced to death and shot during the years he had been Stalin's main prosecutor, in order to make sure his boss was Russia's only deity.

In July of 1940, Russia proclaimed Latvia a part of the Soviet Union by order of the Moscow Supreme Court. In a matter of weeks, Catholic churches were shuttered, and priests were shot or sent to the gulag for Soviet forced labor. Soon after, Estonia and Lithuania became part of the Soviet orbit through the same methods, with the entire Catholic hierarchy and about a third of the entire population of both countries either deported or shot.[122] Such are the methods of Communism eliminating any opposition to their ideology and implementation of government. A fear of many who had to dine with Stalin upon his request, was that they could be driven home in a body bag and dropped off on their front step. Their elimination was intended to reduce the possibility of a coordinated coup. This was not abnormal under Stalin's reign of terror.

The method of embedding Communist people into established positions and then aggressively controlling the narrative reminds one of the words of Aleksandr Solzhenitsyn. He was the famous Soviet dissident and author, who lived under the gulag system, and eventually escaped the USSR to live in Vermont. He sums up Communism in these words:

> We know they are lying,
> they know they are lying,
> they know we know they are lying,
> we know they know we know they are lying,
> but they are still lying.

Solzhenitsyn, who had endured forced labor in the Soviet camps for being a writer on the Soviet Marxist system of Communism, became its most celebrated and articulate critic. He gave the most profound short answer to how it all happened, when he said, **"Men had forgotten God."** Perversion of all kinds have crept into our lives for the exact same reason it has in the past. When God is removed from the public square, all sorts of diabolical thinking will incrementally become mainstream and in time, be accepted and eventually normalized.

Spanish History of Freemasonry and Communism

There were other causal events in Spain taking place behind the scenes in the government before the war. The power is always behind the curtain and the arrow at transition of governments usually points to Freemasonry, dividing to conquer on its terms, to further consolidate power, wealth, and authority. Freemasonry has no religious or political affiliation, other than being in power with a secret controlling government. Ideology is irrelevant, as long as Freemasonry has a seat at the governing table. It has been executed so well, so often, it is no longer a practice, but a science. Class warfare is their *modus operandi* no matter the country. The Masonic motto is *out of chaos comes order,* and the implementation of the plan is executed to perfection upon an unsuspecting public. Civil wars do not just burst on a nation all at once with one action, but thousands of small events contribute to lighting the fuse. The lines of demarcation are drawn and tolerance for the others view is no longer acceptable. Such was the case in Spain, leading to the Civil War in 1936.

Francisco Franco (1892-1975) was an extremely controversial figure on the world stage prior to the Civil War and well after. Battling the dual enemies of Freemasonry, which was a well-known enemy of the Church, and Communism simultaneously, was an internal and external struggle for those bent on dividing Spain for their own interests. Knowing who to trust in light of their affections and allegiances caused insurmountable problems for a way to peace for the Spanish population.[123]

This narrative, and the war with its aftermath, provided the backdrop to what the Blessed Mother said at Garabandal, with her messages specifically about Communism, Russia, and Freemasonry. These messages at Fatima, Garabandal, and other places were central to what Our Lady warned would happen in the world. These evils are what Heaven is fighting. The Spanish Civil War impacted every family there to a larger or lesser degree. No one was immune from what was happening in Spain during the years of the war, prior to Our Lady's intervention. Spain was a mass of contradictions, with conflicting parties seeking to control it.

Francisco Franco had heard from his father about the indignant conversations that he had with colleagues from the naval base, where a defeat was blamed on dark forces such as Freemasonry. An essentially middle-class intellectual movement, Freemasonry was vilified by the Catholic

Church for its anti-clericalism by army officers because of its foreign links.[124] Freemasonry has a global influence and reach into government, military, and corporate board rooms throughout the world. There was no institution Freemasons could not reach. Spanish Freemasons exerting influence in affairs of state had senior French connections in the political establishment.[125]

Leaders in the Republican Communist party cried out the Marxist manifesto, throughout Spain, "It is necessary to spread terror. We have to create the impression of mastery, eliminating without scruples or hesitation all those who do not think as we do. When a peace proposal was offered, leaders said, Negotiate? Never! This war has to end with extermination of Spain's enemies."[126] Communism must eliminate all dissent. It is cruel, raw, savage, deceitful, barbaric, unscrupulous, and has no moral code. It is rebellious and defiant to any civil or ecclesiastical authority, or any fidelity to God as a supreme authority. Christianity is always the early primary target of Communism that must be immediately snuffed out, so the light of Christ may not burn in a heart. Freemasonry and Communism have the same goal — elimination of a moral authority so to place their own structures to govern, absent a Divine role.

The modus operandi of Freemasonry is to create chaos to bring in a system of governance with well-placed members to divide the spoils of conflict. No matter the winner, the Freemasons are situated in positions to govern. As an aftermath of war, "the living nations will gradually encroach on the territory of the dying."[127] When Stalin was finally granted terms for payment, he sent modern aircraft, machine guns, and tanks to the Republican army.[128] Stalin then strong armed and maneuvered for a new Spanish leadership.[129]

Stalin tried to orchestrate a total restructuring of Western Europe. A primary goal of his was to flip France socialist, which would ultimately become Communist. France saw this risk, and gathered an additional 30,000 troops to freeze Stalin's momentum. Stalin clearly had plans for European domination.[130]

Franco backed Vichy France and had the Axis Powers of Italy under Mussolini and Germany as allies under the Nazi flag during the Spanish Civil War. The United States, fearing a Communist take-over in Europe, backed Franco in World War II with loyalties heavily divided in the U.S. This was what the Blessed Mother warned about in her apparitions at Ezkioga, Spain.

Meanwhile, the Soviets were allied with the Americans and the British in the European theater of World War II, and after a long and costly struggle against their common enemy, defeated Nazi Germany in the spring of 1945. As the saying goes, "War makes strange bedfellows." When North Korea invaded South Korea (1950) with help from Mao Zedong in China, world geopolitics became even more complex. Communism was gaining momentum throughout the world.

Franco regarded any foreign pressure for democratic change as the **"Freemason offensive."** He told a cabinet meeting that there were over 15 million Freemasons in England who all voted Labour.[131] He also dismissed foreign criticism against him as the fruit of Freemason conspiracy against Spain.[132] Franco would travel throughout Spain calling for the defeat of "satanic machinations" by perverted Freemasons, and claimed that Spain was under attack from the masonic superstate, which controlled the world press radio stations, as well as key politicians in western democracies.[133] He stated Freemasonry was consubstantial with liberal democracy, conspiring with Communism to destroy Spain.[134] Franco also felt the American government was dominated by Freemasons and ready to open the door to Communism.[135] Well into the 1960's, Franco saw the Freemason threat in the government establishment. He feared Spain's joining the European Economic Community (EEC), believing it was totally run by Freemasons, and in time he felt Spain could be blackmailed into political liberalization.[136] It is for these openly stated views that Franco was branded a right-wing, fascist lunatic by the liberal press.

In 1846, Pope Pius IX wrote about the changes he saw in the future: "That infamous doctrine of so-called Communism is absolutely contrary to the natural law itself, and, if once adopted, would utterly destroy the rights, property, and possessions of all men, and even society itself."[137]

The alleged need for a change in the basic way things are done is consistent with the teachings of the father of Communism, Karl Marx. When he coauthored the *Communist Manifesto* with Frederich Engels, Marx wrote that Communists "Openly declare that their ends can be attained only by forcible overthrow of all existing social conditions."[138]

At the first appearance of the Blessed Mother at Fatima in May, 1917, at Fatima, Russia was not a world superpower. At that time, it was much closer to what could be called a third world nation. Only after the appearances in Fatima did Russia emerge as a blooming world power that would soon become a blight on all humanity through its atheistic doctrine. The messages of Fatima and Garabandal both have the country of Russia central to their warnings — not China, not Islam, not the Persian Gulf, not the Korean Peninsula, not Iran, not Taiwan, **but Russia.** And again, it was about the potential of war and Communism. Our Lady had a message for peace at Fatima and said *"to prevent this,"* meaning the scourge that Russia's Communism would soon bring chaos, changing the political landscape of the world map. People did not respond as requested, and Russia did *"spread her errors,"* as was prophesied.

The Communist Government in Spain Before the War

The dictatorship of Primo de Rivera was overturned in 1930, and brush fires of political dissent were spreading soon to become a raging inferno throughout Spain. Rivera was anti-Communist, anti-mason, and pro-monarch. King Alfonso XIII abdicated his throne in 1932, and the Republic was then led by Manuel Azana Diaz, who was inducted in the Freemason Main Lodge of Spain in 1932. Manuel Azana Diaz introduced oppressive government mandates like those we have seen in the last several hundred years throughout the world — thus, the violent clash between the Nationalists and the pro-Communist Republicans in Spain.

The French Revolution of 1789 was planned to rid France of its monarchy, as was the Bolshevik Revolution of 1917, which overturned in Russia the three-hundred-year-old Romanov monarchy. Spain was the next target of Freemasonry plot to control the populace by abolishing its monarchy. Democracies and republics are much easier to control by outside forces and influences, because a political candidate can be manipulated by a small group of powerful people who finance the candidate's ambitions for their own personal gain — a candidate they select. Thus, all monarchies had to be abolished to make way for Communist domination. If they wish, monarchies report to no inside or outside influences, thus they must be overthrown so the nation or kingdom can be controlled. Under Communism, monarchies are toppled violently if they do not comply with Freemasonic state agendas. Communism and Freemasonry work together as both look to undermine monarchies with similar strategies, so they can be controlled by their chosen cohort of people when these people are well placed in power.[139]

CHAPTER 17

The Apparitions at Ezkioga, 1931, The Kibeho of Spain

In 1981, Our Lady appeared to three young girls in Kibeho, Rwanda. The apparitions of Kibeho were officially recognized in 2001 by the local bishop as authentic. The Blessed Mother came under the title of *Mother of the Word,* and appeared in visions to the children from 1981-1989. She warned of a war and asked the children and the nation to pray for an amendment of life. Our Lady appeared then to others and imparted a special knowledge of the necessity of suffering and repentance. One young girl was worried when asked to spread the devotion worldwide, saying that she did not even have enough money to travel to the next city. Our Lady said, "My child, my grace can do all things. You just do your part." There is the resounding message of authentic apparition sites.

In 1994, war broke out among warring factions of old tribal conflicts, and a terrible atrocity ensued that became known as the Rwandan Genocide. The movie *Hotel Rwanda,* released in 2004 in the U.S., brought attention to the war. Ezkioga and Rwanda have many similarities, before, during, and after the apparitions. Since Rwanda is more well-known than Ezkioga, it is mentioned.

In 1931, the Blessed Mother appeared to young children in Ezkioga, Spain, with a message asking for amendment of life to provide peace for the nation. In the Basque dialect of Spain, this is spelled Ezkioga, and the apparition will be called what the Basque people called it. In an anglicized version, it is sometimes called "Ezquioga." Our Lady gave the reason why she came to Ezkioga, saying "I have come to earth because Satan has taken over the world and wants to put an end to Catholics. The reason for my apparitions in Ezkioga lies in the desertion of My Son's ministers, who do not attend as they should to their churches. That is why I seek other dear souls, so that they labor to do what My ministers forget."

The apparitions began to occur on a nightly basis. At first, there were just two children receiving visions, but the number grew to several dozen children over time, and local clergy said dozens of the apparitions had signs of authenticity. In a matter of days, the crowds grew to 40,000 to hear what the Blessed Mother had to say. In 1931 alone, it was estimated one million people visited the site. That number of people is substantial for the time. Few had automobiles in 1931, the area was remote, the roads were generally inadequate, and it was sparsely populated as a region. In 1930, It was estimated the entire population of Spain was only twenty-four million, yet one million came to hear what the Blessed Mother was saying.

The apparitions came during a confusing time for Spain. Anarchists and socialists in the Basque coastal cities, socialist farmworkers in Navarra, Republican railway officials, school teachers in rural areas, anticlerical poor in the big cities, and socialist and Communist movements worldwide were involved. In this respect, Ezkioga was similar to other modern apparitions.[140]

The Basque area of northern Spain considered Saint Bernadette Soubirous of Lourdes as one of their own for reasons of ethnicity and geographic proximity. Approximately thirty percent of the pilgrims visiting Lourdes were from Catalonia and the Basque area nestled in the Pyrenees of northern Spain at the time of the war. The Catalonians and northern Spain were deeply religious, with cities in the north like Pamplona, Loyola, Vitoria, Burgos, Zaragosa, and others, where the seminaries, universities, and novitiates were mainly located. The camino trail (a walking pilgrimage of reflection and penance) ends up in the Cathedral of Santiago de Compostela in Galicia, along the coast in the north, is part of the region. The city of Santander is the third major stop on the camino del norte (the northern way) and not far from Garabandal.

The walk of the camino dates back to the 9th century and stretches a total of 514 miles. Santiago de Compostela is considered by the Church to be the burial site of the apostle Saint James (the Great). Northern Spain was the birthplace of the priests and religious, and was an integral part of the rural and small-town populations. Spain has a deep and rich heritage of fidelity to the Magisterium of the Catholic Church. Saint Ignatius of Loyola was from Spain, and Saint Dominic was born in Caleruega, Spain. Saint Teresa of Avila, a religious reformer of the Carmelites and Doctor of the Church, was also from Spain. In addition, many orders of nuns and religious headed to the new world after Columbus sailed in 1492. Since the early 16th century missionaries from Spain arrived by the thousands to the Americas, teaching the Faith to all who were already in the New World, building schools and churches, and with those still to come.

Possibly, the most significant event of all, and the reason WHY the apparitions took place in Garabandal versus any other place, is the village long-standing fidelity to the Church and its traditions. *For several hundred years,* the village would ring a bell and the Angelus would be said publicly each afternoon. This would be followed by the custom in which the village would gather for the nightly Rosary. There are similar fidelities that were carried out in the small village in Medjugorje, Bosnia, before the apparitions began there in 1981. Both villages were remote, and very simple. The U.S. landed a man on the moon with Apollo 11 in July 1969, and brought the crew home safely. Medjugorje didn't have indoor plumbing until 1960, nor did Garabandal have central heating in homes at the time of the apparitions. In every sense of the word, both places were remote and simple.

The devout in Spain bore a century of suspicion towards the violent anticlericalism of Spain's large cities and progressive governments. There was over one hundred years of resentment and antagonism between one region towards the other in Spain, thus, the mutual hatred of the Republicans and the Nationalists. With Communism and Freemasonry becoming more entrenched in government, the division and anger over an ideological perspective grew wider among the regions of Spain.[141] These types of divisions are the intellectual breeding ground of wars and civil disturbances throughout history.

From the time the Blessed Mother appeared to Saint Catherine Laboure, a twenty four-year old novice on July 18, 1830, in Rue du Bac, Paris, many clergy publicly undermined the messages. The same can be said for just about every authentic apparition in history. Immediately, there are strident supporters, as well as detractors: the devil is quick to oppose the unfolding of God's plan.

Our Lady then went to a remote mountain village in northern Spain, to young children unstained by the corruption of the world. As Elijah received the voice of God on Mount Carmel, which was also a barren and dry place to hear God's voice, so too Our Lady appears in other remote places to innocent souls. As Elijah rebuked King Ahab and the false prophets of Baal on Mount Carmel, Our Lady brought messages of warning and rebuke to those who oppose God's laws. She announced herself at Garabandal with the title of Our Lady of Mount Carmel. So too, she came to Garabandal a sparsely populated and tiny village conducive and open to her messages.

The same was true for pure souls like Bernadette Soubirous at Lourdes with her simplicity to convey Heaven's messages to humanity, and her inability to fabricate stories about profound theological concepts. People like Saint Faustina of Poland, who had only a third-grade formal education, were also chosen to be the Lord's innocent secretary to present the messages of Divine Mercy to the world. Similarly, it was like this at Fatima to three very young visionaries. Heaven seems to like remote places with unsullied and pristine youthful souls so the world will not see this as a fraud of a learned soul with perhaps deliberate intentions to deceive. Garabandal has no natural explanations on many fronts, which is why it confounds so many people. It can only be understood and explained in the supernatural realm.

The politics inside Spain at the time of the apparitions at Ezkioga were extremely divisive and intense, and civil war broke out five years later. Socially and economically, the country was on the verge of collapse as it grew increasingly divided. Division had grown so great in Spain that thousands of clergy were murdered and churches were closed. People politicized the messages of the Blessed Mother and political parties gave their own interpretation to what Heaven was saying. However, Heaven's messages were about peace and amendment of life — always a sign of authenticity. But, as at Rwanda, some sixty years later, the messages were not heeded.

The apparitions of Garabandal occurred thirty years after those of Ezkioga, and only twenty-two years after the end of the Spanish Civil War. Was Ezkioga, Spain like Kibeho, Rwanada, where the Blessed Mother came to warn the country in 1981 of a horrific war if there was not change? She said, Rwanda *"would become a river of blood"* if the people did not change. Rwanda came to violent war in 1994, where over one million were murdered in just one hundred days. Rwanda had the generational hatred stemming from the genocide of warring factions from 1959-1962, where millions ended up fleeing Rwanda and living in the jungles of the Congo, and neighboring countries for survival. Their children remembered those hardships, and the time came for revenge. With the millions of people in Ukraine and Russia involved in the current war, we will see more of this hatred in the future from that part of the world. Hostilities in Spain brewed for decades, as they have in Ukraine and Russia, where war broke out in 2014, and again in 2022.

Enemies of the supernatural and the Republican regime in Spain from the outset were resolved to deny and destroy the apparitions at Ezkioga. The Bishop at the time was exiled to France, as he opposed the Republican regime and had to flee for his life. The Communist government at the time of the apparitions burned churches, persecuted clergy, and looked to discredit the apparitions as much as humanly possible prior to and during the Civil War of 1936-39. Progressives inside the Church sought to destroy the apparition as soon as the Blessed Mother appeared. Freemason and Communist President Azana said, *"Put an end to everything that has to do with Ezkioga, we don't want another Fatima here."* Azana, using Communist methods to block truth, provided civil and military intervention to create as many obstacles as possible.[142] Clergy feared for their lives, and speaking out on matters of faith contrary to state mandates and laws, resulted in dire consequences.

The young seers sat Ezkioga warned of a civil war coming in a few years and the death of clergy who opposed it (even telling the clergy in advance of their fate). They said the Nationalist side would win the war, there would be three years of famine, Christians would be persecuted, the tyrannical government in Spain would fall, and that plagues and other natural disasters were soon to come. Everything happened as Our Lady said it would.

One of the young visionaries, Benita Aguirre, aged nine, said,

"Our Lady told me that the Communists would soon enter Spain, that they had begun to do evil. There are many who blind, do not realize that **the chastisement will come over and above Communism; and that a fountain of great graces flow day and night from Jesus' Sacred Heart poured out over those with Him**, but that we should try to respond to them, for He will reward us."

"She affirmed that soon the churches would close, that the first to close would be those of Catalonia, where the greatest atrocities would be committed against religion. Because Catalonia possesses treasures in three victim souls, who love her dearly, and have offered themselves to Jesus as victims; and for the sake of these three souls, Catalonia would be chastised less than she deserves. Our Lady ended up telling me, we should set up the arms with which we must defend religion.

"She told me that we who belong to Jesus should **pray hard to save many of those in danger of damnation, and that our supplications, especially now, will be heeded, and that when the famine comes, almost all (true) Catholics will be found outside of Spain, given that Jesus wants to save us from the greater parts of the chastisement, thanks to the prayers said on the Mount of the Apparitions which have been heard.**"[143]

It was said of Benita Aguirre,

> "Leaning slightly backward, resting in the arms of my friends, her head slightly raised, her eyes fixed on a point high up, but not so fixed that they did not move somewhere or blink occasionally. She speaks with the apparition; she smiles, suffers, sobs, but without tears, asks forgiveness with a sad and tender voice. Then she takes one by one the objects lined in front of her, each time raising her arm, presents them to the apparition to kiss and bless them. I have a crucifix about a palm long I bought there that Benita held in her hands that afternoon. It was kissed by the Virgin, Gemma, (whom she saw again today), and the angels. I also have three red rosaries. The medals on the safety pin I wear were kissed by the Virgin and Gemma. All this as said by Benita."[144]

The Blessed Mother taught the young children this prayer: *"O my Jesus, I offer this for the love of thee, for the conversion of sinners, and in reparation for the sins committed against the Immaculate Heart of Mary."*

There was the usual banter and general conversation with the young visionaries about families, their siblings and their general lives at Ezkioga. A relationship developed as the children began to have confidences in what was told to them because so many of the little things they were told came true. People would be told things that materialized just as the Blessed Mother said would happen. These signal graces then gave the young visionaries assurance that what was being told to them would boost their faith.[145] In the anthology of authentic apparitions, this is a normal sequence of events as the relationship between Heaven and the visionary evolves. This is exactly what happened at Garabandal as the four young girls would have casual conversations with Our Lady about events in their lives, and were told things that did happen over the four years of apparitions.

All of the above point to Spain having a rich culture and religious history. This may partially point to **why** Garabandal, of all places on earth, was chosen for such a special reason. There is a saying from Spain:

> Spain the evangelizer of half of the orb;
> Spain hammer of the heretics,
> light of Trent,
> sword of Rome,
> cradle of Ignatius;
> that is our greatness and our unity; we have no other.
> The day we lose those, Spain will return to the cantonalism of the
> Arevacos, and the vectors or the kings of taifas
>
> *Marcelino Menendez Pelayo*

The Messages of Ezkioga Were Ignored

Cardinal Frederick Tedeschini, then Apostolic Nuncio in Spain, in 1932 said, "According to the information I have seen on the events in Ezkioga, it is from Heaven." The martyr Saint Manuel Irutia Almandoz, Bishop of Barcelona, said: "Without sinning by rashness, one cannot deny that there is something supernatural in the Ezkioga business;" and said he "believed in it, and would work privately for it, and said that if I were Bishop of Vitoria, I would work openly to promote it." Several of the young visionaries prophesied the deaths of clergy in advance who opposed Ezkioga. Two bishops who openly opposed the apparitions from the beginning died untimely deaths. Vicar General Echeguren, one of the greatest opponents of the apparitions, died in a car accident as Bishop of Oviedo in 1937. It was also prophesied that Bishop Matthew Mugica would "die exiled from his Episcopal See and completely alone." Bishop Mugica was forced to renounce his bishopric and died blind. It was he who published the biggest attack on Ezkioga, all without any formal study and without sufficient proof of listening to the seers. Despite being required by Canon Law, no Commissions were ever set up to investigate if the alleged messages were either true or false.

As at Fatima, Kibeho, and Bosnia, the Blessed Mother appeared in Ezkioga ahead of bloodshed and chaos to give an alternative to war. When Our Lady appears, some believe, and some do not, and the government usually takes a negative position because they fear what they don't know. The Spanish government tried to kill the apparitions at Ezkioga early on, because they disrupted the plans of warring factions bent on revenge at any cost. In addition, many in government are anti-god and don't want a spiritual element inserted into their plans, as it would disrupt their diabolical agenda. Naturally, the Church sided with the Nationalists as the Republicans were murdering clergy, and the Communists made every attempt to ignore the enthusiasm and authenticity of the apparition from the very beginning.[146]

The stage was being set for the violent eruption that would soon happen in 1936 in Catholic Spain. In 1931, article 26 of the new Republican Constitution ended state funding for the Catholic Church. The state took possession of all church properties, banned the Jesuits and all other religious orders, outlawed Catholic schools, and banned Catholic processions and Catholic teachings. This is the festering hatred of one for another that soon went to the streets in 1936. The fuse was lit, and the hatred grew to a boil, like it has been happening with polarization in the U.S. over the last two generations. What happened in Spain in the 1930s has enormous similarities to what is happening in the USA today, as well as the West in general, mostly due to Communist infiltration of government. If we do not listen to the authentic messages of Heaven, it is to our peril.

There are two pillars that can crush an apparition from the outset. One is a government at the time of Ezkioga. The other is from inside the Church, which has a longer and more devastating impact. Historically, if Freemasonry or the corruption of the clergy is mentioned, the Church will often look at it with a jaundiced eye and attempt to squash the activity immediately. La Salette is one example where the Blessed Mother in 1846 was harsh on clergy, calling them *"a cesspool of impurity."* Melanie Calvat and Maximin Giraud, the two young visionaries at the time, were treated so poorly they never traveled back to La Salette in later years. It was a Bishop in Lecce, Italy who approved the messages, not one from France.

Neither Ezkioga or Garabandal are approved apparitions by the Catholic Church. The issue of Communism and the ravages it brings to any society are an integral part of the messages of Garabandal. Communism is like dye in a garment. The destruction it will bring wherever it goes becomes inseparable over time from the spirit of the culture.

On June 18, 1965, towards the end of the apparitions at Garabandal, the Blessed Mother gave a message of the sort that gives clergy discomfort and often will bring an unfavorable decision by the Church. She said, "Many Cardinals, many Bishops, many priests are on the road to perdition and taking many souls with them."

That is the type of message clergy do not find endearing.

A similar thing happened in Medjugorje, Bosnia, where the Blessed Mother came as the Queen of Peace in June of 1981. She asked again for conversion and fidelity to her Son. The messages deal with living the faith that the Scriptures tell us to live; a joyful, peaceful, and holy life. Our Lady continually spoke over the years that the world was not attentive to what she was saying. Then, in 1992, in what was Communist Yugoslavia under the dictator Marshall Tito (1892-1980), generational hatred between the Serbs and Croats, broke out in a war where an estimated 150,000 people died. Between 1992–1995, the region was destabilized again. The Blessed Mother comes as any caring mother, and does whatever is necessary to help her children. However, the people must listen.

CHAPTER 18

Our Lady Makes Her Move and Intervenes — She is Dismantling Freemasonry

After the United States saw the carnage of World War II, where an estimated 60 million people died, the United States Congress established the National Security Act of 1947. Inside the Act was a clause to monitor world events, and thus not to be caught off guard with any foreign power having ill intent towards the United States. A secret government had just been established, and undoubtedly, the politicians assumed they had America's best interests in mind when they passed the Bill. However, what had just happened unknown to almost anyone, is that a leviathan monster was created, that in time would have no oversight by anyone. The head of the Office of Strategic Services (OSS) during the Second World War was Bill Donovan (often called "Wild Bill Donovan"), and he was commissioned to set up a new agency to monitor these world events. It was called the Central Intelligence Agency (CIA). President Harry Truman, who signed the law creating the CIA, estimated it would have a dozen people researching and handling intelligence passing the findings on to the appropriate government agencies. No one ever dreamed, in 1947, the hydra would grow so many heads.

The more people find out about nefarious intelligence activities, the more likely they will come to know the "conspiracy theorist" was right all along. It has run its course, and Heaven is intervening. The fight is ferocious. Western Civilization itself is on the edge of collapse, Christianity is considered a failed concept by globalists, and the U.S. Constitution is interpreted as a racist document by Communists now in senior levels of government. Existing systems of U.S. governance that were for generations the glue of civilization, are now in the final stages of not functioning as designed. Evil people have a ferocious and diabolical agenda they wish to implement and that is the battle we are witnessing today.

The answer to that is quite simple. It is rooted in what lies in the human heart. There is war in the world because there is war in men's hearts first. It happens when power and authority remain unchecked by another person or entity. The original framers of the U.S. Constitution were aware unchecked authority would ultimately result in the abuse of power, so a system was set up with checks and balances to counter the abuse they knew would come without a system of oversight. As the common adage says, *"Power corrupts, and absolute power corrupts absolutely."* Founding Father and U.S. President James Madison (fourth US. President, 1809-1817) said, *"Men are not angels, and that is why we need oversight of government."* Madison knew Scripture, and was clear the country needed checks and balances to keep tyrants from power, and remain a Constitutional Republic. Madison is known as the "Father of the Constitution" and champion of the Bill of Rights.

A Republic can only endure when there is voluntary compliance with the law. President John Adams wrote that Christianity was mandatory for the survival of the country. The pursuit of virtue combined with sincere religious instruction and belief is necessary. Today, we have little of either in the public square, and especially in government schools (public schools) that have been on the fast track to expunge God from the life of mankind in every way possible. Hitler was clear that if you brainwash the youth, you'll own the next generation. By the time Hitler came along, Germany's population had been thoroughly brainwashed through state indoctrination. Thus, his godless tyranny was generally accepted by the population. It reminds one of the phrase about human nature, "A lie will circle the world, before truth has a chance to tie its boots."

President John F. Kennedy: Understanding the Threat of Secret Societies

On April 27, 1961, President John F. Kennedy addressed the Newspaper Publishers of America at the Waldorf Astoria Hotel in New York City. He spoke about how Secret Societies undermine a democracy. Listening to that speech today on YouTube will send shivers up your spine on the validity of his informed statements concerning a subversive body of people having a profound influence over the U.S. Congress and government in general.

This group exerts control through financial largesse and their loyal secretive interconnected networks, all the while operating with impunity in plain sight, enjoying the sumptuous feast of "easy careers." Even in 1961, just fourteen years after the establishment of the CIA and the birth of the modern leviathan intelligence community, this community had already become entrenched as bloated entities with off the book black op budgets with no oversight. It is for this reason, when President Dwight D. Eisenhower was leaving office, he spoke about the perils to the nation of a "Military Industrial Complex." A body of people had emerged in a short amount of time to stage a behind the scenes coup d'etat to rule government. This National Security State is global. Our Lady sees it — and this is what she is fighting. The National Security State is larger and more interconnected to government than just the Military Industrial Complex. It encompasses social media and technology companies to influence public opinion and further global tyranny through legalized governance structures.

Patrimony and privilege from **The** Secret Society place people in power to ultimately control the government through stealth networks like Freemasonry. At the Waldorf, with speechwriters from The best and the brightest the world had to offer, President Kennedy said, "The very word secrecy is repugnant in a free and open society and we are as a people inherently and historically opposed to secret societies, to secret oaths and to secret proceedings. We decided long ago that the dangers of excessive and unwarranted concealment of pertinent facts far outweigh the dangers which are cited to justify it. Even today, there is little value in opposing the threat of a closed society by initiating its arbitrary restrictions. Even today, there is little value in insuring the survival of our nation if our traditions do not survive with it. **And there is very grave danger that an announced need for increased security will be seized upon by those anxious to expand its meaning to the very limits of official censorship and concealment...**" Kennedy was directly addressing the issue of a body of people who had an agenda of their own outside the constitutional process. One doesn't have to be an historian or Secretary of State to see that a constitutional crisis is in our midst today.

What Exactly is THE Secret Society? The Black Beast?

Before Donald Trump was the GOP nominee for president, former Speaker of the House of Representatives Newt Gingrich said to Bill O'Reilly on The O'Reilly Factor, "Bill, you have to remember, Trump has not been initiated, he is not a member of **The** Secret Society." He used the definite article **THE.** What exactly is **THE** Secret Society? It is Freemasonry. Freemasonry is the most virulent, diabolical, and destructive source of power working against the Catholic Church from within and without, having an active agenda to dismantle the existing form of ecclesial and civic government. The name of the lodge in Rome, is the P2 Lodge, or Propaganda Due in Italian.

The Huge Red Dragon, the Beast Like a Leopard, and the Beast Like a Lamb

In message number **404** of the Marian Movement of Priests, given to Father Stefano Gobbi, titled, the **Huge Red Dragon**, Our Lady says,

> "The huge Red Dragon is atheistic Communism which has spread everywhere the error of the denial and of the obstinate rejection of God. The huge Red Dragon is Marxist atheism, which appears with ten horns, namely with the power of its means of communication, in order to lead humanity to disobey the Ten Commandments of God, and with seven heads, upon each of which there is a crown, signs of authority and royalty. The crowned head indicates the nations in which atheistic Communism is established and rules with the force of its ideological, political and military power *(e)*.
>
> "The hugeness of the Dragon clearly manifests the vastness of the territory occupied by the uncontested reign of atheistic Communism. Its color is red because it uses wars and blood as instruments of its numerous conquests *(f)*.
>
> "The huge Red Dragon has succeeded during these years in conquering humanity with the error of theoretical and practical atheism which has seduced all the nations of the earth. It has thus succeeded in building up for itself a new civilization without God, materialistic, egoistic, hedonistic, arid and cold, which carries within itself the seeds of corruption and death *(g)*."

Immediately after the above, Our Lady gives a message called the **Beast Like a Leopard (405, Secular Freemasonry)**. She says,

"In this terrible struggle, there comes up from the sea, to the aid of the Dragon, a beast like a leopard *(c)*.

"If the **Red Dragon is Marxist atheism, the Black Beast is Freemasonry**. The Dragon manifests himself in the force of his power, the Black Beast, on the other hand, acts in the shadow, keeps out of sight and hides himself in such a way to enter in everywhere. He has the claws of a bear and the mouth of a lion because he works everywhere with cunning and with the means of social communication, that is to say, through propaganda. The seven heads indicate the various Masonic lodges, which act everywhere in a subtle and dangerous way *(d)*...."

In the very next message called the **Beast Like a Lamb (406, Ecclesiastical)** a great deal more insight is provided into the reasons for our peril. It partially reads:

"The black beast like a leopard indicates Freemasonry, the beast with two horns like a lamb indicates Freemasonry infiltrated into the interior of the Church, that is to say, *ecclesiastical Masonry*, which has spread especially among the members of the hierarchy. This masonic infiltration, in the interior of the Church, was already foretold to you by me at Fatima, when I announced to you that Satan would enter in, even to the summit of the Church. If the task of Masonry is to lead souls to perdition, bringing them to the worship of false divinities, the task of ecclesiastical Masonry, is on the other hand, that of *destroying Christ and His Church,* building a new idol, namely a false christ and a false church *(g)*...

"The aim of ecclesiastical Masonry is that of justifying sin, of presenting it no longer as an evil, but as something good and of value. Thus, one is advised to do this as a way of satisfying the exigencies of one's own nature, destroying the root from which repentance could be born, and it is told that it is no longer necessary to confess it. The pernicious fruit of this accursed cancer, which has spread throughout the whole Church, is the disappearance everywhere of individual confession. Souls are led to live in sin, rejecting the gift of life that Jesus has offered us *(m)*."

In the twenty-five years of public messages of the Marian Movement of Priests, the above three are some of the longest and most descriptive ever given. They give reasons for the moral rot destroying the world's political, ecclesiastical, and cultural institutions. This is what Heaven is fighting. The Warning and the Miracle at Garabandal will be the Divine Reset the world needs to restructure its institutions. At this point, nothing else can work for the restoration of the world.

Padre Pio of San Giovanni Rotondo, Italy was intimately aware of Ecclesiastical Freemasonry. After meeting a young priest, Father Luigi Villa, Padre Pio told him his life's work was to expose Freemasonry in the Church. Padre Pio prophesied to him that "The Lord had designs upon him and had chosen him to be educated and trained to fight Freemasonry inside the Church." Father Villa went to meet Pope Pius XII and divulged what Padre Pio had said to him. Pius XII told him since the request was directly from Padre Pio, he would grant this mission to him. However, he said before he was allowed to do this, he had to get his Ph.D. in theology first — which he did.

Padre Pio on a later occasion embraced Father Villa three times while he was on a visit saying to him, "Be brave now, for the Church has already been invaded by Freemasonry," and then stated, "Freemasonry has already made it into the loafers (shoes) of the pope." At the time Padre Pio said this to Father Villa, the reigning pope was Pope Paul VI. This was in the midst of the Second Vatican Council and the messages of Garabandal in 1963.

The connection between Freemasonry, and the secular world and ecclesiastical hierarchy, is made clear here by the Blessed Mother in the book of messages *Our Lady Speaks to her Beloved Sons*, given as locutions to Father Stefano Gobbi. In message 407e, titled the *Number of the Beast: 666*, it says,

> "Ecclesiastical Masonry receives orders and power from the various Masonic lodges and works to lead everyone secretly to become part of the secret sects. **Thus, it stimulates the ambitious with the prospects of *easy careers;*** it heaps up with goods those who are starved for money; it assists its members to exceed others and to occupy the most important positions while it sets aside, in a subtle

but decisive way, all those who refuse to take part in its designs. Indeed, the beast like a lamb exercises all its power from the first beast, in its presence, and it forces the earth and all its inhabitants to adore the first beast."

One can see why young men would join Freemasonry for what the Blessed Mother calls "**easy careers.**" Freemasonry is a fraternal network of individuals promoting and helping people advance in the world, operating in stealth. Catholic priest, Msgr. George Dillon, wrote about this issue in 1885. Pope Leo XIII asked that Dillion's book be translated into Italian and other languages. In 1884, Pope Leo XIII promulgated his iconic encyclical on Freemasonry, *Humanum Genus*. In that document, he asked the Catholic clergy that it "be your first rule of all to tear away the mask of Freemasonry, and let it be seen as it really is."[147]

Dillon elaborates why Freemasonry is so powerful with life-long fidelity by its members. "When Masonry governs, as in France, Italy, and Germany, the only way for youth to obtain a livelihood on entering upon life is being affiliated to masonry; and the only way to secure advancement is to be devoted to the principles, the intrigues, and the interests of the Sect.

"The continuous efforts of Masonry, aided by the immoral and atheistic literature, by a corrupt public opinion, by a zealous propagandism of contempt of the Church, for her ministers and her ministrations, and by a sleepless, able *Directory* devoted to the evil end, and enough in all reason to ruin Christianity if that were not Divine."[148] This able Directory is a very small, yet select committee of people who influence events behind the scenes.

When entire lifestyles and future welfares of families are dependent upon fidelity to the mission of membership of Freemasonry, it is a rare soul that bites the hand that provides all that it has to offer. Members' very future depends on not breaking any pledges made that aided in the early stages of their "**easy careers.**"

Determining the philosophy of Freemasonry through the language used is very difficult. Every aspect of Masonry seems to have an evil interpretation and a benign interpretation. Those who wish to find a Christian interpretation in its symbols can find ample published Masonic justifications. Those who wish to show that Masonry is really a form of Deism — built for all religions and faiths can easily do that as well. It's a classical example of elegant double speak.[149]

Masonic goals are:

1. Creating and vitalizing a New World Order;
2. The **gradual** reorganizing of the social order;
3. The public inauguration of the system of initiation, which will involve the growth and comprehension of symbolism:
4. The esoteric training of disciples and of humanity in this new cycle.[150]

Modernism and Masonry are one and the same. They are conjoined twins with the same agendas. Their goals are identical, using the same methods, tactics, and strategy to overthrow the existing systems of governance and bring in their own leadership and control. Modernism's "trinity of parents" are:

1. Its religious ancestor is the Protestant Reformation;
2. Its philosophical parent is the Enlightenment; and
3. Its political pedigree comes from the French Revolution.[151]

Heaven is Intervening—Their Target

The Lord is hearing the cries of His people who have prayed and fasted. His remnant, God's people faithful to the gospel, have been mobilized and are in spiritual battle. The veil of lies and deceit are presently being lifted, and a joyful and glorious day will soon be upon us. The Lord and His Blessed Mother are now shining a spotlight, exposing the enemies of truth. The Blessed Mother, the prophetess of our age, has been appointed by the Holy Trinity for this role at this moment in time, to expose and dismantle Freemasonry, the same way she won other battles for her children in the past. First, Freemasonry must be exposed and all deeds brought to the light.

So what exactly does the Blessed Mother say about her next target to expose evil? To the Marian Movement of Priests, she identifies her next target of conquest. In message number 456, **In the Name of Mary** (take notice of the name of the message), delivered just before the fall of the former USSR in 1991 from Slovakia, Our Lady says:

"In the name of your heavenly Mother, yes, in the name of Mary, the Turks were defeated, when they laid siege to the city of Vienna, and threatened to invade and destroy the whole Christian world. They were far superior in strength, in numbers and in weapons, and they felt that their victory was assured. But I was publicly invoked and called upon: my name was inscribed upon their banners and shouted out by the soldiers, and thus through my intercession, there took place the miracle of this victory which saved the Christian world from its destruction. It is for this reason that the Pope instituted on this day, the feast of the name of Mary.

> **"In the name of Mary, Marxist Communism, which for decades had been exercising its rule and holding so many of my poor children in oppressive and bloody slavery, has been defeated in these countries. Not because of political movements or persons, but through my personal intervention, has your liberation finally come about.**
>
> **"It will again be in the name of Mary that I will bring to completion my work with the defeat of Masonry, of every diabolical force, of materialism, and of practical atheism, so that all humanity will be able to attain its encounter with the Lord and be thus purified and completely renewed, with the triumph of my Immaculate Heart in the world.**
>
> "It is for this reason that I desire that the feast in honor of the name of Mary be restored, **now that you are entering into the fiercest moments of the struggle and the most painful stage of the great tribulation.**"

Several very important things are being said:

1. This message is about her specific target. It is about Masonry — the power behind the curtain operating in stealth. The average person does not know Freemasonry's hidden agenda. Its tentacles run far, wide, and deeper than most can imagine — always operating in secret. Man hacks at the branches of evil, Heaven attacks the roots of evil.

2. The Christian world defeated the Islamic powers at the Battle of Lepanto (1571), and the Turks at the Siege of Vienna (1683), against great odds after invoking her name. Similarly, under enormous odds, the Soviet Empire was defeated without bloodshed. The USSR collapsed after the fall of the Berlin Wall in 1989, and few saw it coming, other than the Marian devotees following her messages.

3. Victory is swift and decisive if we follow her directives under her mantle. It is her personal intervention that assures this victory, not the words of political rulers and pundits, but because she is the Mother of all Peoples.

4. It is Our Lady who will bring her work to completion with the defeat of Masonry and all that comes with it: every diabolical force, practical atheism and materialism. Will it be the Warning and the Miracle at Garabandal to bring this about?

5. We are in the fiercest moments of the struggle. Much like birth pangs that increase in intensity before the birth of a child, the fierceness of the battle will increase and will be painful for many.

We are witnessing evil versus good, virtue versus vice, God's cohort versus Satan's cohort, children of light versus children of darkness, and the fight is spiritual and involves the highest choirs in Heaven. The reign of Satan as prince of this world is about to be broken by the heel of a woman who steps on the head of the serpent (Genesis 3). Much like Queen Esther interceded to the King on behalf of her people, the Blessed Mother is interceding on our behalf to the King of Kings.

In message 457 to the Marian Movement of Priests, Our Lady says, "**Thus, by means of you,** I am able to continue my motherly work of mercy, which I have begun in these countries, but which I must still bring to completion in every part of the world, for the triumph of my Immaculate Heart."

"**Thus, by means of you.**" Our Lady has said she needs us to participate in her redemptive plan for mankind. Your prayers, your fasting, your sacrifices… Heaven needs you to speak up and stop the lies and deceit. It is your time.[152]

CHAPTER 19

A Kaleidoscope of Gemstones

1. *Needles, Garabandal Magazine, Garabandal Journal,* and Barry Hanratty, More Than Fifty Years

When Joey Lomangino started speaking about Garabandal, his magazine was called **Needles**, which started in the late 1960's. After several years it became **Garabandal** and Barry Hanratty was the editor, as Joey was blind from a young age. In 2002, when Joey developed health problems, Barry became the editor of **Garabandal Journal.** When Joey died on June 18, 2014 (53 years to the day the events started) Barry continued the work of *Garabandal Journal.*

When Joey Lomangino fell ill, Barry Hanratty continued promoting Garabandal, working for the remainder of his life until he died on October 1, 2022, at the age of 84. His fifty-year effort and commitment was herculean, and his work was a benefit to the entire Catholic world. He also stuck to the facts and dismissed some of the hysteria surrounding what many were prognosticating with limited facts. As he continued to tell the same stories, year after year, decade after decade, he branched out to other apparition sites and other inspirational Catholic phenomena in the world.

2. Did Mari Loli Reveal Some Information on the Year of the Warning?

Here again is another piece of information that was released that may be accurate, speculation, or gradually emerged over the years as anecdotally true or false. This should be discerned in light of the statement coming well after Mari Loli's original statements. Tom Fahy, a friend of Garabandal is the source of the letter below. (Tom died in December 2019).

In an email dated March 20, 2015, sent by Tom Fahy to Glenn Hudson, another friend of Garabandal, Tom wrote:

> Dear Glenn,
>
> In the late 1980's or early 1990's, two priests, whom I knew personally at that time, visited Mari Loli in Massachusetts. On their return, one of the priests told me that Mari Loli disclosed to them, when they were leaving, that the Warning would be in an even numbered year.
>
> Several years later, I asked the same priest if Mari Loli said an even numbered year? He said, *"Yes."* I have also read about it or heard the same from other sources, which I do not recall now.
>
> In another situation, I was told by a man in Massachusetts, who knows the pastor of the church that Mari Loli attended, that Mari Loli was speaking to her pastor in Massachusetts. One day, after he came to know about her relation to Garabandal, and told him she could not remember whether it was 3 weeks or 3 months that the Warning would precede the Miracle. **That would confirm that the Warning and the Miracle are in the same year**, as she said in her July 27, 1975 published interview. I take the same year to be the same calendar year.
>
> Fiat,
>
> YES. Actually, I heard this from the priest who was with Fr. Gustavo. I have not been in contact with ether of them for several years now.
>
> Signed: Thomas Fahy

The priest that allegedly heard this statement from Mari Loli was Father Gustavo Morelos who confirmed the statement as true, though she would not tell him the year. Pushing further, he asked if it was in an odd or even year, and she said an **even numbered year.**

This is a sensitive area for many skeptics or those more cautious of apparitions. Many of the seer's families doubt this was ever said.[153] This prediction that both events are in the same year or in an even numbered year should be looked upon with discernment. I also have heard over the years of several mystics who say there is a short duration from the Warning to the Miracle. It may be true, or it may not be true, and beyond the scope of the messages just from Garabandal. However, after the shock of the Warning, several weeks sounds like an incredibly brief amount of time to recover, digest what happened, and journey to Garabandal for the Great Miracle. More importantly, the visionaries never said during the apparitions events were in the same calendar year. The Warning is for the world, but the Miracle and Permanent Sign will be primarily for believers in the messages of Our Lady. People who have been aware of the events will be much more predisposed to travel there for the Miracle.

It will be challenging for someone who wishes to bring a seriously sick or handicapped individual to the site. If an individual has not had past familiarity with the Warning, and what is expected next (Miracle), it will certainly be overwhelming. It will be primarily people familiar with Garabandal who will know what to expect after the Warning. For this reason, this book could have been titled, *What Just Happened, and What Happens Next?*

Over time, more information emerges from visionaries about details of so called *"secrets."* It is just the normal pattern that follows in most instances with apparitions. Due to the grace of the visionaries, Heaven protects the integrity of secrets, as happened with Fatima. However, there is often the emergence of more facts about forthcoming events based upon other data points that materialize.

Irrational exuberance can put unreasonable assumptions on the expected events if nothing happens after speculation, after saying something "will happen," and then doesn't, often results in confusion and doubt. After someone cries wolf too often, it causes prudent and cautious people to fall away from belief, and understandably so. An apparition is often discredited over time with the sincere and devout *sensus fidelium* in the Church, if events do not happen as someone predicted. Continually guessing dates based on irrational statements, emotional cries, or false hope can be harmful to Heaven's plan, and upset or deflate the faithful. It is why Conchita said at one point, let the Lord and Our Lady do as they wish, and the Church will act in time.

3. The Role of the Laity in Our Times, St. Louis de Montfort, Archbishop Fulton J. Sheen

Amen, I say to you, unless you become like a little child, you will not enter the Kingdom of Heaven. Whoever humbles himself like this child is the greatest in the Kingdom of Heaven.

MATTHEW 18:3-4

Saint Lous de Montfort (1673-1716) writes about who will be end times apostles. He is clear it will be the Marian devotees, advocates, and proponents of Our Lady's role. He states it will be the laity that will carry this burning torch, with an interior and perfect practice of Marian devotion. To those with an untrained ear or heart, this may be difficult to process. It reminds one where Bernadette Soubirous said about the Blessed Mother's appearances at Lourdes, France, "To those who believe, no explanation is necessary, to those who do not believe, no explanation is possible."

In his ageless spiritual classic titled, *True Devotion to Mary* (TD), Saint Louis de Montfort gives considerable attention to the role in salvation history of the Marian devotee. He writes,

"It was through her that He will reign in the world. He will intervene with a deluge of fire, love, and justice through the mediation of the Spirit and the manifold acts of Mary. These people will be the apostles of the end times (TD 58). These end times apostles, will be true disciples of Jesus Christ" (TD 59). "These great souls... will be exceptionally devoted to the Blessed Virgin. Illumined by her light, nourished at her breast, guided by her spirit, supported by her arm, sheltered under her protection" (TD 48 & 55). "... her heel will crush the head of the serpent" (TD54). "...the fact that they will be preaching devotion to me, which will make many enemies..." (TD 48).

Archbishop Fulton J. Sheen (1895-1979) echoes this sentiment in a more modern era. While addressing the Supreme Convention of the Knights of Columbus in 1972 he said,

"Who is going to save the Church? Not our bishops, not our priests and religious. It is up to you, the people. You have the minds, the eyes, and the ears to save the Church. Your mission is to see that your priests act like priests, your bishops act like bishops, and your religious act like religious."

4. The Prophecy of Saint Francis of Assisi, Italy

A short time before his death, Saint Francis of Assisi warned of coming troubles saying,

"Act bravely, my brethren; take courage, and trust in the Lord. The time is fast approaching in which there will be great trials and afflictions; perplexities and dissensions, both spiritual and temporal, will abound; the charity of many will grow cold, and the malice of the wicked will increase. The devils will have unusual power, the immaculate purity of our Order, and of others, will be so much obscured that there will be very few Christians who will obey the true Sovereign Pontiff and the Roman Church with loyal hearts and perfect charity. **At the time of this tribulation a man, not canonically elected, will be raised to the Pontificate, who, by his cunning, will endeavor to draw many into error and death. Then scandals will be multiplied, our Order will be divided, and many others will be entirely destroyed, because they will consent to error instead of opposing it.**

"There will be such diversity of opinions and schisms among the people, the religious and the clergy, that, except those days were shortened, according to the words of the Gospel, even the elect would be led into error, were they not specially guided, amid such great confusion, by the immense mercy of God.

"Then our Rule and manner of life will be violently opposed by some, and terrible trials will come upon us. Those who are found faithful will receive the crown of life; but woe to those who, trusting solely in their Order, shall fall into tepidity, for they will not be able to support the temptations permitted for the proving of the elect.

"Those who preserve their fervor and adhere to virtue with love and zeal for the truth will suffer injuries and persecutions as rebels and schismatics; for their persecutors, urged on by the evil spirits, will say they are rendering a great service to God, by destroying such pestilent men from the face of the earth. But the Lord will be the refuge of the afflicted, and will save all who trust in Him. And in order to be like their Head [Jesus Christ], these, the elect, will act with confidence, and by their death will purchase for themselves eternal life; choosing to obey God rather than man, they will fear nothing, and they will prefer to perish [physically] rather than consent to falsehood and perfidy.

"Some preachers will keep silence about the truth, and others will trample it under foot and deny it. Sanctity of life will be held in derision even by those who outwardly profess it, for in those days Jesus Christ will send them not a true Pastor, but a destroyer."[154]

It should be noted that Francis of Assisi (1182-1226) died nearly 800 years ago. There is some room for interpretation concerning this alleged prophecy due to the enormous volume of historical events that have passed in this period of time, namely the Protestant Reformation, the Enlightenment, World Wars, Communism, and many other calamitous events. However, in the history of the Holy Roman Catholic and Apostolic Church, we have never before seen Sacred Doctrine violently undermined by so many leading prelates on a global basis, on issues that have been firmly established as evident and accepted Scriptural truths. This alone speaks to the potential veracity of such a prophecy. Garabandal speaks of perilous times in the world near these events, and the need for correction and reform. This satisfies what is said above may be accurate.

5. The Prophecy of Father Ratzinger (Pope Benedict XVI) of a Church Decimated

As a theologian and professor at Regensburg University, Germany in 1969, Father Joseph Ratzinger (the future Pope Benedict XVI) made an important prediction regarding the Church in our times. (The entirety of the address is much longer and can be found on the internet). He wrote:

"It will become small and start pretty much all over again. It will no longer have use of the structures it built in its years of prosperity. The reduction in the number of the faithful will lead to its losing an important part of its social privileges. It will be a more spiritual Church, and will not claim a political mandate flirting with the right one minute and the left the next. It will become poor and the Church of the destitute. When all the suffering is past, a great power will emerge from a more spiritual and simple Church. The renewed

Church will be a sign of hope for those who have not come to know the love of God."

This thinking regarding the future of the Church corresponds to the messages of Garabandal. Elements of Garabandal involve hostilities in Europe, priests in hiding, hardship, the Church having a great trial, Communism, and generally, "the cup of iniquity is flowing over." Father Ratzinger's thoughts were incisive and accurate, and what he said as far back as 1969 is proving to be true.

6. Divine Mercy: Before the Day of Justice Arrives, I am Sending the Day of Mercy

People today realize the world is in great need of Mercy, and without it, there is no hope for mankind. Are the Warning and the Great Miracle the events that will reverse the course of history?

Saint Faustina's dairy is titled *The Diary of Saint Faustina Kowalska: Divine Mercy in My Soul*. In the chaplet the opening prayer is "….an ocean of mercy opened up for the world. O Fount of Life, **unfathomable Divine mercy, envelop the whole world, and empty the whole world upon us…**" The word unfathomable needs to be contemplated. It means not to be fully understood or incomprehensible. The closing prayer to the chaplet is, **Eternal God in whom Mercy is endless and the treasury of Compassion inexhaustible, look kindly upon us and increase your Mercy in us…"** Also, the phrase, "in whom Mercy is endless and the treasury of Compassion inexhaustible," must be contemplated and what God's love means to the world, and what He will do to save His people.

The Lord said, "Before the Day of Justice, I am sending the Day of Mercy (1588). I am prolonging the time of mercy for the sake of sinners. But woe to them if they do not recognize this time of My visitation" (1160).

"While there is still time, let them have recourse to the fount of My Mercy (848). He who refuses to pass through the door of My mercy, must pass through the door of My justice (1146).

"You have to speak to the world about His great mercy and prepare the world for the Second Coming of Him who will come, not as a merciful Savior, but as a just Judge. Oh, how terrible is that day! Determined is the day of justice, the day of divine wrath. The angels tremble before it. Speak to souls about this great mercy while it is still the time for granting mercy" (635).

Saint John Paul II seemed to have a strong sense of this urgency. In 1981, at the Shrine of Merciful Love in Collevalenza, Italy, he stated that from the very beginning of his ministry, that spreading the message of mercy was his "special task" assigned to him by God. In four of his encyclicals, he stresses that we are now living in a special time of preparation for the new coming of the Lord. He urges us "to implore God's mercy for humanity in this hour of history…to beg for it at this difficult, critical phase of the history of the Church and of the world" (Rich in Mercy, 15).[155]

7. Fatima Continues: The Queen of Heaven and Earth, Gives the Same Message to Humanity at Different Locations Throughout the World

The main visionary of Fatima, Sister Lucia dos Santos reported experiencing apparitions of Our Lady of Medjugorje in the convent. In Sister Emmanuel Maillard's book, *Triumph of the Heart*, she said Sister Lucia's nephew, Father Salinho, a Salesian priest who lives in Portugal, said that Sister Lucia received visions of the Blessed Mother long after 1917. According to Father Salinho, Sister Lucia said the Blessed Mother confirmed her mission in Medjugorje.

Saint John Paul II said on March 25, 1984, "Medjugorje is the continuation of Fatima, it's the completion of Fatima." On several occasions, the seers of Medjugorje have said, "Medjugorje is the continuation and fulfillment of Fatima."

On August 25, 1991, the Blessed Mother, in a message to the world from Medjugorje said, "I invite you to renunciation for nine days so that with your help everything I wanted to realize through the secrets I began at Fatima may be fulfilled."

There is the little-known revelation of Our Lady of Fatima to Sister Lucia in May of 1952, when she said: "Make it known to the Holy Father that I am always awaiting the Consecration of Russia to My Immaculate Heart. Without that Consecration, Russia will not be able to convert, nor will the world have peace."[156]

The most basic and fundamental question of all must be asked. If the promise was there would be peace if Russia (not the world, but Russia by name) was consecrated to the Immaculate Heart as asked at Fatima, would the world now have war in Ukraine, precipitated by an invasion from Russia? The USA is sending hundreds of billions of dollars of assistance and armaments to Ukraine, and 31 NATO member countries are cooperating to varying degrees. China is aiding Russia in known and unknown ways, and Iran is sending state of the art drone technology to Russia. On July 7, 2023, the Biden Administration approved sending cluster bombs to Ukraine. Over 100 nations of the world have signed a treaty condemning the use of cluster bombs. The issue of whether the Consecration of Russia was done as Our Lady originally asked is still a red-hot issue in the Catholic world. If it were done as asked, would we have this war?

The Great Miracle of Garabandal CANNOT achieve the conversion of Russia singularly, solely, independently, or divorced from the Consecration of Russia to the Immaculate Heart of Mary by the Pope together with all the Catholic Bishops. The Miracle and the Consecration *must be* and *are bound to be connected somehow*. This is a matter of *both and, not either or,* as Our Lord and Our Lady cannot contradict each other.

8. Fatima, Medjugorje, and Garabandal

More than thirty years went by where neither the Blessed Mother or a pope commented on the Medjugorje and the Fatima link. However, a message was given by the Blessed Mother on **January 25, 2023,** at Medjugorje while the war was raging in Ukraine that said, "Dear Children! Pray with me for peace, because Satan wants war and hatred in hearts and peoples. Therefore, pray and sacrifice your days by fasting and penance, that God may give you peace. The future is at a crossroads, because modern man does not want God. That is why mankind is heading to perdition. You, little children, are my hope. Pray with me, **that what I began at Fatima and here may be realized...**"

In 1981, at Medjugorje, the Blessed Mother said, "Russia will come to glorify God the most: the West has made civilization progress but without God, and acts as if they are their own creator." Russia has always been the key to the Fatima message, and in 1961 at Garabandal, Our Lady again said Russia was central to her warnings to the world.

Some Sort of Climax Awaits Mankind

In 2016, Mirjana Soldo, one of the visionaries of Medjugorje, released a book that was more than a book of messages, but closer to an autobiography, called *My Heart Will Triumph*. On the very last page of Mirjana's book, she provides a startling, yet subtle story of what we may expect in the future. It is handled tactfully and with elegance to not frighten people, but she also makes a significant point about what may lie ahead. She writes,

"Our Lady told me many things that I cannot yet reveal. For now, I can only hint at what our future holds, but I do see indications that the events are already in motion. Things are slowly starting to develop. Our Lady says, look at the signs of the times, and pray."

"I can compare it to spring-cleaning. If I want my home to be spotless, I know that I first need to turn everything upside down. I move the sofa; I stack the chairs on the table; I open all the cupboards — nothing remains in its place. My home is thrown into chaos and disorder. It's unrecognizable to my children and the peace is gone. But then I clean under everything. I wipe away all the grime. I put every piece of furniture back to its rightful place. In the end, my home is more immaculate than ever."[157]

"This is how I see Our Lady's apparitions and God's plan. A truly clean house starts with a big mess. Will you be like most children who stand back while Mom cleans, or will you not be afraid to get your hands dirty and help her? Like Our Lady said in one of her messages, 'I desire that, through love, our hearts may triumph together.'

"May the triumph of her heart begin with you."[158]

Several things are significant in this message. A theme of Mirjana's book is how through the grace of Heaven, she has dealt with much suffering and still maintains a vibrant life of joy and peace. Few people would have had the grace to wake up morning, noon, and night, since 1981, and have thousands of pilgrims standing outside their front door. And that is just the obvious visible inconvenience.

In addition, Mirjana uses words that are very emotive, like: "upside down, chaos, disorder, wipe away all the grime, and a big mess," where she sees the world headed. Let those who have ears hear.

Women will be able to identify more than men with this, but what we are witnessing on a global basis is like the birth of a baby. As the baby nears delivery, many women experience fear like they have never experienced before. Some feel they could die from delivery. Many don't know what to expect, and the anxiety of what may or may not happen is something the couple has never experienced. There is blood, guts, tearing, shots, screaming, lights, and an unfamiliar environment with people the mother and family don't know, anxiety, fear, cursing (ask any OB-GYN) and just about every emotion and language imaginable for the soon-to-be mother and father. After the birth, there is great fatigue, exhaustion, and relief, yet ineffable joy. The ordeal is over, and the fear and the pain are forgotten, due to the new child and the miracle of life.

Tranquility is there with the triumph of the newborn. The days that we are now in are the like the birth of a child. We are in the late stage of birth pangs. World events may get painful and messy before they get better, but in the end, we will see the promised Triumph of The Immaculate Heart. To get to the other side, as Heaven promises, Satan's plan must be brought to the light first — and this is exactly what we are watching in every genre and milieu of the world. We may see near systemic collapse before the events take place because we have been told, "the Warning will take place when the world needs it most."

9. Mystical Numbers Connect Our Lady's Messages to Humanity.

Numbers in Scripture can be signs from Heaven to communicate to God's people, and a marker for a future event based upon a consistent pattern over time. For the Hebrews of the Old Testament, numbers were important in understanding God's will. As the New Testament fulfills the Old, Our Lady uses numbers as signs to mark time or an event — a signal grace to her people. Numbers are often a signpost to the faithful, while meaningless to the uniformed. Might numbers also be prophetic for future dates? No one can deny the numbers 3, 7, 10, 12, 13, 40 and others, are important numbers in Scripture (Old Testament and New Testament), and you would not have to be involved in numerology to believe it. A person familiar with Scripture knows this to be true.

Fatima is just one example of the consistency of a number, and Our Lady's appearances were on the 13th of each month, from May to October in 1917.

It was on the 13th of the month of Adar, that Queen Esther interceded to save her people from annihilation (Esther 9). Queen Esther is a precursor to the role of the Blessed Mother, where she is interceding with the King of Heaven on mankind's behalf. Heaven uses numbers to communicate messages to their people.

Catherine Laboure was a twenty-four-year old novice in the Daughters of Charity convent at Rue du Bac in Paris when the Blessed Mother first appeared to her on July **18**, 1830. The **18**th of the month was also a prominent date at Garabandal. The apparitions are officially called **The Virgin of the Globe**, but Rue du Bac or Our Lady of the Miraculous Medal, as it is most often called, ushered in the Marian Era as we now know it today.

Likewise, God gave man signs to follow Him from the very beginning of time. Before man was even created Scripture says, "And God said, let there be lights in the firmament of the Heavens to separate the day from the night; **and let them be for signs and for seasons and for days and years,** and let them be for lights in the firmament of the Heavens to give light upon the earth" (Genesis 1:14-15). God is a God of order, and from the very beginning, signs were set up for His people to follow Him. The moon, the sun, and celestial phenomena communicated His will to His people before the world had time pieces and calendars. Things in nature had naturally occurring rhythms the people could follow, and numbers became important for the people.

Our Blessed Mother appeared **18** times to Bernadette Soubirous at Lourdes, France. These apparitions began February 11, 1858 when the Blessed Mother prayed the Rosary with Bernadette. On February **18**, the Blessed Mother spoke and said, "I do not promise to make you happy in this life, but in the next." It was at Lourdes where the Blessed Mother said: "I am the Immaculate Conception." The **18**th and final apparition occurred on July 16, 1858, on the Feast of Our Lady of Mount Carmel, a sacred site to the Jewish people as well as Christians. The Blessed Mother came to Garabandal as Our Lady of Mount Carmel always having on a scapular.

There is significance to the number **18** in both Medjugorje and Garabandal, and **18** is also a number that has meaning to the Jewish people. It signifies **life,** and many observant Jews tithe in increments of eighteen as they feel the number will bring blessings and good fortune if they acknowledge God in their giving. It is also thought that the Miracle of Garabandal will have great significance to the Jews. The 18th of the month is when several important messages were given at Garabandal. On October **18**, 1961, Our Lady said, "Already the cup is filling," and on June **18**, 1965, she said, "Before the cup was filling up, now it is flowing over."

Mirjana Soldo of Medjugorje is one of six visionaries who have been receiving apparitions and/or locutions from the Blessed Mother since 1981. Three of the visionaries have all ten secrets, and the other three have only received nine of the ten secrets as of the date of this writing. A total of fifty-seven secrets have been given thus far by the Blessed Mother to the visionaries. The visionaries themselves don't know if there is overlap in the messages, as Mirjana said they do not discuss the secrets when they are together.

Mirjana Soldo, in her book *My Heart Will Triumph*, states that March **18** will be a date of great significance that we will only understand when the events prophesied at Medjugorje start to happen. She also mentions specifically August 2 as another important date. The Church celebrates August 2nd as the Feast of Our Lady of the Angels. It is also the Feast of Portiuncula, which commemorates a special place in the life of Saint Francis of Assisi. The Blessed Mother used to appear to Mirjana on the 2nd of every month, when she regularly received messages she conveyed to the world, and annually on her birthday of March **18**th. However, with the onset of the Covid 19 pandemic, the 2nd of the month appearances ceased.

Are these dates connected throughout these apparitions? Again, only when these events happen, will we fully understand the importance of the number **18** and possibly the 2nd. It would be presumptuous to say the dates of the **18**th and the 2nd directly link Garabandal and Medjugorje, and also foolish to say they don't. The honest answer is, maybe they do. It is obvious there are many similarities, since **18** has such a thread in both apparitions.

The Blessed Mother appeared daily to Mirjana for only **18** months, yet for three of the other visionaries, the messages are continuing. Mirjana received all of the ten secrets by the **18**th month from the start of the Blessed Mother's appearances. Mirjana emphasized that her secrets deal with the role of the priesthood. She said, "priests will be the bridge to the Triumph." Again, the priesthood was central to the messages at Garabandal.

The Blessed Mother visits Mirjana on her birthday every March **18**, "but the Blessed Mother has never said to me Happy Birthday." Think for a moment how profound that is. Here is a young girl whose mother died when she was young, she had to care for an ill father, and had a brother-in-law who died in the Bosnian War. She has experienced innumerable hardships her whole adult life, and the Blessed Mother never once has said Happy Birthday. Heaven's ways are not our ways. Mirjana said the Blessed Mother promised to appear on her birthday for the rest of her life. Mirjana says the date of March **18** will be very significant for a future event. To date, "the why" of this is a mystery.

Mirjana said, "Only when the things contained in the secrets start to happen will the world understand why she chose the 18th of the month… When everything starts happening, then you will be able to understand why the 18th of March, why every second of the month, and why Wednesdays and Fridays are days of fasting. The significance of the date will be clear." Mirjana's secrets are written on a scroll or parchment. Mirjana said, "I cannot divulge much about the secrets **but I can say this, Our Lady is planning on changing the world."** This is very consistent with the Warning and Miracle prophesied at Garabandal. It is primarily for this reason, there may be overlap in the secrets of Medjugorje and Garabandal. However, what they may be is speculation on anyone's part.

The Blessed Mother said very early at Medjugorje, *"I have a great plan for the salvation of mankind, and I come to tell you God exists."* Heaven has a plan and the Blessed Mother has said time and again, that fear does nothing to enhance our spiritual state. Joy, peace, contentment and laughter are characteristics of Mirjana that emanate from her and her family. She has said that when the visionaries are around each other, the common denominator is joy and laughter.

Mirjana said, "**Our Lady is preparing us for everything that is going to take place in the world.** She is training us for victory. When the events in the secrets begin, everything will be clear. You will understand the importance of these dates, and you will realize why she has been appearing for so long." Mirjana said, "At this moment, according to Our Lady, **we are living in a time of grace.** After this will come the time of the secrets, and the time of her triumph. God willing, you will hear from me then."

Is there a connection of both apparition sites centered around the 18th of the month, when people will understand why the 18th was chosen to release important information? One thing is certain. The language of both

Medjugorje and Garabandal and the magnitude of the prophesied messages cannot be ignored.

10.

A. Moses said to the people: "Ask now of the days of old, before your time, ever since God created man upon the earth; ask from one end of the sky to the other: Did anything so great ever happen before? Was it ever heard of?

"Did a people ever hear the voice of God speaking in the midst of fire, as you did, and live? Or did any god venture to go and take a nation for himself from the midst of another nation, by testings, by signs and wonders, by war, with His strong hand and outstretched arm, and by great terrors, all of which the Lord, your God, did for you in Egypt before your very eyes? All of this you were allowed to see that you might know the Lord is God and there is no other. Out of the heavens He let you hear His voice to discipline you; on earth He let you see His great fire, and you heard Him speaking out of the fire. For love of your fathers, He chose their descendants and personally led you out of Egypt by His great power, driving out of your way nations greater and mightier than you, so as to bring you in and make their land your heritage, as it is today. This is why you must now know, and fix in your heart, that the lord is God in the heavens above and on earth below, and that there is no other. You must keep His statutes and commandments which I enjoin on you today, that you and your children after you may prosper, and that you may have long life on the land which the Lord, your God, is giving you forever" (Deuteronomy 4:32-40).

B. "For when they shall say, peace and security; then shall sudden destruction come upon them, as the pains upon her that is with child, and they shall not escape" (I Thessalonians 5:3).

C. "And Moses said to the people, Fear not, stand firm, and see the salvation of the Lord, which He will work for you today; for the Egyptians that you see today, you shall never see again. The Lord will fight for you, and you have only to be still" (Exodus 14:13).

D. "Be still, and know that I am God. I am exalted among the nations, I am exalted in the earth" (Psalm 46:10).

E. "...Obedience is better than sacrifice..." (I Samuel 15:22).

F. "Jesus answered them, I told you and you do not believe. The works that I do in My Father's name, they bear witness to Me; but you do not believe, because you do not belong to My sheep. My sheep hear My voice, and I know them, and they follow Me; and I give them eternal life, and they shall never perish, and no one shall snatch them out of My hand" (John 10:25-28).

CHAPTER 20

The Personal Testimony of Stanley Villavicencio: He Experienced the Warning, Died for Three Days, and Then Lived to Tell About It

Below are some of the things I have heard over the last thirty years from people who have had experienced a life review similar to Mr. Stanley Villavicencio.

One, people all say, without exception, it is the most dramatic event in their lives — EVER. Nothing can compare to it. **Two**, they all saw the state of their soul as God would judge it at the time of death. **Three**, what they saw is true and they had no response because they were around pure truth, pure love, and divinity. **Four**, it radically changed their perception of life from that moment on. **Five**, it sometimes took years for people to express their view in writing or even to verbally articulate what happened as they had no prior reference point to measure it. Many thought they had gone mad, and felt they couldn't share it with others for a long time. **Six**, all made a profound amendment to their lives for the better. **Seven**, they all had more urgency of living the faith and the sacramental life as given to us by the Church. **Eight**, the event altered every aspect of how they lived from that moment onward. **Nine**, they all had been shown there was accountability for all their actions, and for sins of commission or omission. **Ten**, all were appreciative of the event in retrospect, and saw the event as God's mercy. They were happy they had a chance to make an amendment of life for the better.

The following is the testimony of Stanley Villavicencio from the Philippines. Stanley died and had been on a slab in a morgue for three days and came back to life. The attending physician upon witnessing the miracle, immediately left medicine and entered the seminary and became a priest. Stanley gave his testimony in Washington, D.C., at the Basilica of the National Shrine of the Immaculate Conception, in the year 2000, for *The International Week of Prayer and Fasting.* Mother Angelica founder of the Eternal Word Television Network was also a speaker that year, with approximately 6,000 people in attendance.

Stanley's event is just one of many that could have been provided, albeit few are as dramatic. Stanley's story goes beyond the scope of what the Warning will be as described at Garabandal because Stanley died and came back to life. His testimony shows the direct role and connection to Divine Mercy as articulated by Saint Faustina. The Warning to an individual is an act of the unfathomable Mercy of God to His people. It is for this reason it should not be looked at as something to fear, although it will be more severe for some than others. If a person is distant from God, when there is unconfessed sin, it will be more difficult emotionally and spiritually.

Stanley's testimony has been shortened, with the most salient portion kept in about his life review. Below is what I have consistently heard as it relates to a person's life review. His testimony has not been edited by the author or his language altered in any way. English was not his native language. Stanley had the support of his bishop in writing, and from the Cardinal in the Philippines. Stanley speaks in his own words:

"Before I will give my testimony, I just want to inform you that after what happened to me, I was just going around giving my testimony in my own dialect. You see, the Philippines is composed of more than seven hundred islands and almost every island has different dialect. The Philippines is divided into three major parts; Luzon, Mindano and Visayas. I belong to Visayas because I am living in Cebu. So, I was giving my testimony in Visayas only, until one time Father Seraphim Michalenko, the Spiritual Director of the Divine Mercy nationwide invited me to give a talk in Manila. At first, I am happy because I can go to Manila, but then a day before I was so worried because I do not know how to speak the dialect, because in Manila the dialect is Tagalog and I do not know how to speak Tagalog. I was worried and so I asked the Lord 'What shall I do?'

Then the following day, early in the morning Jesus appeared to me, to my dream and said: 'Do not worry. Just do your best and I shall do the rest.' So, I went to Manila and when I am holding the microphone to give my testimony, I am thinking my testimony in my own local dialect, and it came out in Tagalog. So, they understand me. "And now comes Father

Seraphim, the Head of the Divine Mercy International based in Stockbridge, Massachusetts, U.S.A. He invited me to give a series of talks in the United States, Canada and Mexico and the problem is, I do not know how to speak the English. So again, I was worried and because in Cebu, the owner of the University is a Divine Mercy devotee, so he instructed the English Department to translate my testimony from our local dialect to English and after several months they finished the translation. "They give it to me and it is as thick as this! And they said to me, ' Stanley you memorize that.' And, I said 'No. I cannot memorize it anymore.' Then they said 'Ok you just read it' and I said, 'I cannot read it also because it is my testimony, if I will read it, it will be lifeless.'

So, I went to America leaving behind the translation and upon reaching the States I confided to Father Seraphim everything, so Father Seraphim was so worried because my first testimony will be at the National Shrine of the Immaculate Conception in Washington, D.C. And I will be speaking together with Mother Angelica, the audience is almost seven thousand. Father Seraphim was so worried, so I told him, 'Father don't worry. Anyway, I did not come to America to proclaim my mercy, I am here to proclaim God's Mercy.' So, when I was holding the microphone, I am thinking of my own local dialect, but then it came out English and after that I already know how to speak English.

What I am going to tell you is what happened to me. About my own personal encounter with Jesus Christ of the Divine Mercy. When you hear my testimony, I hope it will increase your faith, and that you know that there really is a God and that God is a living God. What happened to me, happened on March 2, 1993. That was a Tuesday and a birthday of one of my children. By the way, I had ten children, but now I have thirteen. And by the way, I am a member of the Perpetual Dawn Rosary.

It is our practice that whenever there is an occasion at our house, we invite the statue of the Blessed Virgin Mary and it is also our practice that whenever the Virgin comes into our house it is I who has to receive the Virgin. But on that day, when the Virgin is already in our house, whatever they do to wake me up, I cannot be awaken, so it is my mother-in-law who received the Virgin.

At eight o'clock that morning, my mother-in-law said, she heard me moaning and moaning. So, she tried to look at me in my room and she found me lying in bed. Trembling vigorously. Blood coming out of my mouth forcefully. And it was the sister of my father-in-law, who is a nurse, was present, so attended to me immediately. And as she touches my pulse, she cannot find any pulse anymore - and as she touches my chest, my heart beat is already very slow. And when they open my eyes, both eyes are already in white, so they asked help from our neighbors and they brought me to Chong Hua Hospital. At Chong Hua Hospital, we have four specialist doctors and the doctor said that my chance of survival is one in a million, because my heart beat is already slow.

As I enter the Emergency Room I cannot breathe anymore, even with the help of oxygen, so they transferred me to I.C.U. or the Intensive Care Unit, so my breathing can be aided, or forcing oxygen inside. At the I.C.U. my trembling did not stop and the blood was still coming out from my mouth, so the doctor injected me with Valium to control everything.

Because Negros Island and Cebu are just very near, so that day my relatives arrive. Among them is my father who is a doctor and my sister who is also a doctor and the cousin of my wife were already present. By the way, my wife is also a nurse.

The following day, the doctors called up my wife and asked her permission to take me off of all the life support apparatus. So, my wife called up our house and asked that my long sleeve shirt, for my burial be prepared. And my mother-in- law says she has a memorial plan and that her memorial plan is transferable. So, she had it transferred to my name. Meaning! I will be the one using her coffin. And it also happened we had a reservation at the Queen City Garden Cemetery in Cebu, because when my father-in-law died in 1987, we bought three lots, so they process all the papers so they can bring me to the Queen City Garden. Meaning, everything is already ready. I have the long shirt to wear for my burial, I have already a coffin to sleep in, I have already a cemetery to live in.

But God had a different plan, because my wife did not agree to remove the life support apparatus attached to my body. In fact, my relatives, they take in turns to watch over me. But it is only my body present at Chong Hua Hospital, because **I saw a light, a very big bright light but not glaring. You can stare at it. It is like a fountain. It is like a fog as it slowly evaporates, until I notice someone is standing in front of me. And when I look at His face, I recognize Him as Jesus.**

As we are looking at each other, He raised His left hand and when He raised His left hand, the clouds above were sucked downwards and when they reach just above us, the clouds keep on turning and changes in color and when it stops it becomes like a video screen. And He showed me the film of my life, from my childhood up to my present. I notice that every time I do good, it just goes on normally and I also notice that every time I commit a sin, suddenly it would go into slow motion as if He wants to show us that what we have done is wrong, as if He wants to show us that what we have done is a sin. And because I have also committed bigger sins, sins like what we call the mortal sin.

Every time it shows up, suddenly it would stop, came closer and enlarged it. Then I said to myself, 'Why should this be included?' There must be no word of sin saw in Heaven, because it is just too bad to look at, but even if I closed my eyes, I could still see it.

Also, I notice that every time I commit a sin, I could feel the heaviness. I could feel the weight. The more I commit a sin, the more the heaviness, the more the weight. And I also notice that every time I do good, for example, if I give something to the poor, I could feel as if I were floating. So, it is really true what is written in the Bible, 'That what so ever you do to the less of your brethren, that you do unto Me.'

And I also notice that the sins I did not confess to a priest it is too heavy, and also, I notice that the sins that I confessed to a priest, it is lighter. And we cannot deny anything because the screen is so big and very clear and also the pictures are also big and below the pictures are written the day, the month, the date and the year. And below that it is also written the hour, the minutes and the seconds. So, we cannot deny anything, even the seconds are recorded. In fact, He reviewed my film three times and after our long conversation, He tapped my shoulder and as He was tapping my shoulder, He said to me, 'You go back now, because you still have so many things to do. You still have so many things to finish. If I have something for you or if I have a message for you, I will just appear to you in your dream.'

After He say that, I was at the I.C.U. of the Chong Hua Hospital. Suddenly I got up. I could feel my body so light and my head suppressed. That when I got up, I removed the oxygen from my nose. After removing oxygen, there is a tube going down into my intestine, so I slowly remove the tube because it tickles me. And after removing the tube, I slowly remove the I.V. from my hand and because there is a nurse who saw everything, and that she was so afraid that she ran away. In fact, she said, one of the heels of her shoes was broken.

When the nurse returns, she has other nurses, doctors and the technicians, they are all running and when they reach me, they put me to bed again. And one of the doctors put on his telescope and examined me and after a short examination, the doctor put off his telescope, put it beside him and he asked for another. Meaning! He did not believe his telescope. He was given another telescope and he put it on and re-examined me again and after a long examination, the doctor looked at my E.C.G. because every bed in the I.C.U. has its own E.C.G. And he said, since I was admitted at the I.C.U. my E.C.G. was just a straight line, but now they were so surprised because my E.C.G. was working normally and because the technicians were already present, so they subjected me to X-rays, laboratory tests and brain scan. And now, all the results are in negative, meaning, I am not sick.

The doctors were all surprised and they asked permission to have another set of examinations, because they said there might be something wrong with the apparatus. We consented, and they subjected me again to another ultra sound, laboratory tests and brain scan, all except the X-ray. And again, all the results were in negative: meaning, I am not really sick. So, the doctors said 'There is nothing now that we can really do, it is already a miracle.'

When I woke up, I woke up at eight o'clock in the morning of Friday. If you will count from eight 'clock in the morning of Tuesday, to eight o'clock in the morning to Friday, that is exactly three days. And because of that, the media was alerted. The television, the radio and newspaper. And because our Church, the Roman Catholic Church do not easily believe in miracles, so it has to be investigated and the investigation was led by Cardinal Vidal of Cebu.

Cardinal Vidal leads the investigation in March. At the middle of September, Cardinal Vidal released a letter confirming what happened to me. And he gives me an endorsement letter, so that I could give testimony around the world. One of the doctors who was assigned to me at the I.C.U., he is not just an ordinary doctor because when he took his medical examinations, he got the highest score all over the country and when he entered the Chong Hua Hospital, he was awarded as the most outstanding P.G.I. doctor. He was assigned to me at the I.C.U. from the very beginning, until I woke up. **And**

because he cannot sleep anymore, so he entered the Seminary to become a priest, and now he is already a priest.

Also, during my investigation, the doctors asked the Priest, 'Where does all that blood come from?' The blood coming out from my mouth is with force and continuously for several hours and why there was no blood transfusion (Blood count showed no reduced level of blood). So, the Priest prayed and after praying the answer that this blood coming out from my mouth is for cleansing. I have to be cleansed because I have to face the Lord — and they also said that is it also said in the Bible, that whoever sees the Lord will have to die, so I have to die. But because I have a mission, so I have to live again.

Also, they ask me: 'Why you? Why did Jesus choose you?' So, I answered them. 'Maybe because I am nothing. Maybe because I have nothing to be proud of except for my sins.' So, when I have a chance to talk with Jesus, I ask the Lord, 'My Lord, my God, why me? I am a sinner. I am a sinful man.' And Jesus answered, 'You cannot appreciate the beauty of My mercy unless you experience the misery of sin.' And so, I accepted my mission.

Also, so many are coming to me, so I ask the Lord: 'My Lord, my God! So many are coming to me and entrust their problems to me, what shall I do?' And Jesus answered: 'Just let them pray the chaplet unceasingly and they will be guided.'

...He explained it again to them. He explained it again and again. And on the third time that they prayed the chaplet, the children prayed intensely and they finished praying the chaplet. After they finished praying the chaplet, the pig suddenly stood up and one of the children ran and got some food for the pig and the pig consumed everything. And the lesson is, if Jesus answered our prayers for a pig, how much more if we pray the chaplet for a human being...

Wherever I go, so many would ask me how soon is Jesus coming back? Or is the three days of darkness really true? Is the chastisement really true? So, I answered them. Jesus said to me **'Don't be afraid.'** Jesus said to me, **'Don't be afraid because I will take care of your future.** Blessed are those taking advantage of My mercy while it is still the day of mercy but beware, because the day of Judgment is nearer than everyone thinks.' I asked the Lord, 'What are the sins that You cannot forgive?' Jesus said, 'All sins can be forgiven except if you refuse to believe that your sin can be forgiven.' That is the sin He cannot forgive, because Jesus said by refusing His mercy you are also refusing to believe that He is God (That is a sin against the Holy Spirit). That is why Jesus said, 'Before I come as Just Judge I will open wide the doors of My mercy.' But Jesus continued that it is also written in the Diary of St. Faustina, that 'He that refuses to pass through the doors of My mercy will have to pass through the doors of My Justice.'

Now, after a long while that Jesus is opening this door of mercy and after a long while He will close that door of mercy. Then He will open that door of Justice. And if He will open the door of His Justice who can enter Heaven? When Heaven is only for the pure, when Heaven is only for the clean. And who are the clean? And who are the pure? All of us are sinners. All of us are unclean. We can only enter Heaven through His mercy, through His love. Without God's mercy, without His love, it is too difficult to enter Heaven. That is why Jesus now is begging us to go out now and proclaim His mercy. Jesus also said, 'Proclaiming My mercy is not enough, you have to put mercy into action, by living as an example of My mercy.' He said, '**He who will save a soul will save his own.'...**

CHAPTER 21

God's Merciful Judgment, A Priest's True Story: Father Stephen Scheier and His Illumination of Conscience[159]

By Rev. Stephen Scheier

October 18, 1985 will be a date that I will remember until I take my dying breath. At this time, I was a Diocesan priest in the Diocese of Wichita and was stationed in a small town in Southeast Kansas by the name of Fredonia. I was pastor of a parish named Sacred Heart. On that particular day, I decided to go to Wichita, Kansas, about eighty-six miles away to get some advice on a parish problem from one of my brother priests. I didn't have any appointments that day or that evening and I recall that going to Wichita was a first in my stay in Fredonia.

The Accident

I had to travel to Wichita by way of a state highway called 96. This particular highway was one that had no shoulders, was very, very, hilly and went through the Flint Hills. It was traversed by big trucks and semis and was very dangerous, to say the least. I remember returning from Wichita late in the afternoon; and that is the last thing I remember. I was involved in a head-on collision with a truck from Hutchinson, Kansas. There were three persons in that vehicle. Nobody was killed in the accident, thank God! As a result of the collision, I was thrown out of my vehicle (I was not wearing my seatbelt at that time) and landed on the ground outside my car. I suffered a major head concussion at the time and the scalp on the right side of my head was ripped off from my skull. That is, as far as I remember, and I don't clearly remember anything.

Not Expected to Live

Behind me, traveling on the same highway was a Mennonite nurse from Frontenac, Kansas, who stopped and stayed with me until the ambulance came and picked me up. It was because of her expertise that it was discovered I had suffered a broken neck. She informed the drivers of the ambulance when they arrived to treat me accordingly. Had my head been turned either way at the scene of the accident, I would have died of asphyxiation. I later learned that I had suffered a C-2 break of the vertebrae of the neck which they refer to as the "hangman's break", because this is the break of the neck that occurs when a person is hung by the neck. I was taken by ambulance to a nearby town called Eureka, which had a small hospital. The doctor in charge sewed my scalp back on my skull and then, realizing that he couldn't do anything else for me, called the Lifewatch helicopter from Wesley Hospital in Wichita, Kansas to come and pick me up. As the helicopter was lifting off the hospital grounds in Eureka, the doctor said to his sister, who was a nurse, that he didn't expect me to survive the trip between Eureka and Wichita, which was not that far away.

Upon arrival in Wichita, the helicopter landed on top of Wesley Hospital, a Methodist hospital, and I was rushed to the Trauma Center. I was treated there and then admitted to the main hospital in the Intensive Care Unit. I was only about five blocks away from my home in Wichita, so my mother, who was still living at the time, came up to the hospital that night and stayed with me. I was assigned to a neurosurgeon who worked at the hospital and had his office in Wichita; and he treated me according to the damage that I suffered. I did not have to have surgery for fusion; I was put into traction and was also fitted for what is normally referred to as a "halo." The technical term for this orthotic device is called a cervical thoracic orthosis. This orthotic device is used to treat a lot of neck injuries. The "halo" was around my head with four screws, two in the front and two in the back, screwed into my skull, so that I could no bend or move my neck in any way. This device was fitted onto a "jacket" which was irremovable also. I wore these two devices for a period of almost eight months. I do remember that at one time, during visitation hours at the hospital, the screw came out of my head. I have never felt pain like that before or since. Apparently, along with this orthotic device, I was also put in traction so that the bones of the vertebrae could be aligned and start the healing process. I don't remember this procedure at all! The doctors told me that since I lived through this accident, they expected that I would be laying on my back, looking up at the ceiling for the rest of my life, completely paralyzed from the neck down. Apparently, God had other plans!

Prayers of the Faithful

The evening of the accident, a phone call came into the hospital form one of the parishioners at Sacred Heart in Fredonia asking for a nurse on my floor about my condition. The person was told by the nurse on duty that evening that doctors were giving me a 15% chance to live. That was pretty serious! I later heard that on the evening of the accident the doors of my church, Sacred Heart, were opened for people to come in and pray for me. The Christian church and the Methodist church in Fredonia also opened their doors that night so people could come and pray for me. The Assembly of God Minister told me that he spent the entire night in prayer for me. I was also on the Mennonite prayer line. So, I had a lot of prayer support. I later heard that my parish prayed the Rosary twice a day for me: once in the morning and then again in the evening.

Toward the end of my recovery period in the hospital, my neurosurgeon assigned me to a Clinical Psychologist for treatment called Concussive Head Syndrome. This therapy was greatly needed and appreciated. I could stand very little emotional trauma and every very little sound. It was good to talk to a person who seemed to know what I was going through and what I needed. I was released from the hospital December, 2 1985 and then went home to recuperate as best I could with my mom and my younger brother who lived not too far away in Wichita. One of my other brothers was home on leave from the Navy, and so he was in the house night and day — to my benefit. My doctor informed me that I made record time in recovering from my injury and that in the report he could use the word "miracle", but that anyone reading my report would have to come to that conclusion on their own.

My bishop, who was the Bishop of the Wichita Diocese, left my parish in Fredonia vacant as far as a permanent pastor was concerned. A priest was sent to the parish to have weekend liturgies there and at Neodesha until I was completely recovered. I was sent back to the parish in Fredonia in May of 1986. I remember having to shop for another automobile and then travel the same highway back to my parish. I am glad that I had to do it, but I recall that it was a difficult experience at the time. I had gone back to the parish previously in April of the same year for First Holy Communion. Another priest of the Diocese took me down that particular weekend so that I could be there for this special event.

I was treated very well upon my return to Sacred Heart Parish and the city of Fredonia. My parishioners were quick to tell me of their concern and their prayers for my recovery and my return. The people of Fredonia, Kansas, and especially Sacred Heart Parish, are a God-fearing, Catholic people who take their religion very seriously. When I returned, it was noticeable that they did not demand much from me because of my previous condition. This fact was very much appreciated by myself and made a big difference on my performance at that parish there and in Neodesha at St. Ignatius Parish.

One day, not too long after my return to the parish, I was saying morning Mass as I was accustomed to, when something extremely supernatural happened. I was about to read the Gospel for that day, a Gospel that we have heard many times throughout the years. It is from the Gospel according to Luke. To be exact, it was Luke 13:6-9 and it read this way: "And he told them this parable: There was once a person who had a fig tree planted in his orchard, and when he came in search of fruit on it but found none, he said to the gardener, "For three years now I have come in search of fruit on this fig tree but have found none. (So) I cut it down. Why should it exhaust the soil?" He said to him in reply, "Sir, leave it for this year also, and I shall cultivate the ground around it and fertilize it; it may bear fruit in the future. If not, you can cut it down."

When I read this passage from Scripture, it was as if I was remembering a conversation. Besides this, the page itself, from the Lectionary, became illuminated, enlarged and actually came off the Lectionary towards me. I had to finish Mass as normally as I could and when I was finished, I went to my rectory, sat down in my lounge chair with about four cups of coffee and tried to remember why this particular gospel brought back so many memories — memories concerning what?

The Illumination

It did not take long before everything seemed to come back to me. **The following seemed to happen immediately after the accident. I was** before the Throne of Judgment! Jesus Christ was the Judge. I didn't see Him, I merely heard Him. What took place was instantaneous as far as "our time" is concerned. He went through my entire life on earth and accused me of sins of commission and omission that were unconfessed and therefore unforgiven and unrepented sins. To each offense, I said, "Yes, Lord!" I had planned that when this would happen, I would have all kinds of excuses to say to the Lord. For example, "Well, Lord, you know, she was a pretty feisty woman, and one lost his patience very easily with her all the time!" Well, then you are now talking to Truth personified, you don't have any excuses; so all you say is, "Yes, Lord!"

Mother—He's Yours

He reached the end of my judgment and said to me, "Your sentence is hell!" Again, I said, "Yes, Lord, I know!" It was the only logical conclusion that He could have come up with. It was not a shock to my system! It was as if He were honoring my choice, my decision. I had chosen my sentence; He was merely honoring my choice. **It was then, after He had said this, that I heard a woman's voice, "Son, would You spare his life and his immortal soul?" The Lord said, "Mother, he has been a priest twelve years for himself and not for me; let him reap the punishment he deserves!" She, in reply said, "But Son, what if we give him special graces and strengths and then see if he bears fruit. If not, Your will be done!" There was a very short pause and then I heard Him say, "Mother, he's yours!" And then I have been hers both naturally and supernaturally now for the past twelve years. I don't believe that I could have been without her for the length of time that she was absent from my life and my spirituality.**

He Got My Attention

Now, many will say to me, "But Father, you must have had a special devotion to the Blessed Mother before this happened. No wonder she interceded for you!" To this, I have to say no! This is not an indictment against me as a priest, but I have to say that as far as my belief in the angels, the saints, the Blessed Mother, I believed all right, but with my head — 'head' knowledge, not with my heart, a heart knowledge. The angels and saints were to me like imaginary playmates. I believed in them, but they were not real! I discovered by this accident just how real they are! It took the Lord to break my neck just to get my attention! One has to remember the day that Jesus died on Calvary. Mary, His mother and the disciple whom He loved, John, were at the foot of the cross when Jesus looked down upon them and lovingly said, "Woman, behold your son! Son, behold your mother!" It was at this juncture that Jesus gave His mother to all of us, her sons and daughters, as her children. She takes this very seriously! She would come to the aid of anyone and intercede for him or her as she interceded for me; I was not special! I have learned since the accident a very important truth concerning the Blessed Virgin Mary and the Father, Son and Holy Spirit. To whatever the Blessed Mother wants, God — Father, Son and Holy Spirit — cannot say 'no' to her! It is impossible for them to say this!

Another fact that I have learned since the accident is that I was saved from physical and spiritual death for two reasons. The first reason is: hell exists; and secondly, and just as important is the fact that: priests are liable to hell also! In this age, a lot of people tend to dismiss this fact that God is all-just. They think, and wrongly so, that God is love and He wouldn't punish anyone for eternity. This is a fallacy! We are, all of us, liable to keeping God's Commandments and making use of the Sacrament of Reconciliation to have our sins forgiven. If we think we don't sin, then maybe we better do a more complete examination of conscience. One of the truths that I learned in my experience is the fact that God doesn't send anyone to Heaven or Hell, we choose that, we make that decision; He merely honors and confirms our choice.

One must be attuned to the reality that because a priest wears a piece of white plastic in his collar, he is not guaranteed Heaven. The matter is quite the opposite; a priest is just as accountable (and maybe even more so) as any layperson to keeping God's Commandments, and brings the type of priest that he is ordained to be for the people and for Jesus Christ. The Blessed Mother, Mary, has said many times that we are to pray for priests and not criticize them. Now, more than ever, in the age in which we live, it is easy to criticize a priest or a Bishop whom we feel is off the orthodox track. We have to remember the Blessed Virgin's mandate to us!

The Experience Changed Me

I have been asked many times: How has this experience changed me? There is really no way I can answer this question completely. I have to say that, as a priest and a pastor, I shepherded and pastored myself those years. Father Steve Scheier was number one and was of major concern. I never "got into" the priesthood, as such! I was not very spiritual and my prayer life was practically nil. Of course, many others (parishioners and fellow priests) believed quite the opposite; I did not show problem areas very readily to anyone. I was very much surprised during my judgment that Jesus did not take a popularity poll. It was strictly He and I, and He knew me better than a thousand other people. I realized then that I had only Him to please and that my concern in pleasing (or trying to please) countless others, was a total waste of time and energy. I am now t-r-y-i-n-g to be a better priest than I was before. I thank the Lord and His Blessed Mother constantly for giving me a second chance. I try to keep in focus the only thing that matters and that I almost lost for all eternity — the chance to get to Heaven and be with God, the Angels and Saints for eternity!

I would like to preface my remarks from here on by saying to those for whom the following applies, that I love you as my brother priests and as my brothers and sisters in Christ. What I will say does not mean that I was never guilty of such actions, intentions or omissions, it rather points to errors that are still being made today in Jesus' Church by His ministers and by His followers. I see many areas to be addressed today and I can truthfully say that I owe my expertise to the fact that I was judged by Almighty God and was spared in His Divine Mercy. The following is the second part of my experience that I have to address to the Catholic Church worldwide.

Importance of Confession

The first area that needs attention all over the world is the matter of confession. One only has to go to a parish on weekend to see the downfall and collapse of this great sacrament that was instituted by Christ Himself. Jesus instituted this sacrament with His first appearance to His Apostles after He rose from the dead. The first words He said after He came through the bolted door was, "Peace be with you." Jesus said to them again, "Peace be with you." As the Father has sent me, so I send you." And when he had said this, he breathed on them and said to them, "Receive the Holy Spirit. Whose sins you forgive are forgiven them, and whose sins you retain are retained." (John 20:21-22). This is why confession takes place (thus the Sacrament of Reconciliation) and why priests are the recipients of such power to forgive or to withhold forgiveness. So, what's the problem? The problem is there are fewer and fewer who feel any sense of guilt and consequently, feel that they have not sinned! If one does not feel any guilt, there is no need to go to confession — one (in his or her mind) has not sinned. So, where does society get this notion? I blame a great deal on psychiatrists who have told people (and sometimes publicly) that they don't have to feel guilty about this or that, they should put the blame on their parents in bringing them up the way they did, or blame the environment which contributed to the problem — the task or solution is to completely eradicate guilt in a person. This is one of the greatest phenomena that have contributed to the decline in confessions today.

Another reason for the decline is the fact that "some" priests, as well intentioned as they are, advise the penitent that he or she does not have to go to confession "often" and then, when the penitent verbalizes a sin or number of sins, the confessor is quick to tell the penitent that such-and-such is not sinful, but a result of tension, anxiety or over tiredness. Consequently, the penitent is made to feel or think that most or all of his or her sins are really not sinful at all, but merely human weaknesses that are due to some physical abnormality or phenomenon.

Most Catholics do not have a choice in confessors. Some go to other parishes who are more traditional in his treatment of the penitent. But some feel that they cannot leave parish boundaries to attain peace of mind and soul that they are so desperately looking for. The results of the encounters are that people no longer feel a need to go to the confession; plus, they feel that the confessor is not as compassionate and understanding as priests used to be.

One of the biggest atrocities of the priesthood today, and raging rampant in the United States at this time, is the verbalization of opinions by priests to laity about matters of Church doctrine. Priests sometimes forget that they are ordained as representatives of the Church, and therefore, should preach what the Church teaches. If a priest wishes to give his own opinion on a matter that has been strictly defined by the Magisterium of the Church, he should take off his collar and tell those whom he addresses that the following is his opinion regarding the matter. This goes for the pulpit as well. Priests are ordained ministers of the Church!

One of the greatest omissions in parish life the past twenty-five or twenty-six years, is the fact that priests have not mentioned or directed in their homilies the subjects of "hell" and "eternal damnation." If this is the fact, and it is, then the idea of a parishioner feeling or coming to terms with the fact that they should go to confession is totally missing. We have not wanted to upset parishioners! We especially do not want to upset wealthy parishioners who write large checks to the parish and are "good givers." Consequently, what has been addressed in sermons has been peace, love, and joy; these, to be sure, will not upset anyone and consequently, the priest will have given a "good" sermon that weekend! Here again, if there is no guilt, then there is no sin; so why should a parishioner go to confession? The reality, too, is that Father wants to be "popular." He wants people to go away from his parish feeling good, not guilty; and he wants most of all for people to say on their way out of church, "Father, that was fantastic sermon you gave!"

The second area that has to be addressed in our discussion of the misfortunes of the Church today is the area of prayer or non-prayer! The "with it" parish is the one that you can pick up a document form which informs you of all of the organizations in the parish that are there to facilitate healing processes and generally, whatever area of interest or problem area that one is encountering. Organizations for the recently divorced or widowed; for singles, for parents, etc…and the fact is that most of these organizations are nothing more than "socials" where a person is made to feel like he or she can be helped in their situation because there are other people encountering the same situation.

Whatever Happened to Prayer

Whatever happened to prayer? Ever since Vatican II, which was greatly misinterpreted and misunderstood, a lot of para-liturgical services has been unduly dismissed from parishes all over the world — at the discretion of the pastor! Prayer vigils such as novenas and Holy Hours, Benediction and even Perpetual Adoration of the Blessed Sacrament have been deleted from parish activities for quite some time now. It seems as if we are proclaiming, "Prayer is useless, let's have a problem-solving situation or organization to remedy the situation!" Prayer was "needed" in the past, why not now? And then, too, there might be another reason for the demise of prayer situations. These services take "TIME" and that's one thing the priest doesn't want his parishioner to think he has too much of. And too, a prayer service may take away from the priest's TV time or going-out-to-relax time with friend's who are parishioners or who might be other priests. The "sign" that a lot of priests wear is the sign which tells parishioners, "I'M EXHAUSTED, PLEASE DON'T ASK ME TO DO ANYTHING ELSE!" Consequently, the parish priest has more and more time to do absolutely nothing.

Church Being Stripped

Another area where we are seeing a definite decline in traditional spirituality is seen in what is happening or what has happened to many of our churches on the inside. In the name of "ecumenism" a lot is being done that strips us of our Catholic faith and makes us something less than whom we have been baptized to be. Many churches now do not have kneelers — theatre seats are sufficient! There are no Stations of the Cross, no statues, no vigil lights or candles, no pictures of Jesus, Mary, or one of the saints, and no crucifix (there may be a cross, but the crucifix is definitely out.) Also, the "presidential chair" has replaced the tabernacle at the center of the sanctuary. Father is now the focal point, not some non-descript vault that just has "wafers of bread" in it. The tabernacle is now "off to the side" or, unfortunately, in another room in the church, but definitely, but definitely out-of-sight! The actions of "believers" are concomitant with the atmosphere, or lack thereof, of the inside of these churches. Instead of genuflecting in front of the Blessed Sacrament, Father or the parishioners give a little bow. The parishioners have been encouraged, and/or forced, to remain standing for the Consecration. Kneeling is so old-fashioned, don't you know?

One too, might look at how parishioners dress for Mass these days — very casual, if not slovenly! One might mention also that the more fastidious of parishes today have lay ministers who have been commissioned to do almost everything in a parish except say Mass, hear confessions, marry and bury. I know of a certain parish in Washington State where the pastor has a laywoman give the homily at Masses during the weekend for three weekends out of four.

And at some parishes, the priest will sit in the chair at communion time while an extraordinary minister distributes Holy Communion under one or both species. This is forbidden! But it seems that the less Father has to do, the better!

In the 1950's, one heard the comment that there was no greater fraternity than the fraternity of priests. At that time, that was probably a true statement of where the priesthood was, and what priests meant to each other. But things have changed since then, and it is a whole new "ball game." Priests now are not so supportive of fellow priests. In one diocese in the United States, and I suspect that the same holds true to some extent for every diocese throughout the world, there are generally two ways of looking at one's fellow priests: one, is that Father is doing a magnificent job and is really trying and his fellow priests are saying "What is he trying to prove?" The other is the fact that Father may have made some error small or grave, and his fellow priests say, "See, I told you so. What else could you expect from someone like that?" This is sad, to say the least! And then, where is a priest to turn for help? If one goes to a fellow for help spiritually or otherwise, the invitation will come automatically to "have a drink" or to "discuss football or basketball" teams and scores. After all, when priests get together, they shouldn't talk "shop", they should enjoy their golf game or their dinner out and not turn the situation into some counseling session. But, ironically enough, we still have in our dioceses priests who are referred to as "a priest's priest." Other priests see these men as holy and gifted and priests one could go to if needed by any priest who was having difficulties with almost anything.

The final area of concern for our purposes is CCD classes. At least since the beginning of the 70's, our CCD texts have been void of Catholic doctrine and dogma. I have seen primary CCD class text that have a picture of a smiling Jesus on one page and then on the other is the bold-type sentence that says: JESUS LOVES YOU! That is what our children have been learning all these past years. They have been left out learning the commandments, the laws of the Church, mortal and venial sin and the difference between the two. They have been denied learning how to make a good confession by examining one's conscience. They have been denied learning what is short of faith concerning the Real Presence of Jesus in the Blessed Sacrament. The ultra-casual way of receiving Holy Communion by the faithful has added to this dilemma. And many parents do not go to Confession, so their children do not go to either Confession or CCD anymore. Parents, after all, want their children to love them; consequently, they don't make their children do anything they don't want to do!

The list of monstrosities could go on and on, but this gives to the priest and the layperson some idea of the direction that the Church is now heading. Where will all of this lead us? I am not a prophet, but I do know that this most assuredly is not what Christ Our Lord intended. Is it too late to change? Again, what Jesus is saying to us and has always said is that it is never too late to change. He states that we should take advantage of His mercy while we still can, because when He comes as Judge, it will be too late for His mercy! He is patient, He is merciful and He is loving!

Endnotes

1   Schopenhauer, Arthur, German Philosopher.

2   The Marian Movement of Priests, Our Lady Speaks to Her Beloved Sons, Messages to Father Stefano Gobbi, 489d, March 15, 1993.

3   Conchita's Diary, Fahy, Thomas, *Suddenly and Unexpectedly,* Published by the Center for the Divine Will, P.O. Box 415, Jacksboro, TN. 37757, p. 18-20

4   Fahy, Thomas, p. 18-20

5   Signs and Wonders for Our Times Magazine, 2011. Spring/Summer Issue. Sign.org. Message given April 16, 2005. Number 2510.

6   Ibid, June 30, 2007, message number 2857.

7   Ibid, December 30, 2006 message number 2779.

8   Ibid, October 24, 2007, Message number 2907.

9   This story on abortion above is from the Garabandal Journal, January/February, 2004, page 11. This is completely understandable for a young girl to ask this question before abortion was a common practice and legal, although the word abortion was probably never used or Conchita would have used the word to describe what she heard.

10 The Call of Garabandal — April/June 1984, Reprinted in Garabandal Journal, November/December, 2003

11 Marian Movement of Priests, MMP, Our Lady Speaks to her Beloved Sons, 383d

12 MMP message 478h

13 Gloria.tv/post/BBQy3N2TEmwo3SomnlGCQ61gA

14 Garabandal Journal November-December 2021. The original source is from Pesquera, Eusebio Garcia de, OFM, Cap. *She Went in Haste to the Mountain,* St. Joseph Publications. 17700 Lorain Ave, Cleveland OH. 44111, 1981. Other source material is originally from Father Pesquera. The English version (Dr. Miller) is a three-volume set that is 8.5 X 11 in size, and the first translation into English of the classic work *Se Fue Con Prisas a la Montana,* that was originally published in Spain in 1972 and 1979 by Father Pesquera, OFM. When the

first printing in English ran out, there was no reprint. The book was written by Father Pesquera and is considered a classic due to the volume of the material it covers, and is often quoted. Brian Miller, MD gave the book free of charge to The Workers of Our Lady of Mount Carmel for the 2000 edition coming out by the same title all in one volume. The three-volume set of Dr. Miller edited and updated by Barry Hanratty and Irene Dutra, was published by The Workers of Our Lady of Mount Carmel, P.O. Box, 606, Lindenhurst, New York, 11757, under Our Lady of Mount Carmel de Garabandal, Inc. The author is in possession of the translated work of Pesquera to English (3 volumes) by Gerard Buel and Otto Miller. Original copyright of the book is Father Pesquera, OFM, and was a source for this book. Photos are from the three-volume set cited above from Dr. Brian Miller. These photos have been circulated for over 60 years across all forms of global media with no known identifiable or registered copyright.

15 This is the end of the interview from the Garabandal Journal November/December 2021, that was taken from *She Went in Haste to the Mountain,* by Eusebio Garcia de Pesquera, O.F.M., CAP., Pages 4-11

16 Flynn, Maureen, *The Global Warning, The Illumination of the Conscience of the Mankind*, pages 2-3, 2011, Signs of the Times Apostolate, Sign.org

17 The Flame of Love apparitions were approved by Cardinal Peter Erdo (1952 –), Hungary. Elizabeth Kindelmann (1913-1985), *The Flame of Love,* Children of the Father Foundation, *Nihil Obstat:* Monsignor Joseph G. Prior, Censor Librorum. *Imprimatur,* Elizabeth Kindelmann.

18 *Weber, Albrecht, Garabandal: Der Zeigefinger Gottes, p. 132, 2000.* Barry Hanratty contacted Mr. Weber to confirm the authenticity of this statement. Weber responded that Conchita mentioned it in the presence of her mother, and himself, and that her mother wrote it down word for word.

19 The above stories of Padre Pio are from *She Went in Haste to the Mountain,* other sources of the author gathered over the years, and Garabandal Journal, January-March 2023. The first issue to be published since Barry Hanratty died.

20 This is from Barry Hanratty's interview, see footnote below for the source.

21 Hanratty, B, *Garabandal Journal,* September-October 2022, p. 7-9.

22 Pesquera, Father Eusebio Garcia, OFM, Cap., *She Went in Haste to the Mountain,* p. 654.

23 Flynn, Maureen, The Global Warning, *The Illumination of the Conscience of Mankind,* Pages 133-135. 2011, Sign.org

24 Barry Hanratty, Garabandal Booklet, 2018 edition, p. 48.

25 Father Pesquera, Eusebio Garcia de, O.F.M., CAP. *She Went in Haste to the Mountain.* Translated from Spanish by B. & O. Miller, Gerard Buel. Second English Edition of 1981, Original Translation published unaltered in one volume in 2000. PDF p. 632.

26 Garabandal Journal January/February 2006

27 Garabandal Journal January/February, 2006

28 Flynn, Ted and Maureen, *The Thunder of Justice, The Warning, The Miracle, The Chastisement, The Era of Peace,* pages 88-89. Maxkol Communications, 1993, revised 2010

29 Workers of Our Lady of Mount Carmel, July-September, 1993, p. 9-10

30 Quoted in the Milan-based daily Italian newspaper *Corriere della Serra,* p. 7, of its issue dated October 14, 1977

31 Serre, Jacques, Caux, Béatrice, Apparitions of the Blessed Virgin Mary, p. 234.

32 Father Joaquin Alonso (Official Archivist at Fatima); *La Verdad sobre el Secreto de Fatima* 1976. See also Frère Michel de la Sainte Trinité, The Whole Truth About Fatima – Vol. III, p. 687, 704-705. See also De nuevo el Secreto de Fatima, 1982 Ephemerides Mariologicae p. 93.

33 Alonso

34 Alonso

35 Pope Paul VI on December 7, 1968 during an Address to the members of the Pontifical Lombard Seminary https://w2.vatican.va/content/paul-vi/it/speeches/1968/december/documents/hf_p-vi_spe_19681207_seminario-lombardo.html

36 Pope Paul VI, June 29, 1972 on the 9th Anniversary of his coronation during the homily given at Mass for the Solemnity of St. Peter and St. Paul with 30 cardinals in attendance https://w2.vatican.va/content/paul-vi/it/homilies/1972/documents/hf_p-vi_hom_19720629.html

37   *Gabandal The Village Speaks* by Ramon Pérez. Translated from the French-1977 by Annette I. Curot Mathews. Translation published in 1981, p. 206

38   Cardinal Luigi Ciappi 1995 (Papal Theologian to Popes Pius XII, John XXIII, Paul VI, John Paul I and John Paul II) from a personal letter to Professor Baumgartner of Salzburg, Austria; Father Gerard Mura, "The Third Secret of Fatima: Has It Been Completely Revealed?", the periodical Catholic, (published by the Transalpine Redemptorists, Orkney Isles, Scotland, Great Britain) March 2002

39   https://www.lifesitenews.com/blogs/how-the-smoke-of-satan-entered-the-second-vatican-council/
https://archive.fatima.org/news/newsviews/2016/newsviews0517.asp
https://web.archive.org/web/20200630011042/http:/archive.fatima.org/crusader/cr92/cr92pg7.pdf
https://web.archive.org/web/20200630010207/https://archive.fatima.org/crusader/cr93/cr93pg3.pdf
https://onepeterfive.com/cardinal-ratzinger-not-published-whole-third-secret-fatima/
https://onepeterfive.com/cardinal-ratzinger-not-published-whole-third-secret-fatima-2/
https://onepeterfive.com/confirmation-father-dollingers-claim-cardinal-ratzinger-fatima/
https://voxcantor.blogspot.com/2016/05/fatima-secret-not-all-released-alleged.html

40   Mother Angelica Live, Eternal Word Television Network (EWTN)

41   William Thomas Walsh, *Our Lady of Fatima* 4th printing, (1947) p. 226; See also Louis Kaczmarek, *The Wonders She Performs,* 1986, p. 160

42   https://onepeterfive.com/chief-exorcist-father-amorth-padre-pio-knew-the-third-secret/

43   The interview is from *Garabandal,* January-March-April-June, 1983

44   Frère Michel de la Sainte Trinité, *The Whole Truth About Fatima: The Third Secret, Vol. III.*

45   Pacepa, Lt. General Ion Mihai, *Disinformation, Former Spy Chief Reveals Secret Strategies for Undermining Freedom, Attacking Religion, and Promoting Terrorism,* page 93, WND Books, 2013.

46 Pacepa, page 350.

47 Flynn, Ted & Maureen, *The Thunder of Justice, The Warning, The Miracle, The Chastisement, The Era of Peace.* Maxkol Communications, Inc. P.O. Box 345 Herndon, VA 20170, 1993, and revised and updated in 2010, 357 pages. Although the book was a mini anthology of major apparitions in the world, Garabandal became the heart and soul of the book. The original source material for Garabandal — The Divine Reset was drawn heavily from *The Thunder of Justice,* and subsequent books on the subject. Much of the above material was from the Thunder of Justice as it relates to Judaism, and its roots. The body of material was given to me by a good friend, the late Mr. Stanley Karminski, of Wayne, PA. In the late 1980's, Stan was an early supporter of Garabandal and had written articles on Garabandal for our magazine, *Signs and Wonders for Our Times* (Sign. Org), prior to the publication of the book. Stan had a unique gift of capturing Our Lady's intent in her messages and putting them in context of what it meant for the world.

In addition, some material now incorporated in many different publications that was distributed throughout the world for decades was a small pamphlet by Father Philip Bebie and his work on *The Warning.* The material was from his personal diary when he was in the last stages of terminal cancer. Father Bebie had a deep Marian devotion, but because Garabandal had not been approved by the Holy See, the order in which he was a member would not endorse his diary or pamphlet, so it does not have a copyright. Information on Anna Maria Taigi is from *The Warning.* The Warnings of Garabandal are quoted by Father Joseph A. Pelletier, A.A., who wrote on Marian apparitions for many years in journals and books. Some other sources are *O Children Listen to Me* by Robert Francois, *Star on the Mountain* by Father Laffineur and M.T. Pelletier.

Some of the material from Garabandal and the Synagogue is from a talk that was given by the French Dominican Father Francois Turner in a barn near the pines on August 8, 1988. It has been used with permission and changed only in grammar and style for readability from the French translation. The Book of Exodus speaks of the pillar of smoke by day and the fire by night guiding the Jews into the promised land. Father Turner was considered a credible witness and scholar on Garabandal. The remainder of the material is taken from Scripture and the many places of the elements of the Exodus of the Jews in the desert for 40 years. Every Jew, no matter their belief in the Shekinah, will know of the pillar of smoke by day and fire at night, called the Shekinah Glory.

48   Francois, Robert, *O Children Listen to Me, Our Lady Teaches at Garabandal,* Originally published in French under the title, Tout le Peuple l'Ecoutait, 1975. Translated and published in English in 1980 by The Workers of Our Lady of Mount Carmel, Inc., Lindenhurst, NY, 11757

49   Rose, Michael, *Goodbye! Good Men,* pp. 298-299.

50   Pesquera, Eusebio Garcia de O.F.M., Cap., *She Went in the Haste to the Mountain.*

51   Pesquera

52   Pesquera

53   Sanchez, Ventura y Pascual, F. *The Apparitions of Garabandal,* The entire article is from: Our Lady and The Priesthood, this ends the article from Garabandal Journal, July/August 2018, B. Hanratty, p. 8-12.

54   Conchita's Diary has been printed by several different entities, and publishing firms over the years. The same is true for Mari Loli's Diary.

55   *Eucharistic Miracles of the World, Presented by the Real Presence Eucharistic Education and Adoration Association,* Inc, by The Institute of St. Clement I, Pope and Martyr, 2016, page 355.

56   Pelletier, Father Joseph, A.A. *Fr. Luis A Vital Person in the Garabandal Event.* Hanratty, Barry, Garabandal Journal, January-March 2015, p. 9-10, Reprinted by B. Hanratty.

57   Pesquera, *She Went in Haste to the Mountain,* p. 261.

58   Pesquera, OFM, Cap., *She Went in Haste to the Mountain,* p. 4-7.

59   *Needles: Interview granted by Mari Loli,* July 27, 1975.

60   https://garabandalnews.org/2017/06/03/in-memory-of-albrecht-weber/
https://garabandalnews.org/2023/02/10/from-albrecht-to-aviso-about-the-pope-in-moscow-soon-online/

61   Weber, Albrecht, *Garabandal: Der Zeigefinger Gottes,* 2000, p. 130

62 Casorosendi.com, as reported by TASS Pope Francis asked for a meeting at the airport in Moscow.

63 Madrid, May 2014.

64 Gerard O'Connell, October 9, 2021, internet article.

65 The Spanish website *InfoVaticana* interview translated into English.

66 Kwasniewski, Peter, *How This Dissident Jesuit Theologian is the Key to Understanding Pope Francis*, Lifesite News, September 12, 2023.

67 Lifesite News, June 20, 2023, Michael Haynes, an internet article.

68 *Archbishop Vigano on the Conclave, Provocations & Schism: Fernandez is to Bergoglio what Zelensky is to Biden,* by Aldo Maria Valli, July 15, 2023. Article found on the internet.

69 This homily was transcribed from Spanish to English by a friend, and sent to me via email.

70 Lifesite News, Raymond Wolfe, July 21, 2023, found on the Lifesite News web site.

71 Perez, Ramon Garabandal, *The Village Speaks,* Translated from the French by Annette I. Curot Mathews. Translation published in 1981, p. 350-351.

72 The Gateway Pundit, *Controversial Synodal LGBQT Agenda Set for Global Approval — Byzantine Catholic Patriarchate Calls Bishops of Asia and Australia to Rise Up.* June 14, 2023

73 *Akita: The Tears and Message of Mary,* edited by Teiji Yasuda, O.S.V., translated by John M. Haffert, 101 Foundation, Asbury, NJ, 1989, pp. 77-78.

74 Ferrara, Christopher, *The Secret Still Silenced, 2008, p..41-42*

75 Published in "Avvenire" August 19, 1978; "*The Fourth Secret of Fatima*" 2006 by Antonio Socci, footnote #350

76 Tosatti, Marco, *Ratzinger, Tyconius, and Fatima, An Interpretive Key for the End Times,* September, 2022.

77 Declaraciones de Sor Lucia al R.P. Augustin Fuentes hace 61 anos

78 From a personal letter to Professor Baumgartner of Salzburg, Austria; Father Gerard Mura, "*The Third Secret of Fatima: Has It Been Completely Revealed?,*" The periodical Catholic, (published by the Transalpine Redemptorists, Orkney Isles, Scotland, Great Britain) March, 2002

79 Our Lady of La Salette to Mélanie Calvat, September 19, 1846
    The La Salette Controversy Part 6.

80 Cardinal Henry Edward Manning, *The Present Crisis of the Holy See,* 1861, London: Burns and Lambert, p. 79, 88-90.

81 Works of the Seraphic Father St. Francis of Assisi (London: R. Washbourne, 1882), Part V, Chapter XIII – The Saint Prophesies Great Schisms and Tribulations in the Church, pp. 248-250.

82 Rev. E. Sylvester Berry, *The Church of Christ: An Apologetic and Dogmatic Treatise,* 1927, page 119.

83 Rev. Herman Bernard Kramer, *The Book of Destiny,* 1975, pgs. 277-279.

84 Father Linus Clovis, May 18, 2017, excerpt taken from an address given at the fourth annual Rome Life Forum, organized by Voice of the Family. *The Anti-Church has Come, But Don't Be Afraid,* video, Daily Motion.

85 Catechism of the Catholic Church (1992), Paragraph #675 – The Church's Ultimate Trial.

86 The Virgin of Revelation Vision to Bruno Cornacchiola, 24 February 1968, Saverio Gaeta, *Il Veggente. Il Segreto Delle Tre Fontane* The Seer. The Secret of the Three Fountains), Salani editore, Milano, 2016, p. 73.

87 Father Paul Kramer, Facebook quote, May 2016.

88 http://www.vatican.va/content/john, xxiii/es/apost_ constitutions/1962/documents/hf_j-xxiii_apc_19620222_veterum-sapientia.html

89 Major insight from this citation is from the *Bible of Garabandal,* Se Fue Con Prisas a la Montaña *(She Went in Haste to the Mountain)*

90 Pesquera, Eusebio de Garcia, *She Went in Haste to the Mountain,* 2003, pdf, pgs. 577-578.

91 Pesquera, Eusbio Garcia de, O.F.M., CAP. *She Went in Haste to the Mountain.* Page 566, footnote numbers 27 and 28 are the inclusive quotes from this narrative. Translated from Spanish by Dr. B. Miller, Gerard Suel and Otto Miller. Second English Edition of 1981 original translation published unaltered in one volume in 2003 pdf p. 577-578. The PDF version was used for this footnote.

92 Pesquera, *She Went in Haste to the Mountain.* Page 566, footnote number 28

93 Interview with Bishop Francisco, Garmendia Auxiliary Bishop of New York, and Conchita, Garabandal Journal. March-April 2004.

94   Interview with Conchita conducted by Monsignor Francisco Garmendia, Auxiliary Bishop of New York (1981), Garabandal Journal, March-April 2004.

95   Garabandal Journal/Special Edition. The letter was printed in the Special Edition.

96   Kelly, Ed, *A Walk to Garabandal, a Journey of Happiness and Hope,* Revised Edition, Good Books Media, 2017

97   Catholic News Agency, internet article on the position of the Bishops over time.

98   Interview With Conchita, 1973, Garabandal Journal January-February 2004. Conducted by Dr. Jeronimo Dominguez, pp. 12-15

99   *The 8 March Principles for Human Rights-Based Approach to Criminal Law Proscribing Conduct Associated with Sex, Reproduction, Drug Use, HIV, Homelessness, and Poverty,* page 22.

100 European Conservative, June 30, 2023, Chris Tomlinson, internet article.

101 Zindulka, Kurt, Breitbart, *The Future is Digital — EU Chief Calls for Global Digital ID's and New U.N. Body to Govern Artificial Intelligence,* September 10, 2023.

102 Aldous Huxley, *Brave New World,* 1931

103 Benjamin Franklin to the Pennsylvania General Assembly and a tax dispute of the Penns family.

104 Kissinger, Henry, *World Order,* Penguin Press, 2014, page 1.

105 Flynn, Ted *Hope of the Wicked — The Master Plan to Rule the World.* P.100, MaxKol Communications, 2000.

106 Flynn, Ted, *Hope of the Wicked,* MaxKol Communications, p. 7, 490 pages, 2000.

107 *WEF Says CBD's Must Be implanted Under your Skin if You Want to Participate in Society,* July 25, 2025, The Second Smartest Guy in the World, Sean Adl-Tabatabai.

108 The Gateway Pundit, *The Annual Meeting of New Champions,* July 3, 2023, internet article.

109 Obama wants digital fingerprints, Fox News, June 16, 2023

110 Fortune Magazine online, Finance/Blackrock, by Will Daniel, January 17, 2023.

111 Hyde, Douglas, *I Believed, the Autobiography of a Former British Communist,* William Heinemann, LTD, 1951, page 56.

112 Hyde, pgs. 57-58.

113 Hyde, pgs. 59-60.

114 Hyde, p. 280

115 Hyde, p. 284

116 Hyde, p. 274

117 Hyde, p. 281

118 Chambers, Whitaker, *Witness*, p. 81, 1952. Copyright and renewed 1980 by Esther Chambers. Gateway Editions, A Division of Regnery Publishing, Washington, D.C.

119 Meyer, Frank, S., *The Moulding of Communists: The Training of the Communist Cadre*, p. 58, 1961, Harper & Row, Publishers, and Hamish Hamilton Ltd.

120 Pacepa, Ion Mihai, Lt. General, and Professor Ronald Rychhlak, *Disinformation: Former Spy Chief Reveals Secret Strategies for Undermining Freedom, Attacking Religion, and Promoting Terrorism*, WND Books, Washington, D.C., 2013, page 50. Pacepa had been head of Romanian intelligence previously and knew all of the tactics of the former USSR and their satellites. Seeking political asylum he became a defector to the United States in July, 1978, and wrote a book about his experiences. His reports are considered a treasure trove of information how the Soviet Union operated to over-throw governments throughout the world. Lt. General Pacepa exposes the science of Soviet disinformation.

121 Pacepa, p 50.

122 Pacepa, p 51

123 Hispanist scholar Paul Preston in his book, *A People Betrayed, A History of Corruption, Political Incompetence and Social Division in Modern Spain*. Preston is the author of 14 books on Spain covering primarily the 20th Century. He provides history how the country evolved with its complicated and corrupt past to today. He has been a professor of Spanish history at the London School of Economics. This book could be considered his magnum opus of culminating complexities of Spanish politics. He writes on the Iberian peninsula before, during, and after the Spanish Civil War.

124 Preston, Paul, pages 47, 48

125 Preston, p. 63.

126 Preston, p. 304.

127 Preston, p. 48.

128 Preston, p. 317.

129 Preston, p. 323

130 Preston, p. 328

131 Preston p. 372.

132 Preston p. 370.

133 Preston, p. 374

134 Preston, p. 378.

135 Preston, p. 420

136 Preston, p. 423

137 Flynn, Ted, *Hope of the Wicked, The Master Plan to Rule the World,* MaxKol Communications, 2000, page 4. Original is from: Pope Pius IX Encyclical: *The Dangers and Evils of Our Times,* quoted by Rev. Clarence Kelly, *Conspiracy Against God* and Man, American Opinion, Appleton, Wisconsin, 1974, page 210, in A. Ralph Epperson, The New World Order, Tucson, Az., Publius Press, 1990, page xvi.

138 Flynn, Ted, *Hope of the Wicked,* MaxKol Communications, 2000, page 4, Marx, Karl, Engels, Friedrich, *The Communist Manifesto,* reprint edition, American Opinion, Appleton, Wisconsin, Originally issued by the Communist League, 1848, p. 36

139 We are also seeing more of these methods being used more aggressively in the USA today — which leads one to think violence awaits us as sides become more strident with their views. The agendas are now in the open with little hidden at this point. What was once beneath the surface is now visible. All the while dialogue is non-existent between the parties with differing views. Common ground for negotiation is elusive. Communist views on social welfare programs, education, healthcare, and laws protecting the guilty are at odds with those of a Christian nation.

140 Christian, William, Jr. *The Spanish Republic and the Reign of Christ,* University of California Press, page 7, 1996, 544 pages.

141 Christian, p. 18.

142 The Apparitions of Ezkioga, Iglesia Catolica, Palmariana, found on the internet.

143 Palmarianchurch.org, Internet

144 Christian, page 91

145 Christian, pages 81, 83, 91, 95, 99, 102, 123, 256, 257.

146 Apparitions of Ezquioga, Iglesia Catolica Palmariana. Internet

147 Dillon, Msgr. George, DD, *The War of the Antichrist with the Church and Christian Civilization,* reprinted by TAN Books, Gastonia North Carolina, 2023 from the original in 1885. Edited by Joshua Charles, page xvii.

148 Dillon, page 182-183.

149 Flynn, Ted, *Hope of the Wicked, the Master Plan to Rule the World,* p. 136, MaxKol Communications, Inc, 2000

150 Flynn, p. 141

151 Flynn, p. 148

152 Flynn, Ted, *Diabolical Disorientation, The Roots of the Crisis in the Church, Family, Nation, and Culture,* MaxKol Communications, Inc. pages 17-22, 2020.

153 This source is from a friend who has lived in Garabandal for nearly ten years.

154 Works of the Seraphic Father St. Francis of Assisi [London: R. Washbourne, 1882], Part V, Chapter XIII – *The Saint Prophesies Great Schisms and Tribulations in the Church,* pp. 248-250.

155 *The Divine Mercy, Message and Devotion,* Revised Edition, Quotes from Faustina, Marian Press, Stockbridge, MA. 01263, pages, 79-80.

156 Pellegrinaggio Della Meraviglie, p. 440, Rome, 1960. This same work, published under the auspices of the Italian Episcopate, affirms that this message was communicated to Pope Pius XII. Also, Canon Barthas mentioned that the apparition in his communication to the Mariological Congress of Lisbon-Fatima in 1967; See De Primordiis cultus-mariana, acta congressus mariologici -marianae in Lusitania anno 1967 celebrati, p. 517. Rome, 1970. See Frere Francois de Marie des Anges, Fatima: Intimate Joy World Event, Book four, *Fatima: Tragedy and Triumph.*

157 Soldo, Mirjana, *My Heart Will Triumph,* Catholic Shop Publishing, 2016, page 369.

158 Soldo, 369.

159 *Signs and Wonders Magazine;* Summer of 2002. Vol. 14 No. 2, p.50-55. Father Scheier's story is well known, especially when he went

on EWTN and told his story post the interview of him speaking in the documentary, *Prophecy and the New Times,* released by MaxKol Communications in 1995. His story was a center piece of the documentary I did in 1995. Father Scheier was just one person telling his story of experiencing the Warning. The interview is in his own words, and no language has been changed. His story is very similar to others that have had an Illumination of Conscience. A common occurrence after the Warning is people tell the truth about events in their life like they never did in the past, because there is a total transformation in their lives. It is clear based upon this interview, that Father Scheier has strong opinions on the proper role of a Catholic priest versus how he lived his life prior to the Warning. A layperson will see their sins one way, and a priest will naturally look through the prism and say "was I a good priest?" Father Scheier did not feel he was a good priest, and he speaks in those terms after his Warning. Father Scheier passed away on April 16, 2020 at the age of 72.

Bibliography

BOOKS

1. Albright, Judith, M. *Our Lady at Garabandal.* Faith Publishing Co., P.O. Box 237, Milford, OH 45150. 1992.

2. Apolito, Paolo. *The Internet and the Madonna.* Religious Visionary Experience on the Web. Chicago: The University of Chicago Press. 2005.

3. Bebie, Rev.Philip, C.P. *The Warning: To be Read as Though the Warning Had Just Come.* The Queen's Press. P.O. Box 189, Washington, NJ 07882. 1981?

4. Christian, William, Jr., *Visionaries, The Spanish Republic and the Reign of Christ,* University of California Press, 1996.

5. Daley, Harry. *Miracle At Garabandal.* Ward River Press, Ltd., Knocksedan House, Swords, County Dublin. Ireland. 1985.

6. Fahy, Michael T. *Suddenly and Unexpectedly, Non-Fiction. Unprecedented-Certain-Imminent-Irreversible, The End of Our Times.* The Center for the Divine Will, P.O. Box 415, Jacksboro, TN 37757 USA, August 5, 2019.

7. Flynn, Maureen. *Signs, Secrets and Prophecies.* Signs of the Times Apostolate, Sign.org. P.O. Box 345, Herndon, VA 20172. 2014.

8. Flynn, Maureen. *The Global Warning: An Illumination of the Conscience of Mankind,* Signs of the Times Apostolate. Sign.org. P.O. Box 345, Herndon, VA 20172-0345.

9. Flynn, Ted. *Diabolical Disorientation.* Maxkol Communications, Inc. P.O. Box 345 Herndon, VA 20172-0345. 2020.

10. Flynn, Ted. *Garabandal and Its Secrets.* Maxkol Communications, Inc. P.O. Box 345 Herndon, VA 20172-0345. 2022.

11. Flynn, Ted. *Hope of the Wicked.* Maxkol Communications, Inc. P.O. Box 345 Herndon, VA 20172-0345. 2000.

12. Flynn, Ted. *Idols in the House.* Maxkol Communications, Inc. P.O. Box 345 Herndon, VA 20172-0345. 2002.

13. Flynn, Ted. *The Great Reset.* Maxkol Communications, Inc. P.O. Box 345 Herndon, VA 20172-0345. 2022, 42 pages are on Garandalal.

14. Flynn, Ted. *The Great Transformation.* Maxkol Communications, Inc. P.O. Box 345 Herndon, VA 20172-0345. 2015.

15. Flynn, Ted & Maureen, *The Thunder of Justice: The Warning, The Miracle, The Chastisement, The Era of Peace.* Maxkol Communications, Inc. P.O. Box 345 Herndon, VA 20172-0345, revised and updated in 2010. Although the book was a minor anthology of major apparitions in the world, Garabandal became the heart and soul of the book. The original source material for *Garabandal—The Divine Reset* was used heavily from *The Thunder of Justice,* and subsequent books on the subject. The body of material was given to me by a good friend, Mr. Stanley Karminski, (deceased) of Wayne, PA. in the late 1980s. Stan was an early supporter of Garabandal and had written articles on Garabandal for our magazine called, *Signs and Wonders for Our Times* (Sign.Org), prior to the publication of the book. Stan had a unique gift of capturing Our Lady's intent in her messages and putting them in context of what it meant for the world. In addition, some material now incorporated in many different publications was a small pamphlet by Father Philip Beebie, titled *The Warning.*

    The material was from his personal diary when he was in the last stages of terminal cancer. Father Beebie had a deep Marian devotion, but because Garabandal had not been approved by the Holy See, the order in which he was a member would not endorse his diary or pamphlet, so it does not have a copyright. Information on Anna Maria Taigi is from *The Warning.* The Warnings of Garabandal are quoted by Father Joseph A. Pelletier, A.A., who wrote on Marian apparitions for many years in journals and books. Some other sources are *O Children Listen to Me* by Robert Francois, *Star on the Mountain* by Father Materne Laffineur and M.T. Pelletier. Some of the material from *Garabandal and the Synagogue* is from a talk that was given by the French Dominican Father Francois Turner in a barn near the pines on August 8, 1988. It was used with permission and changed only in grammar and style for readability from the French translation. Father Turner was considered a credible witness and scholar on Garabandal. The remainder is taken from Scripture and the many places of the elements of the Exodus of the Jews in the desert for 40 years. Every Jew, no matter his belief, will know of the pillar of smoke by day and fire at night, called the Shekinah Glory.

16. Flynn, Ted, *Prophecy and the New Times,* DVD, Interviews with leading mystics of the day. 1995. Writer, Producer, Director. Editor: Pam Tyrrell.

17. Flynn, Ted, *Key to the Triumph, The Fifth Marian Dogma of Co-Redemptrix, Mediatrix, Advocate,* DVD, 1997. Writer, Producer, Director. Editor, Pam Tyrrell.

18. Francois, Robert. *O Children Listen to Me, Our Lady Teaches at Garabandal,* The Workers of Our Lady of Mount Carmel, Inc. P.O. Box 606, Lindenhurst, NY 11757. 1982. Originally Published in 1975 as Tout le Peuple l'Ecoutait, Copyright 1975, Fr. A. Combe, Notre Dame du Carmel, La Graviere 01480 Jassuns-Riottier, France.

19. Garabandal Journal, P.O. Box 1796, St. Cloud, MN 56302-1726. 2019, notation provided.

20. Garza, Janie. *Heaven's Messages for The Family,* Vol. 2, 1999. *Messages to Janie Garza.* St. Dominic's Media, P.O. Box 345, Herndon, VA 20172-0345. Signs and Wonders of Our Times is publisher of Janie Garza books. See Sign.Org.

21. Gobbi, Fr. Stefano, *To the Priests, Our Lady's Beloved Sons.* The Marian Movement of Priests. P.O. Box 8, St. Francis, ME 04774-0008. Final English Edition. 2016 edition.

22. Gonzalez, Conchita, *Garabandal, Conchita's Diary,* Translated from the original Spanish version by Father Adolf Faroni, SDB. Published date not provided.

23. Gonzalez, Conchita. Mazon, Mari Loli. *Conchita's Diary, Mari Loli Mazon's Diary.* Our Lady of Garabandal messages. The Work of God. org, Diary from October 1961 to June 1965.

24. Hyde, Douglas, *I Believed: The Autobiography of a Former British Communist,* William Heinemann, LTD., 1951.

25. Kelly, Ed. *A Walk to Garabandal: A Journey of Happiness and Hope.* Goodbooks Media. 3453 Aransas, Corpus Christi, TX 73411. 2017.

26. Kowalska, Saint Faustina, *Divine Mercy in My Soul, The Diary of Sister Faustina.* Marian Press, Stockbridge, MA. 1987.

27. Laffineur, Fr. M. & Fr. Pelletier, M.T., *Star On the Mountain.* Our Lady of Mount Carmel de Garabandal, Inc. P.O. Box 606, Lindenhurst, NY 11757. 1992.

28. Libietis, Fr. Helmuts. *St. Louis de Montfort's True Devotion. Consecration to Mary.* Angelus Press. P.O. Box 217, Saint Mary's, KS 66536. 1998. There have been many versions of this book over the years. Originally it was printed as a small book, then all books necessary for the Consecration were packaged into one book including the Scripture verses for recommended reading.

29. Moynihan, Jeffrey, L. *Sister Mary Mediatrix. A Mystic in America.* Queenship Publishing Co, Queenship.org. P.O. Box 220, Goleta, CA 93116, 2013.

30. Pacepa, Ion Mihai, Lt. General, and Rychlak, Prof. Ronald J., *Disinformation: Former Spy Chief Reveals Secret Strategies for Undermining Freedom, Attacking Religion, and Promoting Terrorism,* WND Books, Washington, DC. 2013.

31. Pelletier, Joseph, A, A.A. *Fr. Luis A Vital Person in the Garabandal Event.* Garabandal Journal. January-March 2015.

32. Pelletier, Joseph, A, A.A. *Garabandal Prayer and Rosary.* Our Lady of Mount Carmel Inc. P.O. Box 606, Lindenhurst, NY 11757. 1970.

33. Pelletier, Joseph, A, A.A. *God Speaks at Garabandal,* An Assumption Publication. 500 Salisbury St. Worcester, MA. 01609. 1978.

34. Pelletier, Joseph, A. A.A. *Our Lady Comes to Garabandal: Including Conchita's Diary.* An Assumption Publication. 500 Salisbury St. Worcester, MA 01609. 1971.

35. Perez, Ramon. *Garabandal: The Village Speaks. Translated from the French original Garabandal ~ le village parle.* By Annette I. Curot Matthews. Lindenhurst, NY: The Workers of Our Lady of Mount Carmel. 1981.

36. Pesquera, Eusebio Garcia de, OFM, Cap. *She Went in Haste to the Mountain,* St. Joseph Publications. 17700 Lorain Ave, Cleveland OH. 44111. 1981. It is a three-volume set that is 8.5 X 11 in size, that is the first translation into English of the classic work *Se Fue Con Prisas a la Montana,* originally published in Spain in 1972 and 1979 by Father Pesquera, OFM. When the first printing in English ran out, there was no reprint. The book was written by Father Pesquera and is considered a classic due to the volume of the material it covers, and is often quoted. Brian Miller, MD gave the book free of charge to The Workers of Our Lady of Mount Carmel for the 2000 edition coming out by the same title all in one volume. The book was then edited and updated by Barry Hanratty and Irene Dutra, and published by The Workers of Our Lady of Mount Carmel, P.O. Box, 606, Lindenhurst, New York, 11757, under Our Lady of Mount Carmel de Garabandal, Inc. The author is in possession of the translated work of Pesquera to English (3 volumes) from the Spanish by Gerard Buel and Otto Miller. Copyright of the book is Father Pesquera, OFM, and was a source for this book.

37. Petrisko, Thomas, *Twilight of Marxism: Medjugorje, the Downfall of Systematic Evil, and the Fulfillment of the Secret of Fatima,* Saint Andrew's Productions, 2022.

38. Preston, Paul, *A People Betrayed: A History of Corruption, Political Incompetence, and Social Division in Modern Spain,* Liveright Publishing Corporation, First American edition, 2020. A History of Spain in the 20th Century. Preston is the author of 14 books on Spain, largely centered on the 20th Century.

39. Rolla, Gregory M. *Of Queen and Prophets, The Garabandal Events and the End of Times.* 2011, and revised 2013. Create Space, Charleston, SC. 29418.

40. Saavedra, Jose Luis, *Garabandal, Message of Hope,* Association Elizabeth Van Keerbergen, 2016.

41. Sanchez-Ventura y Pascal, F. *The Apparitions of Garabandal.* Eighteenth edition. Pasadena, CA: St. Michael's Garabandal Center. (First published in 1965 as Las Apariciones Son un Mito el Interrogante de Garabandal. 2000.

42. Serre, Jacques & Caux, Beatrice. *Garabandal. Apparitions of the Blessed Virgin Mary as Our Lady of Mount Carmel*. Vol. 1. From Beauty to Truthfulness. Ferny Hills, Qld: The Workers of Our Lady of Mount Carmel of Garabandal. 2001.

43. Soldo, Mirjana, *My Heart Will Triumph,* Catholic Shop Publishing, 2016.

44. Weber, Albrecht, *Garbandal — Der Zeigefinger Gottes* (German edition), 1993, 2000, Translated into English: *Garabandal — The Finger of God.*

WEBSITES

1. Britannica, The Spanish Civil War

2. Conchita's Diary. http://www.stjosephpublications.com/books

3. Garabandal Clarification. http://www.garabandal.com Garabandal Journal.

4. Garabandal http://www.garabandal.org Garabandal US.

5. Holocaust Encyclopedia, The Spanish Civil War

6. Iglesia Catolica Palmariana, The Apparitions of Ezkioga, Spain. It is spelled Ezquioga for an English-speaking audience versus the Basque spelling used in the 1930's.

7. Our Lady of Garabandal Messages. http://www.theworkofGod.org/apparitions/garabandal/apparitions.htm

8. Signs and Wonders for Our Times, US. http://www.sign.org

Magazines Among Others Where Interviews Were Used

1. Garabandal Magazine Staff. *Garabandal. The Message of Our Lady of Mount Carmel.* The Workers of Our Lady of Mount Carmel, P.O. Box 606, Lindenhurst, NY 11757. October-December 1990.

2. Hanratty, Barry. *Garabandal Journal.* Vol. 20, No. 4. P.O. Box 1796, St. Cloud, MN 56302-1796. July-August 2021.

3. Garabandal Journal, Barry Hanratty, September- October 2022. The last issue of Garabandal Journal published by Barry Hanratty before

he died. Issue was used with notation. Soon after Barry Hanratty died, Garabandal Journal resumed under the leadership of Dick Kodet, Editor.

4. *Needles* magazines from 1972-1978

5. Selected issues of *Garabandal* from 1980-2002

6. Selected issues of Garabandal Journal from 2003-2023. In total over 100 over the years.

VHS TAPES

1. Everson, Richard. *The Events at Garabandal.* Richard Everson. P.O. Box 130425, Roseville, MN 55113. 1971.

2. *The Message of Garabandal.* The Workers of Our Lady of Mount Carmel. P.O. Box 606, Lindenhurst, NY 11757-0606

3. *Village Life in Garabandal,* 1990-1991

4. *Joey Lomangino on Mother Angelica Live,* EWTN release

5. *Garabandal, Then and Now,* Part II, *The Prophetic Messages Revealed by Eyewitness,* Maria Saraco

6. *Garabandal Reflections,* www.garabandal.org, Saint Michaels Center, 30 main Street, Middletown, Co Armaugh, B.T. 60 Northern Ireland, England. MFJ Productions, PO Box 385, Orewa, Auckland, New Zealand.

7. *Garabandal, After the Visions, The Message of Garabandal,* The Workers of Our Lady of Mount Carmel PO Box 606, Lindenhurst, New York, 11757.

DVD

1. *San Sebastian of Garabandal. The Eyewitnesses.* St. Michael's Garabandal Centre. 889 Palo Verde Ave, Pasadena, CA 91104. St. Michael's Garabandal Centre, 20 Main Street, Middleton, Co. Armagh, B.T. 60. Ireland. DVD Released by MFJ Productions P.O. Box 385 Orewa Auckland, New Zealand. Garabandal.org. 2002.

Index

Fahy, Thomas: 263

Families: 1, 10, 49, 60, 164, 179, 213, 223, 228

Fasting: 60, 105, 180, 226, 235, 240, 244, 296

Father of the Constitution: 218

Fatima, Portugal: 3, 93, 106

Faustina, Saint: 34

FBI: 191-192

Feast of the Visitation: 19, 153, 166

Fernandez, Cardinal Victor Manuel: 146

Filipino: 3

Fink, Larry: 192

Fire by Night: 78, 110-111, 113, 267

Flame of Love: x, 14, 64, 264

For Whom the Bell Tolls: 195

Four More Popes: 6

Francis of Assisi, Saint: 152, 231-232, 239, 270, 274

Franco, General: 195-197, 204-206

Franklin, Benjamin: 185, 271

Freemasonry: xiii, 7, 146, 149, 204-207, 210, 215, 217, 219-224

French Revolution: 16, 207, 224

Fulda, Germany: 97

Gallagher, Christina: x, 64

Garabandal Journal: viii, 31, 45, 70, 118, 135, 169, 227, 263-265, 268, 271, 280-283

Garabandal Magazine: 227, 281

Garmendia, Bishop: xii, 157, 159, 160, 270-271

Garza, Janie: 278

Gates, Bill and Melinda: 180, 190

Gingrich, Newt: 220

Global Digital Health Certificate: 189

Gobbi, Father Stefano: 40, 81-82, 104, 146, 220, 222, 263, 280

Gorbachev, Mikhail: 35-36

Great Chastisement: 32, 56, 75, 153-154

Great Depression: 37

Great Event: 6, 156

Great Miracle: i, xi, 1, 15, 17, 19, 25-26, 29, 32, 34, 60, 70-71, 77-78, 80, 83-88, 94-95, 105, 109, 113, 123, 128, 131, 147, 154, 193, 229, 233, 235, 295

Haffert, John: 3, 269

Hanratty, Barry: vii, 5, 31, 45, 70, 72, 88, 118, 135, 227, 264-265, 268, 281, 283

Haverhill, Massachusetts: 36

Heaven: v, vi, viii, ix, xi, xii, xiii, 1, 3-5, 7, 9-10, 12, 15-18, 20, 22-24, 26-30, 43, 45, 47, 51, 58, 64, 74, 78, 81-82, 89-90, 92, 104, 107, 109-114, 117, 123-124, 131, 149, 151, 153-154, 158, 183-184, 187, 193, 199, 204, 211, 213-215, 217, 222, 224-226, 229-230, 234, 236-238, 240, 247, 250, 256-257, 294

Previous Works by the Author

- 1993, (revised in 2010), **The Thunder of Justice** – *The Warning, The Miracle, The Chastisement, The Era of Peace.* A book on the major apparitions of the Blessed Mother. It has been translated into 6 languages. 427 pages.

- 2000, **Hope of the Wicked** – *The Master Plan to Rule the World.* A best-seller on the political philosophy of the New World Order. 1,200 footnotes of world leaders in their own words where they wish to bring the world. We are now living what they said. A book detailing the agenda of the Deep State, before the phrase was used. 504 pages.

- 2002, **Idols in the House.** A book that shows what happens when a nation abandons God and the 1st Commandment. 282 pages.

- 2015, **The Great Transformation** – *Finding Peace of Soul in Troubled Times.* A book showing where the culture is headed and how believers are to conduct themselves from an historical and Scriptural perspective in times of stress. 334 pages.

- 2020, **Diabolical Disorientation** – *The Roots of the Crisis in the Family, the Church, the Nation, and the Culture.* It is a collection of essays on what Heaven has told us what we can expect to see what happens in the world, and the battle between good and evil reaches its apex. 198 pages.

- 2022, **The Great Reset** – *The Globalist Plan vs. Heaven's Victory.* A book on what the Great Reset means for mankind. A narrative on the battle we see around us for supremacy of a global elite politically and in every area of our life. A great deal is said about the Deep State and the Deep Church, and how believers are to navigate the times in which we live based upon Scriptural and time-tested principles. As much as the subject is a serious theme, it is a book of great hope that will inspire. 277 pages.

- 2022, **Garabandal and Its Secrets** – *The Warning and the Miracle of Garabandal, Like Nothing Before in History, Two Supernatural Events That Will Change the World, The Global Reset—Heaven Resets on Their Terms.* A pocket booklet that explains the significance of the apparitions of Garabandal from 1961-1965, and how it is Heaven's plan to reset the world from its present state of grave sin to one that will be God's ultimate act of mercy for humanity. Time in the future will be measured before the Warning and Miracle, and after the Warning and Great Miracle. 78 pages.

- 2024, **Garabandal – The Warning and the Great Miracle,** *The Divine Reset That Will Correct the Conscience of the World.* A book on the apparitions at Garabandal in northern Spain from 1961-65. Chronicles the history and major points of the 2,000 apparitions, and the life changing prophecies that the Blessed Mother made to four young girls, over more than four years. 300 pages.

Film documentaries:

- **Prophecy and the New Times** (1995), on visionaries and apparitions that were in the book the Thunder of Justice.
- **Key to the Triumph** (1997), about the Fifth Marian Dogma

About the Author

Ted Flynn has been a Washington, D.C resident for 47 years and has been involved in various apostolates and businesses during that time.

In 1979 he was a Fellow of the Fellowship Foundation, an organization that sponsors the National Prayer Breakfast, with a mission of discipleship to young leaders throughout the world.

In 1984 he and his wife Maureen co-founded a crisis pregnancy center, and in 1987 founded Teen Choice, a program designed to teach teen chastity. After counseling thousands of young woman and men on the physical, spiritual, and psychological effects of abortion, they decided teaching and forming people in the faith would have a greater impact in the culture to stop the scourge of abortion. Thus, Signs of the Times was started in 1989.

Signs of the Times Apostolate (Sign.org) has been teaching and informing people on the faith providing resources through its magazine, product distribution, conferences, and web site. Seeing the lack of progress in politics providing an answer to the country's moral decline, the International Week of Prayer and Fasting (IWOPF.ORG) has been held annually at the Basilica of the Shrine of the Immaculate Conception since 1990.

Ted has been in management consulting, real estate development, Chief Economist for a government agency, energy development, a consultant, he lived in Warsaw and Krakov, Poland, to retrofit power plants after the fall of the Berlin Wall in 1990/1991. He distributed U.S. AID and Agriculture commodities near Chernobyl to the Republic of Belarus in 1992/93 after the fall of the Soviet Union. He has been the President and founder of MaxKol Communications since 1993, a publishing company.

He has traveled to over 50 countries of the world on business and pleasure, spoken in over 700 venues of the world, and done over 300 radio, TV, and podcasts on political philosophy, religion, and culture—topics addressed in his books.

He has attended the University of Massachusetts, Amherst, American University, Washington, D.C., the University of Fribourg, Switzerland, and the London School of Economics, England.